INTRODUCTORY PSYCHOLOGY

This series of titles is aimed at introductory-level psychology students in sixth forms, further education colleges and on degree courses and those wishing to obtain an overview of psychology. The books are easy to use, with comprehensive notes written in coherent language; clear flagging of key concepts; relevant and interesting illustrations; well-defined objectives and further reading sections to each chapter; and self-assessment questions at regular intervals throughout the text.

Published

INDIVIDUAL DIFFERENCES
Ann Birch and Sheila Hayward

DEVELOPMENTAL PSYCHOLOGY (Second Edition)
Ann Birch

BIOPSYCHOLOGY
Sheila Hayward

COGNITIVE PROCESSES
Tony Malim

SOCIAL PSYCHOLOGY (Second Edition)
Tony Malim

RESEARCH METHODS AND STATISTICS
Tony Malim and Ann Birch

COMPARATIVE PSYCHOLOGY
Tony Malim, Ann Birch and Sheila Hayward

PERSPECTIVES IN PSYCHOLOGY (Second Edition)
Alison Wadeley, Ann Birch and Tony Malim

SOCIAL PSYCHOLOGY

Second Edition

Tony Malim

palgrave

First edition 1989
Reprinted 3 times
Second edition 1997

Published by
PALGRAVE
Houndmills, Basingstoke, Hampshire RG21 6XS and
175 Fifth Avenue, New York, N. Y. 10010
Companies and representatives throughout the world

PALGRAVE is the new global academic imprint of
St. Martin's Press LLC Scholarly and Reference Division and
Palgrave Publishers Ltd (formerly Macmillan Press Ltd).

ISBN 0–333–67048–5

This book is printed on paper suitable for recycling and made from fully managed and sustained forest sources.

A catalogue record for this book is available from the British Library.

10   9   8   7   6   5   4
06   05   04   03   02   01   00

Copy-edited and typeset by Povey-Edmondson
Tavistock and Rochdale, England

Printed and bound in Great Britain by
Antony Rowe Ltd, Chippenham, Wiltshire

Cartoons by Sally Artz

Contents

List of Figures and Boxes

FIGURES

BOXES

Preface to the Second Edition

It is now seven years since the first edition of *Social Psychology* was published in this series and a great deal has happened during this time. In the first place there have been changes in the content of the syllabus for A-level both with the Associated Examining Board and the Northern Examinations and Assessment Board. Furthermore, the Oxford and Cambridge Board has introduced a syllabus for A-level. This book attempts to accommodate these changes.

As well as this, the emphases within the field of social psychology have altered fairly radically. The focus is presently much more upon social cognition: that is, the way in which social events are stored in memory and used subsequently to determine social behaviour. This focus has been more clearly represented in the new edition with clear explanations of such concepts as schemata and scripts, social representation and social identity.

Traditionally, social psychology has been dominated by American theory and research. There has been an attempt here to introduce more of the work done in Europe, as well as in Australia and New Zealand.

The aim has been to set out theories and the research which underpins them in as clear and succinct way as possible, using illustrations and boxes to focus attention on the detail of important pieces of research. Important concepts are highlighted and explained throughout the book and each chapter starts with a set of objectives for that chapter so as to make it easier for those who are working largely on their own to focus upon the relevant ideas. In addition, there are self-assessment questions at the end of each section to enable students to check their understanding.

Social psychology is a fascinating study and one which has relevance to everyday life. These relevances have been highlighted also. Some areas have received more attention than in the first edition, notably affiliation, love and marriage. Self-concepts and self-perceptions have been examined more fully, while persuasive communication, much of the research into which now seems rather dated, has had less attention. In general, the intention has been to provide an up-to-date picture of social psychology for students who are studying psychology at a fairly basic level, particularly for A-level and for GCSE. We hope that you will find the book understandable and above all enjoyable.

Tony Malim

Acknowledgement

The author would once again like to thank Sally Artz for the cartoons at the beginning of each chapter.

"THE HECK WITH 'REALISM' — NEXT TIME I'M OPTING FOR 'MANIPULATION'!"

Introduction and Methods

At the end of this chapter you should be able to:

1. Identify some of the perspectives used by social psychologists as they study people's behaviour in a social context.
2. Describe some of the aims of social psychology.
3. Show an appreciation of the difficulties which are frequently thrown up by researchers' choice of participants in their studies.
4. Highlight some of the ethical problems which are specific to social psychology.
5. Illustrate the balance which needs to be struck between **realism** and **rigour.**

SECTION I SOME PERSPECTIVES ON SOCIAL PSYCHOLOGY

Social psychologists attempt to provide a framework within which to understand the interactions between people. Perspectives which have been taken correspond quite closely to those adopted in other branches of psychology. They include:

Social Role Perspective

The idea of **role** is probably the oldest perspective on the ways in which people interact. It envisages a world in which everyone plays a part or, more likely, several parts. In every part or role a person plays, expectations are aroused in terms of behaviour. Let us take an example:

> Jane is a mature student who has come back into college, now that her children are at school. She plays a whole series of interrelated roles. Figure 1.1 shows a few of them, together with some of the expectations which are aroused as she plays out these

FIGURE 1.1
Roles and Expectations

Role	Role Partner(s)	Expectations
Wife	Husband	Loving, caring, nurturing
Mother	Children	Loving, providing
Student	Tutor	Paying attention, doing assignments etc.
Student	Other students	Joining in, supplying mutual help
Badminton club member	Other members, the team	Good play, co-operation, training, enthusiastic playing.

roles. In each case there will also be a **role partner** or **role partners** who observe her from the outside and interact with her.

Stryker and Statham (1985) have shown that the idea of role is shared by a number of perspectives, but the main components of role theory as a framework for explanations of how people behave, concentrate on three things:

1. The roles themselves;
2. The social context in which these roles are played out;
3. The expectations engendered.

Social psychologists such as Cooley (1902) and Mead (1934) have used role theory in their attempts to explain **self-concept**. More recently Snyder (1987) made use of it in his work on **self-monitoring**; that is, how people continuously pay close attention to the way in which they are perceived by others and change their behaviour in response to it.

Learning Perspective

A second perspective is that of learning, which concentrates upon **stimulus** and **response**. This goes back to behaviourist theory and in particular to the work of Watson (1913) and later to Skinner (1953) and others. A stimulus can be defined as an event which results in a change in someone's behaviour. This may be either internal or external. As far as a social stimulus is concerned it is most likely to be something which someone else does or says.

Reinforcement is a further important element, a favourable outcome related to the stimulus which makes a particular response
more likely to re-occur. This seems highly technical but in practice it
is simple enough. Suppose our boss comes to us and remarks how
well we dealt with that difficult customer. Our behaviour has been
reinforced and we will be more likely to treat a future customer in a
similar way. Learning has occurred. If, however, our behaviour goes
unrewarded there will be no such impulse to behave in the way we
did.

If the same positive outcome results from more than one social
stimulus, a person will be likely to group these social stimuli
together as having some common feature. Being polite to a difficult
customer, trying to see his or her point of view and not responding
in kind to abuse come to be **generalised**. Stimulus generalisation is
very useful in allowing learning theorists to explain behaviour which
otherwise might be difficult to explain if each behaviour had to be
reinforced separately.

Stimulus discrimination occurs when we learn to respond differently to different stimuli. Perhaps a different tone might be adopted
towards a customer with a legitimate grievance from that shown
towards someone who is just 'trying it on'. Different reinforcement
in each set of circumstances results in learning to discriminate
between one stimulus and another.

Learning theorists tend not to be much concerned with what is
going on in the mind of the learner, but just with relationships
between stimuli and responses, the argument being that they can see
different stimuli and can observe and measure different responses
but there is no way to account for what thoughts are going through
the mind. It is all the language of cause and effect.

Examples of the use of a learning perspective include the following:

- The work of Miller and Dollard (1941) who explained the
  socialisation process in young children in terms of stimulus–
  reward and reinforcement.
- From this basis Bandura (1973) developed **social learning theory**
  claiming that learning can occur by observing the behaviour of a
  model, that is by imitation.
- Homans' (1958, 1974) **social exchange theory** and Thibaut and
  Kelley's (1978) development of it are manifestations of learning
  theory as applied in social psychology. According to this theory,

social behaviour can be explained in terms of costs and rewards. Any interaction with another person (a dyad) depends on the rewards it offers and the costs it incurs. Box 1.1 distinguishes the approaches which have been employed:

BOX 1.1
Learning Theory and Social Learning Theory

As a reaction to introspective and psychoanalytic methods which were employed in the early years of this century, Watson attempted to apply scientific method to the study of psychology. Publicly-observable behaviour became the proper subject matter for psychology. Watson and the other 'behaviourists', as they became known, rejected consideration of the internal mechanisms of the mind, concentrating instead upon observable behaviour.

Skinner (1974) was a leading exponent of this approach who developed **operant conditioning**. A key principle of operant conditioning was that where behaviour is reinforced – that is, where people are rewarded when they behave in a particular way – it will tend to be repeated under similar circumstances.

Bandura (1969) extended this by proposing that imitation plays a significant part in human learning. People learn by observing what others are doing. Thus a **social learning approach** to human behaviour proposes that the main determinants of an individual's behaviour are not any internal characteristics or traits that individual may possess, but what happens to that individual in the environment, both observing the behaviour of others and finding that particular kinds of behaviour are reinforced. Observed behaviours may be stored and only introduced when individuals feel that they will be reinforced. Thus Bandura reintroduced some element of cognition, that is the build-up of patterns in the mind though stored experience.

Social Cognition

The social cognition perspective has tended to be the dominant one in recent years as it seems to have greater applicability to a wider range of topics within social psychology than do the others. It is this perspective which we have used to provide a unifying framework for this book. It is analogous to ideas put forward by Tolman and others (Tolman, 1948) relating to **cognitive maps**.

The suggestion is that an internal representation is built up, through learning and memory, which provides a framework for our understanding of external events. Altman and Chemers (1980) investigated cognitive mapping in the physical sense. The places in which we spend the most time are 'mapped' in the greatest detail and are used as a kind of shorthand for orientation. Cognitive maps are in essence personal, reflecting our own experiences as individuals. Milgram (1977) took a structured approach to cognitive mapping. New Yorkers were shown colour slides of their city and asked to identify locations. This revealed that people had a very uneven picture of their city – just enough of a map for them to get by – reflecting their individual needs and experience. For British people, cognitive maps of the world tend to show Britain and Europe dominant against a background of the rest of the world and looking larger than, say, Africa or South America, in spite of the fact that Africa is five times the size of Western Europe, and South America is three times the size. This illustrates the point that the pictures built up in cognition represent what is important to us as individuals from the point of view of our experience.

Schemata

Similar processes are at work when people interact with others. Patterns are developed which provide some consistency in the way in which they behave. It is almost as though they were actors playing their parts on a stage. In the same way that you would not expect a performance in the theatre to be impromptu and unscripted, so one way in which social psychologists attempt to impose order upon the apparent chaos which is people's interactions with each other is to visualise them as performing a role and following a script. In very much the same way as an actor learns his or her 'lines' and then rehearses them, an individual acquires a cognitive framework of social interaction with others over the course of a lifetime.

Crocker *et al.* (1984) have described the structure of knowledge which results as networks of **schemata**. They may be representations, stored in memory, of types of people, of social roles to be played out or of events to be re-enacted.

Functions of Schemata

1. *Interpretation*. When we meet someone else and he or she either says something or behaves in a particular way, how do we know how to react? We will draw upon our stored schemata to make

sense of it. At a very simple level, suppose we meet someone and in response to the usual, 'Hello, how are you?' he or she says, 'Much better now, thank you', we draw upon our knowledge, gained from previous encounters, that the individual concerned has been in hospital and is now recovering. If, however, the response is, 'I'm OK now, no thanks to you', different schemata are drawn upon, involving memory of some less than totally pleasant incident. They help us to interpret more effectively and with greater speed the social events which we encounter.

2. *Inference.* The schemata are also gap-fillers. They not only provide us with a means to interpret stimuli, but also the context within which that stimulus occurs; a set of inferences which allow us to arrive at judgements about people and about social events. Schemata allow us to fill in the gaps in information which we acquire in social encounters. We are thus able to build up much more rapidly a more complete picture of the context in which an encounter occurs than would be possible if we were to rely just on the stimuli in front of us.

Scripts

Schemata do not arrive singly, but in battalions. Scripts could be described as sequences of schemata. How do children in school know how to behave? They develop a 'classroom script', a set of rules governing what you do when you are in a classroom. If the script developed is a good one, this might involve sitting quietly in one's place, putting a hand up and waiting to be asked before volunteering an answer, and so on. On the other hand a script might develop that was unhelpful to the progress of learning, a 'shouting out' script or even a 'baiting the teacher' script. The idea of cognitive **scripts** was developed by Schank and Abelson (1977) and Abelson (1981) takes the social cognition perspective further. A 'script' relates to a set of rules for behaving in a particular context or class of context.

Langer (1978) draws a distinction between mindful and mindless behaviour. Behaviour which conforms to an established script is mindless, carried out and responded to without conscious thought. The pattern has been set according to a cognitive map and becomes automatic. Unscripted behaviour, on the other hand, requires more thought.

Prototypes

In the same way that a script is a sequence of schemata, a prototype is a cluster of schemata relating to an individual person or to a group of individuals. For instance, you might have developed the **prototype** of a 'yuppie'. The prototypical yuppie might display a number of characteristics, trendiness in dress, perhaps, an ostentatious display of prosperity and a particular style of life. An observer who establishes a prototype of a yuppie, that is a particular pattern in his or her mind which represents in shorthand-form all the characteristics that experience has shown represent 'yuppie', would classify him/her as a yuppie after identifying at least some of the characteristics. Once identified, the observer might ascribe to him or her other 'yuppie' characteristics, pushiness, perhaps, or self-advertisement. In much the same way as schemata and scripts speed up and facilitate the responses made to situations we may find ourselves in, prototypes enable us to make judgements and responses easily and quickly about individuals or groups of people on the basis of experience

The idea behind prototypes, as behind scripts and schemata, is that by establishing a pattern or framework in knowledge and memory, individual social interactions become easier to manage.

We shall continue to compare different explanations of social phenomena and relate them back to these three perspectives, though increasingly the social cognition perspective is tending to predominate.

Self-assessment Questions

1. What are the essential features of social cognition? Why do you think it has become important in the study of social psychology?
2. List the essential elements of learning theory. What is meant by stimulus generalisation?
3. What are meant by schemata in relation to the understanding of social interaction?

SECTION II METHODS IN SOCIAL PSYCHOLGY

You want to investigate something. Where do you start? Investigation starts with theory. Theory in turn is firmly based upon the

Independent and Dependent Variables

Beyond this starting point lies the means of testing predictions. In many instances, perhaps in most cases we are talking about setting up experiments. This will involve the identification of variables – **independent variables (IV)** which may be manipulated deliberately by an experimenter, and **dependent variables (DV)** which may be measured. The IV is some condition which the experimenter may deliberately alter and which is presumed to be likely to have some effect on participants' responses; the DV is a measure of these responses. For instance, a researcher might be interested in the relationship between what young people watch on TV and aggressive behaviour. The independent variables might consist of a series of TV programmes, varying in the level of violence displayed and in realism (as opposed to fantasy). The DV might be a measure of the aggressive behaviour shown by the young people. The prediction might be that young people who watched the TV programme which contained the greatest violence, combined with the greatest realism, would display the highest level of aggressive behaviour.

Reliability and Validity

These variables, both IV and DV must really represent the theoretical concepts they are supposed to represent or the whole endeavour is meaningless. They need to have **validity** and **reliability.** Validity refers to the extent to which a variable actually does represent what it says it represents; reliability refers to the consistency with which it represents it.

Deaux *et al.* (1993) have used a study by Doob and Gross (1968) to illustrate this point. They were investigating the relationship between two concepts, frustration and aggression. For frustration they needed to find something which got in the way of a person achieving his or her goal. They chose the case of a car which had stalled at a traffic light, obstructing the progress of the cars behind. This seems to be a valid case of something likely to produce frustration. A person's goal (in one of the cars behind) is to make progress and get past the lights. The stalled car certainly frustrates this and we could say that it consistently frustrates the progress of the cars behind. As an IV it is both valid and reliable.

For the DV (aggression), Doob and Gross had to find something which measured (reliably and validly) aggression which might result from a person's progress being obstructed. They chose the honking of a horn. We could say this was aggressive in that it was designed to irritate the driver of the stalled car. Perhaps this was valid. Whether it was reliable is a little more questionable. Is the horn honked *only* to annoy the person in front? Could there be another purpose? Perhaps to attract the attention of a friend who might be walking by on the pavement? But we are much less likely *in the circumstances* to honk to greet a friend if we are waiting at traffic lights than to signal our irritation. So perhaps it does pass the test of reliability and validity.

A third variable (the IV) was the **status** of the individual causing the frustration. Doob and Gross chose to use the quality and cost of the stalled car to represent the status of its driver. They predicted that the status of the stalled car's driver would affect the amount of aggression displayed. It was not hard for the postgraduate students conducting the study to find battered old low-status cars; the high-status car was more difficult for them. They hired a Chrysler. It is worth considering whether this was a valid and reliable variable representing the 'status' of the individual causing the frustration.

Experimental Factors

Demand Characteristics

Orne (1969) has suggested that any cues which may be introduced indicating to participants what behaviour is expected by the researchers will make it more likely that this behaviour will be exhibited. If those taking part in Doob and Gross's study had been aware that horn-honking was being taken as a measure of aggression this would have distorted the results. Instead of aggression, horn-honking might have come to represent co-operation with the researchers. These cues have been described as **demand characteristics**. They are particularly easy to introduce into social psychological experimentation.

Evaluation Apprehension

A further problem to be aware of is that of the effect on participants of being aware that they are taking part in an experiment. Any kind of awareness of being evaluated (or of an evaluation taking place) tends to have an effect upon performance. This is **evaluation**

- *College students as participants.* Sears (1986) has argued that excessive reliance upon college students can produce distortions. College students are, compared to the general population, more cognitive, more concerned with material self-interest, less crystallised in their attitudes and more responsive to situational pressures which are less likely to effect other people.
- *Untypical participants.* Students are also untypical. The laboratories are usually on the university campus, and it is convenient to have student participants readily available, but this can cause distortion.
- *Volunteer participants.* Students form a volunteer sample. Ora (1965) has shown that volunteers tend to be insecure, influenced by others, dependent, aggressive, neurotic and introverted in comparison to a cross-section of non-volunteers. This might be acceptable if the experimenter's intention was only to generalise to a population of volunteers, but not to a population of people who do not share these characteristics.
- *Realism/rigour conflict.* This is in effect the conflict between **realism** and **rigour**. Experiment with its careful use of controls, remains the best way to test cause and effect. By carefully controlling and isolating one set of variables, problems are created in relation to the divorce between what is happening in the laboratory, and in reality. After all, how many people in their ordinary lives find themselves judging the length of a line in comparison with a 'test' line, as Asch had his participants doing in his classic experiment on conformity (Asch, 1956). To put it in another way it is the conflict between internal validity, that is the extent to which controls can ensure that measures of the dependent variable really are due to the independent variable manipulated in the experiment, and external validity, the similarity of the situation to anything in real life.

Some Other Research Methods Used in Social Psychology

Deaux *et al.* (1993) have listed the following:

- Quasi-experimental research;
- Field research;
- Archival research; and
- Simulation research.

Quasi-experimental Research

This includes those cases where a complete control over the manipulation of the independent variable is impossible, either for ethical or for practical reasons. Cross-cultural and medical research are two areas which fall into these categories. In the first case it is clearly not possible for an individual participant to change from belonging to one culture to belonging to another. An example can be found in a study by Hui *et al.* (1991). The hypothesis under test was that Chinese culture, with its greater affiliation, nurturing and so on, tends to be more collective than American culture which tends to be more individualistic.

Students from Chinese and American cultures were asked to divide the rewards for a completed task between co-workers. Half the students in each culture they had completed 80 per cent of the work, with the co-workers completing only 20 per cent. For the other half of the students the situation was the reverse of this, co-workers contributing 80 per cent as opposed to a 20 per cent contribution by the students. The Chinese were found to be more generous in sharing the rewards than the Americans.

It is clearly not possible to manipulate the culture of the individuals concerned, but you can manipulate 'culture' as an abstract idea so that this is quasi-experimental research or it could be described as a natural experiment. This method allows variables to be studied which are not amenable to true experiment, where conditions are manipulated relating to a specific set of participants. In doing this, however, a certain amount of control is lost.

Field Research

In these cases the researcher observes and records as much information as possible about a situation as it exists, without attempting to manipulate the variables in any way. This observation may be either participant or non-participant, and the settings may be very varied. Deaux and her colleagues mention exotic locations such as 200 feet below the surface of the Pacific Ocean (Radloff and Helmreich, 1968), in a space station orbiting the earth (Stewart, 1988) and in Antarctica (Harrison *et al.*, 1990). We shall mention just two examples here. In a study by Ainsworth and Bell (1969) 26 babies were observed in their own homes. The independent variables were the promptness with which the mothers responded to their babies

The principal advantage of simulation and role-play is that it allows the study of areas which might otherwise be inaccessible to study. Appropriate experimental controls can be incorporated into the simulation. Participants also have a greater degree of involvement than in a more typical experimenter/participant study.

There are problems, though, and simulation has proved controversial. Principally there is doubt expressed in some quarters as to whether the participants in simulations really would behave the same in a real situation as they do in the simulation. Do they do only what they *think* they would do in the real situation, rather than what they would actually do?

There can be ethical problems too. Zimbardo's well-known simulation (Haney *et al.*, 1973, described in more detail in a later chapter) put participants into the role of prisoners or warders and this had to be discontinued after six days because of the distress that was being caused.

Survey Methods

This includes interviews or questionnaires. In the interview type of survey a set of questions is presented to participants and the answers recorded. In a questionnaire it is done in written form. To design a survey well is extremely difficult. The wording of the questions may well bias the answers. The survey can either be highly-structured with fixed alternative answers, or more open-ended, with participants free to express their views. The former is more difficult to construct but analysis is perhaps less complex, while in a more open-ended survey it is the analysis which may prove difficult with much of the data being of a qualitative rather than a quantitative kind.

Rutter's survey of London schools (Rutter *et al.*, 1979) is an example. The researchers examined academic attainment, attendance and delinquency in 12 secondary schools. There were structured interviews as well as some observation of events in classrooms. Variables considered included the status and sex composition of the pupils; the size, space and age of the buildings; the number of sites and staffing; and class size and organisation.

An example of a questionnaire type survey is that of Abdalla (1991) who examined questions of social support and job stress in Kuwait. Where there were high levels of support from co-workers, both men and women achieved greater job satisfaction than where the levels of support were lower. Women generally enjoyed lower levels of support than men owing to Arab culture, but they made better use of what support they had, perhaps because they had greater experience using such support in their home environment.

Self-assessment Questions

1. List some of the sources which give rise to the formulation of research hypotheses in social psychology.
2. Identify some of the factors which may cause a conflict between 'realism' and 'rigour' in research in social psychology. How do you think a balance may be struck?
3. What is meant by quasi-experimental research? What are its limitations?
4. Identify some of the problems associated with simulation. Do you think that the controversies which have arisen over simulation are justified?

SECTION III   SOME ETHICAL CONSIDERATIONS

In this country, the British Psychological Society has issued guidelines on ethical questions in research (British Psychological Society, 1990). In the US, similar guidance is offered by the US Department of Health and Human Services, which all recipients of grants must follow. Additionally, papers have been written both here and in the US. In particular, Wadeley (1991) has outlined some of the salient points and the Association for Teaching Psychology has produced an issue of its journal devoted to Ethics (*Psychology Teaching*: New Series No. 2, 1992). There is also a section on ethics in research in *Perspectives in Psychology* (Malim *et al.*, 1992) to which the reader may refer.

In this book it seems sufficient to highlight some of the ethical issues which relate specifically to social psychology. The issues are related to the following:

- *Informed Consent* It is important that any participant in a psychological study should be fully informed as to what the study is about and should have given consent for his or her involvement in it. Menges (1973) looked at 1000 studies in the USA. In 80 per cent of these, participants were given less than complete information about what the study entailed. Epstein and

Lasagna (1969) found that only one-third of participants volunteering for an experiment really understood what it entailed.

If at any stage in the progress of an experiment participants feel they want to withdraw they should be able to do so, without any pressure being exerted on them to continue. In Zimbardo's experiment, mentioned above (also see Chapter 6, Section I), the study was aborted after six days although it had been scheduled to last a fortnight. The increasing realism with which the participants were role-playing prisoners and guards was causing excessive stress.

- *Deception*   Social psychological research is littered with cases where participants have been deceived as to the real purpose of the experiment. There may be occasions when this is inevitable. 'Blind' and 'double-blind' experiments depend upon participants ('blind' experiments) or both participants *and* those administering the tests ('double-blind'), not having full knowledge of what the study is about. Designing experiments in this way is an important strategy to avoid demand characteristics or experimenter effects distorting results. Where the use of single or double-blind techniques is necessary, full debriefing afterwards is essential.

- *Confidentiality*   Research records should be regarded as confidential and not released to the public without the consent of participants. Numbers, initials or pseudonyms should be used to protect the identity of participants when research is reported. There may well be ethical dilemmas created. Psychologists may, in the course of their work, be told of criminal activity or child abuse. They are of course bound by the law of the land, but it is not always clear cut where their responsibilities lie.

- *Competence*   The important thing here is that researchers should work within their own limits of competence. For instance, before using psychometric tests they should have had appropriate training. Advice should always be sought if there is any doubt.

- *Conduct*   Embarrassment, pain and stress should be avoided. Illegal acts should also not be involved. Plagiarism or the creation of fraudulent data is also unacceptable.

From the above factors there are a number of well-known studies in the field of social psychology where deception in particular has been an integral part of the design of the study. We shall single out two studies where deception has been central or where the ethics were dubious.

1. Milgram's Experiments on Obedience

First, Milgram's experiments (Milgram 1963, 1965, 1974) which are described in full in Chapter 6. As regards ethics, Milgram appears to break all the rules. The consent given to take part was certainly not informed consent. Attempts to withdraw were rebuffed and pressure was applied for participants to continue long after they wanted to withdraw, and there was massive deception. As a result of adverse public reaction to the original study and to Milgram's follow-up studies (Milgram, 1965, 1974), he made attempts to justify himself. Pain and distress was caused to participants which Milgram attempted to justify in terms of:

The careful debriefing which followed the study

After the study procedures were undertaken to ensure that the subject would leave the laboratory in a state of well-being. A friendly reconciliation was arranged between the subject and the victim, and effort was made to reduce any tensions that arose as a result of the experiment.   (Milgram, 1963, p. 374)

Interviews were also arranged with psychiatrists. Follow up questionnaires also indicated that no long-term harm had been done.

The care he took to protect the interests of participants and the theoretical and practical advances in knowledge which resulted.

In other words the ends justified the means. Before the study he asked 14 psychology students and no fewer than 40 professors how far they thought participants would obey him and what degree of discomfort it might cause them. Their answers apparently satisfied him. There was no way of knowing beforehand, he claimed, how far participants would go or what degree of stress or discomfort might be caused. However, ignorance is not really a defence.

As regards confidentiality, too, there was some problem. Milgram's research was videotaped and the videos released not only in the USA but in the UK as well. There remains the question of whether all the participants gave their consent for this.

Baumrind (1964) has been a vociferous critic of Milgram's experiments. His criticisms include the following:

- That Milgram did not do enough to protect his participants from harm.
- That the procedures participants were subjected to were found by some of them to be extremely stressful; that is, they were compelled to inflict pain on someone else.
- That they were not given the chance to withdraw when they clearly wanted to; he actively prodded them to go on.
- That he found it necessary to deceive them.

2. Sherif's 'Robber's Cave' Study

This second example (Sherif *et al.*, 1961; Sherif, 1966), which is described in full in Chapter 4, involved manipulating the group feelings of adolescent boys attending a summer camp in Oklahoma. The issues raised are somewhat different:

- There are ethical issues which arise from the very fact that questionable attitudes were deliberately induced in the children.
- There was certainly a problem of informed consent. Where children are concerned parents should have been fully informed of the true purposes of the study before the experiment took place. It seems unlikely that a cross-section of middle-class parents would have given their consent to prejudice deliberately being induced in their children.
- The children had no inkling as to what the whole thing was about. They were manipulated.
- There is no evidence that any of these children could have withdrawn from the experiment at any time during it.
- There is no doubt at all that pain and stress was caused at various stages in the experiment.

The experiment was justified by the experimenters in that a great deal of insight was gained into the way in which intergroup tensions arise, and that it all ended happily. There did not appear to have been any permanent damage done. However, there clearly were risks which it is hard to justify.

Summary

Ethical experimentation in social psychology rests upon several fairly simple principles, including:

- *Informed consent* – all participants or their parents (or perhaps those in *loco parentis*) should be fully informed of all the issues involved before a request is made for consent to take part.
- *Freedom to withdraw* – all participants must be free to withdraw, and no pressure must be placed on them to continue once they want to withdraw.
- *Deception and withholding of information* – deliberate deception or deliberately withholding information is unethical unless it can be demonstrated that there are exceptionally good reasons and that no more ethical method can be found. Advice should first be sought from colleagues.
- *Debriefing* – There should be full debriefing after the study in all cases.
- *Pain and stress* – it is not ethical to cause pain and stress even when the outcomes seem to justify it.
- *Confidentiality* – all participants are entitled to their privacy and there should be strict rules of confidentiality, particularly when the results are reported.
- *Competence* – researchers should be fully aware of what they can and cannot do and should work within their own competence. This particularly concerns psychometric testing.
- *Conduct* – there are rules of professional conduct which should be observed, including causing pain and stress, creating fraudulent data, plagiarism and the like.

Self-assessment Questions

1. What is meant by informed consent? How do Milgram's and Sherif's studies appear to breach the ethical rule of informed consent?
2. In what circumstances do you think deception or the giving of less than full information can be justified?
3. What steps should researchers take to ensure that they always work within their own competence?

FURTHER READING

J. R. Eiser, *Social Psychology: Attitudes, Cognition and Social Behaviour* (Cambridge: Cambridge University Press, 1986).

K. Deaux, F. C. Dane and L. S. Wrightsman, *Social Psychology in the 90s*, (6th edn) (Pacific Grove, Cal.: Brookes Cole, 1993).

British Psychological Society (1991) 'Code of conduct, ethical principles and guidelines', *The Psychologist*, 3, pp. 269–72.

Association for Teaching Psychology, *Psychology Teaching, New Series, No 1, Ethics* (Leicester: British Psychological Society).

"THEY'RE PERFECTLY HARMLESS — I'VE LOCKED THE HOUSE AND THE GARAGE, AND NOTIFIED THE LOCAL POLICE."

Self and Others   2

At the end of this chapter you will be able to:

1. Describe how people store information about themselves and about others as schemata.
2. Outline the self-perception theories put forward by Bem, Weiner and others.
3. Identify what is meant by the **attribution process** in the judgement of a person's character.
4. Describe models of the attribution process as they apply both to a person's perception of 'self' and of others.
5. Describe some of the influences of **social cognition** in how we perceive ourselves and others.
6. Identify some of the factors which may cause us to be attracted to another person.
7. Describe some of the theories put forward to explain attraction to others, including **social exchange theory, interdependence theory** and **reinforcement/affect theory.**
7. Identify some of the factors involved with the growth of **prejudice**.
8. Describe some other attempts which have been made to explain prejudice, including the **frustration–aggressson hypothesis, authoritarian personality** and **belief-congruence theory.**

SECTION I   THE PERCEPTION OF OTHERS

In this section we shall review the social cognitive approach to the way in which we appraise other people, including the use of schemata, scripts and prototypes. Then we shall discuss the attribution process as it relates to person perception. There is a full account in Chapter 1 of social cognition and it may be useful to refer back to it.

Social Schemata

It is necessary for us to be able quickly to make sense of persons, events, situations or places which we meet in our lives. The building up of schemata fulfils this need. Effectually, we are making a cognitive plan of whatever or whoever it is we meet to represent our knowledge of it. This plan will include the characteristics we are aware of and the interrelationships between these characteristics. This forms a schema, stored in memory and activated by a particular cue.

Let us put flesh on some of these rather nebulous ideas. We meet and get to know someone. Characteristics of that individual register in our memory; for instance, that he or she is very intelligent, fond of reading serious books, but at the same time is something of an adventurer who likes to go to wild and sometimes dangerous places to walk and to climb. At the same time, he or she is politically quite aware and has a very active social conscience. All these traits and pieces of information are stored away and form a schema. Every time you meet this person the schema of old information is activated by some cue (perhaps the recognition of his or her face) and new information is added. Then gaps are filled in by means of prior knowledge or preconceptions, both about this particular individual or those you have met with similar characteristics. This pattern fits all the different kinds of schemata, the most common of which include:

- *Person schemata*   This is what has been mentioned above. These amount to impressions formed of either a particular person we have personal knowledge of, a friend, a neighbour or a work-mate, or someone well-known to us of whom we may not have personal acquaintance, a politician, perhaps, or a television personality.
- *Role schemata*   These structure the knowledge we have about the occupants of particular roles. Teachers, for example, have been categorised in our minds as having certain defined characteristics. This pattern of characteristics is formed from experiences we may have had of teachers, either first-hand or via information from someone else. Some cue will trigger this teacher schema (perhaps meeting someone carrying a pile of books), and inferences are made about the way in which this particular teacher will behave. Gaps in this pattern of knowledge

are continually being filled through direct experience. The schema of 'teacher' is thus modified in the light of what we know.

- *Scripts* These are schemata about events. We might perhaps have developed a schema relating to going to a restaurant for dinner which might involve waiting for a waiter to seat us at a table, being presented with a menu and so on. This schema has developed as result of our stored experience of restaurants and what happens in them. The fact that we know what is going to happen when we go to a restaurant makes it much easier for us to cope. In situations where these established scripts do not exist there can easily be disorientation or frustration. We might, for instance, have been invited to a royal garden party at Buckingham Palace. We have no script for such an event so that it is difficult for us to cope. If, however, we were the Queen, a royal garden-party script would be well-developed through long experience.

Impression Formation

Social psychologists have a long history of attempts to make sense of the impressions we form of those we meet. When we meet someone for the first time **physical appearance** is probably the first source of information we have about that person. Gender and race are immediately evident. It may not even be necessary to get a good look at someone to determine gender. Berry (1990) has suggested that the way in which people walk or the way in which they move their faces and heads while talking enables us to decide whether they are male or female. Then we notice other physical features, such as height, weight, or facial expression. These initial pieces of information about race or gender or about outward physical appearance enable us to categorise a person as belonging to a particular kind of schema. For any category of people, from very broad categories like male or female, young or old, black or white, or narrower categories such as teacher or doctor, perhaps a set of characteristics comes to mind.

Prototypes

These characteristics represent a **prototype,** a fairly fuzzy and ill-defined set of images we have of people belonging to a particular category. Though usually the prototype represents the average member of a category of people, Chaplin *et al.* (1988) have said that there are occasions where the prototype is the ideal or perhaps an extreme member of a category. An individual who is concerned deeply about animals might form a prototype of a vivisectionist as a person who derives satisfaction or even pleasure from inflicting pain on animals. The prototype is what immediately comes into our mind when we think of a category of people. Particular instances we meet will not fit our prototype exactly, because that prototype of some category of people or other is something we have constructed in our minds, but all instances are more or less prototypical.

Finally, there will be considerable similarity between the prototypes formed about a particular category of people by members of a particular social group. For instance, the prototypes formed of 'teacher' by a group of school children are likely to be very similar.

Exemplars

There is a suggestion that as people become more familiar with a particular category of people they tend to alter their mental representation of the category from the fairly fuzzy prototypical representation towards a more clear-cut representation of the group in terms of **exemplars** (specific instances of the category which they have met). Brewer (1988) takes this view, while Judd and Park (1988) suggest that as far as **in-groups** are concerned, that is to say members of a group of which the observer is a member, mental representation is in terms both of prototypes and exemplars fairly indiscriminately, whereas **out-groups** (groups of which the observer is not a member) use only exemplars.

There is a great deal in common between schemata, prototypes and exemplars. They are all part of the network of mental representations of the world based upon memory and experience which enables us to respond quickly and easily to people and events which we meet.

Social Stereotypes

Prototypes and exemplars are essentially personal. Each individual's network of social cognition is different from that of each other individual and is firmly based in the experience of that individual. There are cases, however, where the prototypes established by individuals are widely shared. In these cases it can be said that there is a **social stereotype**. The term originates from Lippman (1922) who described stereotypes as 'pictures in our heads'. This seems not unlike the schemata which we have been discussing with this distinction. Whereas schemata tend to be neutral, stereotypes often seem to have a pejorative connotation. Lippman saw stereotypes as a means whereby people protect their relative standing in society. In a white-dominated society, for instance, white people may use negative stereotypes of black people to justify their dominance. However, it would not be correct to say that all stereotypes are negative. A stereotype will reflect the whole range of our information about a particular group of people. This information is likely to be positive and neutral as well as negative. Deaux and Lewis (1983) studied stereotypes of men and women. Commonly men were stereotyped as being independent and competitive; women warm and emotional. Whether these characteristics are regarded as positive, negative or neutral reflects the attitudes of the individuals who are making the judgment.

Formation of Stereotypes

Stereotypes are easily developed and can be pervasive in their effects. Hill *et al.* (1989) found that they were able create stereotypes in a very short time. A description of their study is given in Box 2.1.

Quite often stereotyping embraces national characteristics. Linssen and Hagendoorn (1994) studied European students' stereotypes of northern and southern European nations. Participants in this study were 277 16–18-year-old students in Denmark, England, the Netherlands, Germany, France and Italy. A questionnaire was administered to participants by means of which 22 characteristics were identified which clustered into four general dimensions:

1. Dominant – proud, assertive, aggressive.
2. Empathic – helpful, friendly.
3. Efficient – industrious, scientific, rich.
4. Emotional – enjoying life, religious.

Participants were asked to indicate the proportions of each national group who possessed each of these characteristics. Results showed a polarisation between northern and southern nations. The northern

32   *Social Psychology*

BOX 2.1
Formation of Stereotypes. A Study by Hill *et al.*, 1989

Participants in their study were shown six videotaped episodes, each less than two minutes long. A voice-over indicated that the person speaking had a personal problem related to the episode, but none of the participants knew the nature of the problem. Half the participants were shown episodes where it was always a man who had the problem; the other half were shown episodes where the person with the problem was a woman. Two weeks before they saw the episodes and again two weeks after the viewing, participants were asked to rate on various traits including 'sadness'. such people as their boy or girl friends or other men and women they knew well.

Results, illustrated in Figure 2.1, showed that before the viewing participants did not feel that the men and women they rated differed in 'sadness'. After they had seen the videotaped episodes, however, there was an apparent difference. Those who had seen episodes where there was a male voice-over which seemed to be sad, rated males they knew as sadder; those who had seen episodes where there was a female voice-over which seemed to indicate sadness, rated the females they knew as sadder. Participants were interviewed afterwards and indicated that they had not even realised that it was men or women who had more problems in the episodes they watched. In spite of this, the viewing of manipulated gender differences between people who were quite unknown to them, had altered their judgements about people they knew well.

nations were characterised as being more efficient; the southern ones as being more emotional.

Hogg and Vaughan (1995) have identified a number of clear findings which result from research into stereotyping going back several decades. These are as follows:

- People show an easy readiness to characterise vast human groups in terms of a few crude common attributes.
- Stereotypes are very slow to change.
- Stereotype change is generally in response to wider social, political or economic changes.
- Stereotypes are acquired at a very young age, often before the child has any knowledge about the groups which are being stereotyped.

FIGURE 2.1
Creation of Stereotypes

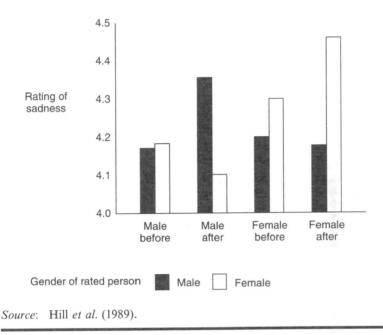

Source: Hill *et al.* (1989).

- Stereotypes become more pronounced and hostile when social tensions and conflict arise between groups, and then they are extremely difficult to modify.
- Stereotypes are not necessarily inaccurate or wrong; rather they serve to make sense of particular inter-group relations.

Implicit Personality Theories

As a result of socialisation during childhood as well as through experiences later, each of us arrives at his or her own **implicit personality theory**. This comprises a set of unstated assumptions about what personality traits will tend to go together. Frequently these implicit personality theories are extended to include beliefs about what sorts of behaviour goes with particular personality traits. It is important to note that these theories are rarely made explicit, or stated in formal terms; quite frequently we are not consciously aware of them at all. In spite of this they dominate the way in which we make judgements about other people. Rosenberg and Sedlak (1972) found that college students, when they described people they knew used only a limited number of terms – intelligent, lazy, self-centred, ambitious and friendly. However, they were unlikely to use all these terms to describe the same person. 'Intelligent' frequently went with 'friendly'; rarely with 'self-centred'. So that individuals have an implicit personality theory where intelligence goes with friendliness, but not with self-centredness.

Rosenberg and Jones (1972) used archival methods (see Chapter 1) in an analysis of *A Gallery of Women* by Theodore Dreiser (1929), a collection of sketches of 15 women. In their analysis, the investigators tabulated all the trait descriptions which Dreiser used in his sketches. By means of statistical analysis they arrived at three basic dimensions of personality used by Dreiser – hard/soft, male/female and conforms/does not conform. Hardness was found to go together with maleness (though they were not identical traits), but maleness/femaleness were not closely associated to conformity/non-conformity.

Implicit Social Theories

In much the same way as we have developed implicit personality theories or constructs about the people we meet, so we develop **implicit social theories** which inform our behaviour. Typically, implicit social theories embrace cause and effect relationships, explanations as to why events happen. For instance, a social theory might embrace the relationship between lack of discipline in schools and the rise in crime; or, alternatively, unemployment and the rise in delinquency. This has been investigated by Anderson and Sechler 1986). These implicit theories are different in at least two ways from more formal social theories developed by social psychologists:

1. They are unstated and so are not subjected to public scrutiny in the way in which formal theories are.
2. While formal theories are based firmly in logic and tested in research, implicit social theories are based upon casual observation. They are essentially personal and idiosyncratic.

When we only have a limited amount of information to go on we tend to fill in the gaps to make people and events more comprehensible. Anderson and Sechler found that when presented with two random events and asked to imagine a link between them, people more often than not found a relationship. Both implicit personality and implicit social theory help individuals to make sense of what is otherwise a chaotic world.

Personal Construct Theory

Kelly (1955) devised yet another approach which has some similarities to implicit personality theory. He suggested that individuals construct a cognitive theory which mediates the way in which they see the world (and this, of course includes other people). **Personal constructs**, as he termed them represent each individual's guide to interpreting the world. Kelly's view was that we are all scientists, struggling to understand and predict events. To this end we build up constructs (sets of assumptions which form the basis for our view of the world). What motivates us primarily is validation of our construct systems. We need proof that the way in which we view the world is the right one.

Kelly rejected the possibility that there might be some absolute or objective truth in favour of a phenomenolgical approach. This suggests that the world does not have any meaning outside our own perception of it. Constructs he thought of as having bipolar dimensions. For instance, an individual might have developed a construct of *disciplined* as an expression of personality; the opposite pole to this might be *scatterbrained*. Impressions formed of other people would use this dimension (amongst others). When we meet people they are categorised according to where they seem to be on this dimension. The effect is to impose some kind of framework on what otherwise might be chaotic impressions formed of other people. But it is an idiosyncratic order; no one person's constructs are likely in total to be the same as any other person's. Moreover, it is not just impressions of other people, but every facet of life which is affected by our construct system.

Let us take as an example. We are in the market to buy a car. Within our construct system we have established certain constructs about cars, which might for instance have the following bipolar dimensions:

fast–slow
cheap to run–costing a lot to run
keeping its re-sale value–depreciating quickly

These are the terms in which we see the cars we are in the market to buy, ignoring, perhaps, someone else's constructs which might include:

providing a smooth ride–giving a harsher ride
having soft seating–having firm seating
resistant to corrosion–prone to rust

Kelly developed a way in which personal constructs might be uncovered and this has been extensively used in a wide variety of fields. This was known as the Repertory Grid Technique. A fairly large number of the people, events or objects under investigation are assembled and arranged in threes. Participants are asked in what way two of the three are the same and the third one different. From the responses, constructs (the ways in which two are the same) and opposites emerge. Taken together they provide a picture of the participant's personal construct system as it relates to what is under investigation. There is a full discussion of Kelly's theory in Birch and Hayward (1994) *Individual Differences* in this series.

Self-assessment Questions

1. What are meant by social schemata? In what way do the social schemata we have developed affect the impressions we form of people?
2. What is a script? Describe some of the ways in which scripts serve to facilitate our interactions with other people.
3. How are social stereotypes formed? How does stereotyping influence the perceptions we have of others?
4. Describe the basis for personal construct theory. What practical means have been developed to uncover an individual's personal constructs?

SECTION II   ATTRIBUTION

This section deals with the ways in which we draw inferences about people we meet from the behaviour we observe. Human beings operate as scientists, trying continually to find explanations for observed phenomena. This enables us to attempt to predict the behaviour of people and maybe exert some influence over it. In this way we are more in control of our lives and less prone to be blown randomly this way and that. To find causes for things is quite a powerful tool in our attempts to control events. If a tower block collapses it is immensely valuable to find out the cause of that collapse if we are to stop it happening again. Much the same applies to human behaviour. If we understand why people behave in the way they do, it might be possible to predict and control behaviour. This is what lies at the root of **attribution processes**.

Heider (1958) believed that left to themselves most people attempt to construct their own theories about the causes of human behaviour. The following principles lie behind Heider's ideas:

- Human behaviour is motivated. If we can discover their motives we can predict how people are likely to behave.
- The search for causes for things pervades most human thought. In an experiment Heider and Simmel (1944) asked participants to describe the movements of abstract geometric figures. The researchers found that they did this as though the figures were humans with intentions to act in particular ways.
- We are trying all the time to predict and control elements in the environment which may impinge on us. Because of this we look for causes which are stable and enduring; personality characteristics in people which are consistent in many situations; stable environmental circumstances.
- When we attempt to explain why people behave as they do, we distinguish between internal and external causes. Internal causes include such things as individuals' personality characteristics or abilities; external causes include social pressures or environmental circumstances. An individual is caught shoplifting. Internal causes might include the suggestion that he or she is dishonest or not very bright. External causes might be that he or she is out of work, has lost his or her home through repossession.

Correspondent Inference Theory

Jones and Davis (1965) and Jones and McGillis (1976) claimed that individuals make **correspondent inferences**. That is to say, the assumption is made that the behaviour we are witnessing is the result of a corresponding dispositional trait. The brusque behaviour of someone we meet is explained by inferring that the individual concerned is naturally grumpy or irritable. Irritability is a stable trait which enables us to explain his or her behaviour and allows us to predict how that individual will behave next time we meet him or her. In this way we are able to control our world better.

To make a correspondent inference about someone's behaviour, Jones and Davis suggest that people need to take account of the following:

- How *freely chosen* is the behaviour? Clearly, if there are external constraints upon behaviour (threats or inducements for instance) it is less easy to infer that the behaviour is due to some dispositional cause.

- Does the behaviour observed have *non-common* effects? These effects have been defined as those which could only be achieved by behaving in this particular way In other words, does the observed behaviour have effects in common with other behaviour? If that is the case, then it is going to tell us less about the *disposition* of the individual than would be the case if there were few behaviours which might produce the same effect. Take an example. It is John's girl-friend's birthday. There is a variety of things he could do, send her a bunch of flowers, take her out to dinner, arrange a surprise party and so on. But he met her at a performance of *Carmen* and knows that is special to her. So he takes her to the opera to see *Carmen*. It is behaviour on his part which demonstrates his love for her in a way in which none of the other possibilities could. It has the fewest non-common effects.

- How *socially desirable* is the behaviour? If it is socially desirable it may be social roles (that is, what society demands of us in the particular role we are playing) which produce it rather than our disposition. Correspondent inference is more easily made if the behaviour observed is 'out of role'. Edward comes to a funeral dressed in a flowery shirt, shorts and sandals. He is behaving out of role and that fact will tell observers more about his disposition than if he arrives in a dark suit. Edward's role as 'mourner' carries certain social expectations and obligations (see Chapter 1). This includes dressing soberly. Jones *et al.* (1961) found that where people behaved 'out of role' (in a way which did not fit with what was expected), more inferences were made about their disposition than when they conformed.

- Correspondent inferences are more likely to be made about behaviour which has *hedonic relevance*. How does the behaviour which we are observing affect us? It has hedonic relevance if it involves rewards or costs for the observer. An extension of this may be referred to as *personalism*; that is, where the *intention* of the person performing the action we observe is to help or to harm us.

One difficulty with this theory is that a great deal hinges upon intention. Yet an equally strong source of correspondent inference is unintentional behaviour. A person could easily be characterised as slapdash as a result of acting in a careless manner. It is unlikely that he or she would *intentionally* behave in a careless or slapdash manner. Nisbett and Ross (1980) and Ross (1977) have highlighted a problem with the issue of non-common effects. People simply do not pay regard to behaviour which is not observed; that is, all those other ways in which an individual *might* have behaved. The issue of whether there might be other behaviours which would produce the same effect simply does not arise.

Kelley's Co-variation Model

This is probably the best known model of attribution. Kelley (1967, 1973) maintained that people use the principle of co-variance to decide whether to attribute behaviour they observe to internal (dispositional) causes or external (environmental) causes. Kelley refers to the 'actor' as the individual who is behaving in a particular way and the 'observer' as the individual who is affected by this behaviour, who observes it happening. When a particular action and a cause are seen to co-vary (or occur together) repeatedly in the case of a specific person, conclusions tend to be drawn about that person. For instance, whenever there is a party Charlie is found sitting in a corner drinking by himself. There is co-occurence of action (sitting alone, drinking in a corner), a specific person (Charlie), and a possible cause (extreme shyness). Attributions which are made by an observer depend upon three factors:

1. **Consistency** Does Charlie always go off into a corner at parties or only at this particular one? If there is high consistency (it

happens every time or at least most times), the observer will tend to attribute this behaviour to Charlie's disposition (shyness). If there is low consistency (it is only at this party that Charlie behaved like this) the potential cause (shyness) will tend to be discounted and the observer will look for some other cause.

2. **Distinctiveness**   Is it just at parties that Charlie behaves in a shy manner (high distinctiveness), or does he display the same kind of behaviour in all kinds of environments (low distinctiveness)? In the former case the observer will tend to discount shyness and look for another cause.

3. **Consensus**   Does everyone behave like this or is it just Charlie? There might be a strange party, perhaps, where everyone goes off by themselves, but if that did occur there would be high consensus. If it were just Charlie it would be low consensus.

Figure 2.2 shows the co-variation model of Kelley

FIGURE 2.2
Kelley's Co-variation Model

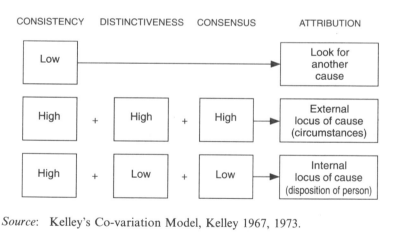

Source: Kelley's Co-variation Model, Kelley 1967, 1973.

Discounting or Augmentation of Cause

In general terms, behaviour is likely (in Kelley's model) to be attributed to Charlie's disposition where the following apply:

- Consistency is high;
- Consensus is low;
- Distinctiveness is low.

Kelley's model also allows for what he terms the **augmentation principle**. The way he expresses this is as follows:

> When there are known to be constraints, costs, sacrifices or risks involved in taking an action, the action is attributed more to the actor than it would be otherwise.   (Kelley, 1973, p. 114)

What this means is that where the action observed has costs involved for the actor, an observer would be more likely to attribute it to the disposition of the actor than to some environmental circumstance. Let us consider an example of how this might work. There is a strict embargo in the office against any one of the secretarial staff releasing details in advance of proposed redundancies, on pain of dismissal. Mary knows that James' wife is expecting her first baby and they have just bought a new house. The list for redundancies is going before the board the next day and James' name is on it. In spite of the extreme risk involved, Mary leaves James' name off the list the Chief Executive Officer (CEO) has drawn up in the hope that it will not be noticed, and James' will get a reprieve. Because of the risk involved to herself, an observer would be much more likely to attribute this to Mary's sympathy for James than to any other cause.

The opposite effect is termed **discounting** which results in one possible cause being reduced in importance by other plausible causes. Suppose there are several possible causes for an action which is observed. Mary might have been very tired at the end of a long day and have left James' name off the list inadvertently. Two of the names the CEO gave Mary might have been very similar and James' name might have been left off because Mary could not read the CEO's writing. The CEO might have confused the issue. He might have listed James Sturt rather than James Stewart when there was a John Sturt working for the firm. This situation represents what Kelley terms a **multiple sufficient cause schema**. A number of factors are there in the observer's mind, any of which might be sufficient to be the cause of James' name being left off the list. Which cause we select depends upon the information we have available. Mary might have expressed concern at James' possible inclusion. The CEO might have made a habit of getting names wrong and getting very cross when mistakes are pointed out to him. Mary's expression of concern might cause the observer to **discount** the CEO's mistake or Mary's tiredness.

Causal Schemata

In common with other schemata, mentioned earlier, **causal schemata** are mental representations built up as a result of experience and stored memories. In this case, to use Kelley's words,

> a causal schema is a conception of the manner in which two or more causal factors interact in relation to a particular kind of effect.
> (Kelley, 1973, p. 152)

In the course of our observations of people we have developed certain beliefs about causes and effects. These beliefs then form the basis for our explanation of a particular person's behaviour.

As well as the multiple *sufficient* cause schema, mentioned above, we might have a **multiple *necessary* causal schema** which could be applied. More than one cause might be necessary to explain the event. A combination of the CEO's confusion of names and Mary's tiredness at the end of the day, perhaps.

Bias in Attribution

There is evidence that attribution is biased towards dispositional explanations of behaviour. Unless there is some situational cause staring us in the face, we tend to attribute observed behaviour to some internal characteristic of the individual observed. Jones and Harris (1967) showed that even where students had been clearly told that the author of a particular essay had been assigned to take a particular political viewpoint, they made inferences about the author's political attitudes from the content of the essay. Fiske and Taylor (1984) have called this pervasive tendency to explain behaviour in terms of disposition, **fundamental attribution bias**. Gilbert (1989) has claimed that it is automatic for us to attribute behaviour to disposition and we cannot avoid doing it. All we are able to do is to amend it once we have made the attribution. Miller and Lawson (1989) go so far as to maintain that fundamental attribution bias can only be overcome when additional, objective, information convinces us that the disposition of the actor could not possibly be the cause of the action. People in Western society have a very strong sense of personal responsibility, according to Jellison and Green (1981); people have to be held accountable for their actions so that internal attributions of cause are much more highly valued than external ones.

Cross-cultural Evidence for Attributional Bias

While American children were found by Miller (1984) to place increasing reliance upon disposition as an explanation of events they observed, as they grew older the Hindu children of India by contrast based their attributions more on situations. This suggests that the fundamental attribution bias may not be universal.

Actor/Observer Effect

Another explanation of the fundamental attribution bias is that it depends upon whose perspective it is taken from. While Jones and Nisbett (1972) confirmed that as far as the *observer* was concerned dispositions play a much more central role in explanations of behaviour than situational factors, *actors* place more emphasis upon the situation. This has become known as the **actor–observer effect**. Storms (1973) conducted an experiment which provided strong confirmation that this was in fact the case. Pairs of participants (the actors) were asked to converse while another pair of participants (the observers) watched on closed-circuit television. The actors were found to place greater emphasis upon the situation when the conversations were rated, while the observers placed more emphasis upon disposition. There was an apparent actor–observer effect. Then, when Storms showed the actors a videotape of their conversation (in other words turning them into observers of their own conversation) greater emphasis was placed upon disposition. Subsequent investigations as to why this should happen have concentrated upon self-focus. Gibbons (1990) reviewed this research. What seemed to happen was this: in normal circumstances we tend to pay more attention to the situation than to ourselves. However, when we are watching ourselves on videotape we tend to focus more on ourselves. The interpretations of behaviour we then make are those which best confirm our self-concept. So long as the behaviour observed is consistent with the way in which we see ourselves, we are likely to attribute it to dispositional rather than situational causes. But if we observe ourselves acting in a way which is inconsistent with our concept of ourselves, then the situation becomes more important when we come to attribute cause

False Consensus

As we have seen, alongside information about consistency and distinctiveness 'consensus' information helps us to attribute cause to the behaviour we observe in people. Ross *et al.* (1977) has demonstrated that we do sometimes create our own consensus effect. We regard our own behaviour as typical. Given the same set of circumstances, we assume anyone else would behave in the same way! Ross demonstrated this **false consensus effect** experimentally. Students were asked to walk around their campus for 30 minutes wearing a sandwich board proclaiming 'Eat at Joe's'. Those who agreed to do so estimated that 62 per cent of their peers would also have agreed. Those who refused estimated that 67 per cent of their peers would also have refused. Why does this happen? Marks and Miller (1988) have suggested several possibilities:

1. Consensus is artificially inflated by the habit people have of associating with other people who have similar views. In one group of people, the consensus might be that it is lax discipline in schools which is the root cause of the upsurge in crime. Because they tend to meet only people with similar views they assume that everyone thinks the same. There is consensus. Among a different group, the rise in crime is thought to be due to unemployment. Again there is consensus because they tend not to associate with people who think differently.
2. Another possible explanation is that our own views are so salient as to displace any consideration of alternatives.
3. Yet a third possibility is that exaggerating the consensus behind our own views justifies us in maintaining they are correct.

In this way we manage to maintain a stable perception of reality – at least of reality as we see it! Factors which research has thrown up which appear to influence false consensus include:

- How important beliefs are to us and how certain we are about them (Granberg, 1987);

- External threat;
- Status as a member of a minority group;
- Cause and affect – we get what we deserve.

Another source of bias lies in the rooted belief that the world is essentially a just place. This is the **just world hypothesis**. Lerner (1966) put it like this:

> There is an appropriate fit between what people do and what happens to them. (p. 3)

When we see apparent injustice happening, that is something which threatens our belief in a just world, we make attempts to put the situation right. This may involve one or more of several expedients:

- We may compensate the victims; raising money to alleviate suffering – Band Aid for instance.
- We may attempt to mete out justice to those who are to blame; trying to ensure that someone is convicted of the Lockerbie bombing, for instance.
- We may try to convince ourselves that no injustice has in fact occurred. A girl is attacked and raped late at night in a sleazy part of town. 'Why was she out at night in that neighbourhood alone? It was just asking for trouble.' There was no injustice; she only had herself to blame!

We make attributions of cause to support our belief that we live in a fundamentally just world. There must be a logical explanation for injustice occurring. Symonds (1975) has interviewed hundreds of rape, assault and kidnapping victims. Many received not help and sympathy but censure from friends, family and the police.

Some Applications and Extensions of Attribution Theory

Cognition and Emotion

In an experiment which has now become very well-known, Schachter and Singer (1962) demonstrated that there were two separate components in emotion:

1. The arousal which produces such effects as an increased heart rate, changes in breathing patterns and in the distribution of the

blood, and similar physiological effects. These have been well described elsewhere (for example, Hayward, 1996, *Biopsychology*).

2. The cognitive component which allows us to interpret the physiological changes we are experiencing as feelings of fear, anger or other emotions.

Box 2.2 shows the details of Schachter and Singer's experiment.

BOX 2.2
Attribution of Emotion. An Experiment by Schachter and Singer (1962)

Schachter and Singer injected some student participants with epinephrine (adrenalin) which had the effect of inducing physiological arousal. Others were injected with a placebo (a saline solution which had no physiological effect and so acted as a control. Different groups of participants were given different information about what they would experience as a result of the injections they had been given. For one group, the effects of an adrenalin injection were accurately described (though they were not told it was adrenalin, but a drug called suproxin which was supposed to improve their visual acuity). For a second group the information given was that they would experience numbness and itchiness. A third group were given no information as to what they would feel. The fourth group (which had the placebo injection) were also given no information. A confederate then attempted to produce feelings of euphoria in some of the participants and anger in others as they waited in an ante-room. The misinformed group experienced the strongest emotional feelings. The informed group searching for an explanation for their physiological state attributed it to the injection they had had. The misinformed group and the uninformed group had no such explanation and so attributed their bodily changes to strong emotion (anger or euphoria). In the absence of a situational cause, a dispositional cause came to the fore.

Schachter and Singer's work led Valins (1966) to test what was termed the **misattribution paradigm**. Where we experience physiological arousal which does not *particularly* indicate a cause, we will search for a cause to attribute to it. Valins saw therapeutic implications in this. For instance, if someone feels depressed for no apparent reason, then by supplying a plausible cause for the feelings experienced we can alleviate them by a process of reattribution.

However, Valins' initial hopes have not been fully realised. There are two reasons for this:

1. Maslach (1979) has shown that it is not as easy as was thought to manipulate emotional feelings. Unexplained arousal is not easily explained by superimposing environmental cues. Because it not pleasant to feel emotionally aroused, there is a strong tendency to attribute negative causes for it.
2. The misattribution effect which Schachter and Singer and Valins noted seems to be confined to the laboratory and it was in any case short lived.

Self-assessment Questions

1. Outline two models of the attribution process.
2. List some of the sources of error in causal attribution.
3. What is meant by 'fundamental attribution error'?

SECTION III SELF-CONCEPT

The way an individual perceives him or herself is immensely important. The information we store about self represents our **self-concept**. We have already come across self-schemata in Chapter 1 where it was used to illustrate the social cognitive approach to social psychology. It has been applied to the way in which self-concepts are built up.

Schemata and 'self'

In much the same way that schemata influence the way in which we perceive and react to social events, established schemata relate also to our perceptions of ourselves. Markus (1977) has referred to **self-schemata**. Networks of knowledge about ourselves are built up and come together to form the **self-concept**. Markus distinguishes between people who are **schematic** in relation to certain attributes of themselves, and those who are **aschematic**. Schematic individuals are intensely concerned with a particular aspect of themselves and have therefore built up very well formed schemata in relation to these aspects. Markus *et al.* (1982) have applied this to masculinity and femininity. They classified individuals as:

1. *Schematic*   Those whose self concept was stereotypically masculine (masculine schematics) or stereotypically feminine (feminine schematics). These were people for whom being masculine or feminine assumed an overwhelming importance in the way which they perceived themselves.
2. *Androgynous*   Those with a strong set of schemata relating to masculinity or femininity, but whose self-schemata included a combination of masculine and feminine attributes.
3. *Aschematic*   Those without a strong set of schemata relating to masculinity or femininity; those who were effectively neutral.

Self-schemata as a Context-specific Network

Breckler *et al.* (1991) have portrayed these self-schemata as a net composed of nodes which are context-specific. In some contexts of their lives people have developed very clear concepts of themselves; in other contexts their self-concepts are nothing like as clear. To put this in terms of schemata, they are aschematic in some contexts of their lives; schematic in others. It all depends upon what is important to an individual; that is, his or her own value system. Some people, for instance, set great store on sporting prowess and on sporting interest. Sport occupies a prominent place in their value system. It is likely that they would be schematic in that area of their lives; they would have developed a very clear concept of themselves within the context of sport as a result of their life experiences. These same individuals might very well find that the appreciation of fine art was much less important to them. They would be likely to be self-aschematic within this context; no very clear view of themselves would have developed.

Most individuals' self-concept is complex. There are a relatively large number of self-schemata. Linville (1987) has suggested that this fact is beneficial in that it provides a buffer to limit damage to a person's self-concept resulting from negative life events. If a person's self-esteem takes a knock in one area of their life (for example being thrown out of the football team in which they were playing), this is much less damaging if there are a large number of other areas in their life which are important to them. An individual whose whole life seemed to revolve around playing football (a person with a very limited number of self-schemata) would find it much more damaging.

Self-schemata and Aspiration

It is just as important that self-schemata indicate what we aspire to as what we are at the present time. Higgins (1987) has suggested that we have three types of self-schemata:

1. Actual self – that is, how we currently see ourselves to be;
2. Ideal self – how we would like to be;
3. Ought self – how we think we should be.

Where there are discrepancies between these sets of self-schemata, motivation to change may come to reduce the discrepancy. If efforts are made to reduce the gap which are not successful, then emotional difficulties may arise. Failure to resolve the gap between the actual and the ideal could result in disappointment, dissatisfaction or sadness. Failure to close the actual/ought gap results in emotions such as fear, anxiety or anger.

A Humanistic View of Self

This is not dissimilar to the view of self-concept taken by Rogers (1951, 1961). In his view a person's self-concept arose from his or her interactions with other people which resulted in internalised **conditions of worth**. It was necessary for psychological health for people to receive **unconditional positive regard** from others. Where this unconditional positive regard was there, the ideal self and the actual self were not too far apart. On the other hand, where this unconditional positive regard was not forthcoming, the fear was always present that their behaviour might not receive approbation from others and their self-development was impaired. The conditions of worth which they internalised were reflections resulting from other people's reactions to them. To put this into simpler terms, they were always 'looking over their shoulders' at what others were thinking of them, rather than being secure in their knowledge of their own self-worth. They had very low self-esteem. Rogers' solution was **client-centred therapy**. This non-directive therapy allowed clients to explore themselves without any sense that the therapist was directing them to think or behave in a particular way.

Self and Attribution

Attribution theory, which was more fully described in the previous section, refers to the way in we observe the behaviour of those with whom we come into contact, and from our observations make inferences about what they are like. For instance, we might characterise an individual as 'mean' on the basis of his or her reluctance to contribute a full share of the cost of an outing. The behaviour we have observed is said to have an **internal locus of cause**. It results (we surmise) from a character trait. Bem (1967, 1972) has suggested that this attribution process might equally be applied to the judgements we make about ourselves. This **self-perception theory** proposes that there is no essential differences between judgements arising from *self-attribution*, and the attributions of character we make of others. We are aware of what we do and as a result of that awareness we make judgements about the kind of people we are. For instance, we go jogging every morning and quite frequently find ourselves in the gym having a 'work-out'. It is quite possible that someone whose opinion we care about has remarked that we are getting fat. In that case, the self-perception theory does not apply. But in the absence of any such **external locus of cause** we would infer that it is a facet of our character to like to keep ourselves in trim.

Self-attribution and Motivation

Bem's theory has quite strong implications for motivation. We can either do something because there is an external pressure exerted on us to do it, or because we enjoy it and are committed to it. There is evidence (Deci and Ryan, 1985) that in the latter case, motivation increases; while in the former, motivation to perform is reduced. An employer offering a large bonus as an inducement for someone to finish a job on time or, alternatively, threatening to sack the employee if they do not, does not result in that employee being as strongly motivated as they would be if they were doing the job simply because they liked doing it. There is even evidence (Condry, 1977) that being given an external reward for doing something which had previously been done because enjoyment was obtained from it actually worsens performance. This has been termed the **overjustification effect**.

Weiner's Extension to Self-attribution

Weiner (1979, 1985, 1986) was interested in success or failure in a task, and the causes and consequences of attributions which are made for this success or failure. There are three factors which may have a bearing on future performance of the same task:

1. *The locus of cause.* Did a person fail their driving test because they were not yet ready for it (in their own estimation)? This would be an internal locus of cause. Or because they had a poor instructor? Or again because the traffic on the day of the test was horrendous? These would be external causes.
2. *The stability of the cause.* The same person could hire another instructor next time; could make sure that the test was not held in the rush hour; or they could prepare themselves extra well by masses of practice. Each of which indicate a cause which is not stable. It can change. If, on the other hand, they felt they had failed because they were so nervous that they could not control what they were doing, that would be a much more stable cause.
3. *Controllability.* If the traffic on the test route was always horrendous, that might be beyond the person's control. If they were subject to panic attacks, that too might be beyond their control.

It could be argued that controllability and stability are really two facets of the same thing. But Weiner claims that these three dimensions are independent of one another and can help individuals understand their successes and failures. However, it is at least doubtful whether we actually undertake an analysis like this of the cause of our success or our failure outside the confines of a social psychology laboratory.

Rotter (1966) did some work in this area on what was termed **attributional style**. The suggestion was that individuals differ in the amount of control they feel they have over the outcomes of their actions. A distinction is made between those with **external locus of control** and those with **internal locus of control**. Internals have a tendency to attribute the outcomes of actions (in particular rewards or punishments) to some facet of their own character; externals, on the other hand, impute causes of these outcomes to external factors. Let us consider how this might work. Two individuals, Jeremy and John, take their A-level psychology examination and fail. Jeremy, having an external locus of control, claims that he had a very poor teacher, the paper was exceptionally difficult, and not only that but all through the examination there was a pneumatic drill digging up the road outside the hall where the examination was taking place.

John, with an internal locus of control, blamed failure on the fact that he had always had difficulty understanding the subject – after all, he had always been regarded as a borderline candidate. Two other candidates, Janet and Jane passed with flying colours. Jane, whose locus of control was external, said it was a very easy paper and, besides, all those questions which she had just revised came up. Janet realised that it was all down to the hard work she had put in during the previous months and in any case she always did well in examinations; she had an internal locus of control. Just consider the differences in their self-concepts. The externalisers, Jeremy and Jane, saw themselves as so much flotsam, tossed hither and thither by the storms of life. There was little that they could do to influence events. John and Janet were able to take much more active control of the outcomes.

Self-esteem

Yet another facet of self-concept is **self-esteem**, the value which we place on ourselves. There are two sides to this:

- *Self-image* is factual. A person may see themselves as fat or thin, clever or not so clever, athletic or not athletic. There is a basis in fact for this. A person came last in the race. Another person can no longer get into the clothes they bought for themselves last year.
- But this is only half the story. If someone sees being fat as something disgusting and dislikes themselves for it, their self-esteem is low. If they see being fat as something comfortable or cuddly they have a positive view of themselves.

Coopersmith conducted experiments into self-esteem with a group of ordinary American 10 to 11-year-old boys (Coopersmith, 1968). He measured the self-esteem of the boys in three ways:

1. The boys' own self-evaluation;
2. Teachers reports;
3. Psychological tests.

There was high degree of agreement between these three measures and the boys were allocated on the basis of these tests to three groups, high, medium and low self-esteem. Differences were observed between the three groups in that:

- The high self-esteem group were active, expressed themselves well, and tended to succeed in what they were doing. Their parents were generally interested in their children, were fairly strict and set clear limits on the boys' behaviour
- The low self-esteem group contrasted strongly with this. Their parents were less interested in their sons, and had lower aspirations for them. They tended not to set themselves such high targets and their success rate was lower. They also suffered from ailments of one kind or another, headaches, stomach upsets or insomnia.
- The middling group did nearly as well as the high self-esteem group, they were optimistic and took criticism well. However, they were the most conventional of the three groups and tended to rely more on the opinions of others.

The conclusions which Coopersmith came to were that the sources of high self-esteem were complex, but that parental styles were important as was the setting of targets. It seemed to be important that children should receive respect, they should have well-defined values and guidance to achieve competence in surmounting problems.

Culture and Self

It is difficult to divorce what an individual conceives himself or herself to be from that individual's cultural context. Culture is quite a complex thing. It might be related to something as local and individual as membership of a family group which defines an individual's aspirations and values. On a broader level, it could embrace religious affiliation, or social class. From a different perspective, gender or ethnicity are important elements in culture. There is little doubt that African, Japanese, Chinese or Hindu cultures are distinct and different from one another, and in their turn distinct and different from those of Western Europe or America.

Bharati (1985) has described how Hindus equate a person's innermost self, not with community or social contexts, but with the one-ness of God. Access to this innermost 'self' can only be through meditation and self-discipline.

Devos (1985) describes how the self in Japanese culture is intimately linked with social interaction and social relationships. Perhaps this is the influence of Buddhism which sees each and every one of our actions and experiences as linked in a chain of cause and effect. If we commit some injury to another, a bad *karma* will be the result and we shall reap the reward for it, if not in this life then in a future incarnation (Gruber and Kersten, 1995). Japanese children learn from a very early age to be aware of the effect that their actions will have on others. In this way the Japanese have their ultimate satisfaction in belonging to a group. Their sense of self is intimately associated with an awareness of the ways in which what they do impinges on others.

Summary

The social cognitive approach describes self-schemata, a network of constructs relating to self which have been built up as a result of experiences in life. In some individuals these experiences will cover a very wide range and so their self-schemata will be complex and embrace a great many different contexts. There will be few contexts which are aschematic; that is, where self-schemata have not been developed. In other individuals the contextual range of their experiences is much narrower, so that the self-schemata developed will be related to fewer contexts and more of the contexts in which they may find themselves acting will be aschematic. In other words there will be more areas of their lives where an individual view of self has not been fully developed.

The humanistic approach to the self-concept centres upon unconditional positive regard from important other people. Where this unconditional positive regard was available to an individual, their actual self was closely aligned to their ideal self and the result was a good state of mental equilibrium. Where unconditional positive regard was not available a person would need continually to seek to obtain the approbation of others. This would result in low self-esteem.

Bem developed the self-perception theory which suggested that we observe what we do and infer from these observations what we are like. Our behaviour is seen to have either an internal or an external locus of control; that is, what we do is either the result of something external to us or else it stems from something within our own character.

Self-esteem is seen as another facet of self and is concerned with the evaluations we make of ourselves; while self-image is concerned with factual observations made about ourselves. Self-esteem can have a profound influence on behaviour.

Self-concept is also culturally dependent. Culture may influence profoundly the way in which an individual sees himself. Included in culture are such things as gender, ethnicity, family, tribe and community.

Self-assessment Questions

1. Distinguish between schematic and aschematic self-schemata. How do the contexts in which we perceive ourselves acting have an affect upon self-concept?
2. Bem has developed an attributional theory of self. Describe in simple terms how this attributional process works.
3. What did Carl Rogers conceive of as being the source of mental well-being? What did he mean by *unconditional positive regard?*
4. What is meant by *self-esteem?* How do you think that Rotter's locus-of-control theory relates to self-esteem?
5. Outline ways in which self-concept may be different in the context of different cultures. How do you see gender or ethnicity affecting the way in which we see ourselves?
6. What is social identity? What does it add to the concept of self?

FURTHER READING

M. A. Hogg and G. M. Vaughan *Social Psychology: An Introduction*, Chapter 3 (London: Harvester Wheatsheaf, 1995).
N. Hayes *Foundations of Psychology*, Chapter 13 (London: Routledge, 1994).

"HEY! REMEMBER THE BAD OLD DAYS, WHEN THEY MADE US WEAR SCHOOL UNIFORM?"

Relationships with Others 3

At the end of this chapter you will be able to:

1. Describe why it is that humans have a need to affiliate.
2. Identify some of the factors which influence our choice of people with whom to affiliate.
3. Show an understanding of balance theory and social exchange theory in relation to affiliation.
4. Distinguish between friendship and love and between different kinds of love.
5. Understand how relationships develop.
6. Appreciate some of the factors which may lead to the break up of a relationship and the consequences of such a break up.

SECTION I   AFFILIATION

No man is an island entire of itself.

(Donne 1571–1631: *Devotion*)

Human beings have a need to affiliate. There is some evidence that we cannot easily cope with being out of contact with other human beings for prolonged periods. Schachter (1959) conducted a study in which participants (five male students) volunteered to put themselves into a situation where they had no contact at all with other people. One of these students lasted in his isolation cell a mere 20 minutes before he had an uncontrollable desire to leave. Isolation did not affect them all equally but even one who remained isolated for eight days admitted feeling nervous and uneasy. Schachter put forward four possible reasons why we should have such a strong urge to affiliate with others:

1. Anxiety is less when we are together with other people; we feel more secure in a group. Cutrona (1986) found that there was a significant relationship between social interaction and stress.
2. Our own immediate concerns assume less importance to us, which again reduces the anxiety we feel.
3. We have need of the information which association with others can provide; it provides us with **cognitive clarity**. Our minds become clearer. Kirkpatrick and Shaver (1988) have noted that when people are in a stressful situation they look for someone to help them cope with stress, either a competent intelligent person who will help them assess the situation clearly, or somebody warm and supportive
4. Being with others provides us with a yardstick against which we can evaluate ourselves. **Self-evaluation** is a mechanism for anxiety reduction.

Patterns of Affiliation

We develop systematic links with other people so that a **social network** is formed. Berscheid (1985) has used this term to refer to those people with whom an individual is in actual contact. Social networks are not static, particularly when people move. New people join and some of the old associates drop out of the picture. Much of the research which has been done in this area has been done on college campuses. It is necessary to bear in mind that samples of college students are not typical of people as a whole. Nevertheless, these kinds of studies do provide insights. Hays and Oxley (1986) studied differences in affiliation patterns between first-year students who remained at home and commuted to college, and those who lived in. In American universities this generally means dormitories. Commuting students generally retained connections with friends and relatives more easily and their relationships tended to be more intimate. The social networks established by the resident students included many more new acquaintances and centred more upon what was going on in the university. We could say that resident students integrated more deeply into the life of the university than those who retained links with home by living there. Hays and Oxley found some gender differences too. Men included more friends of the opposite sex. Women provided more social support for their friends, both informational and emotional. These gender differences did not obtain in the non-resident students in their contacts with friends and relatives outside college. The origins of these gender differences have been studied by Wheeler *et al.* (1983) who suggested that women have been socialised to express their emotional feelings more than men. They found that interactions between women were more 'meaningful' – measured by such things as self-disclosure, other-disclosure, intimacy and pleasantness – than those between men.

Choice of Relationship

The question which needs to be answered is this; on what basis do we choose those with whom we affiliate? What makes someone attractive to us? Deaux *et al.* (1993) have listed six factors which may influence choice:

- Proximity; the propinquity factor.
- Similarity in beliefs, values and personality characteristics.
- Complementarity of needs.
- Pleasantness or agreeableness.
- Physical attractiveness.
- Reciprocation of attraction.

The Propinquity Factor

It is suggested that when everything else is considered we like people better with whom we are frequently at close quarters than those at a distance. Festinger (1950) showed that people who lived on the same floor of an apartment block liked each other better than people who lived on other floors or in another building. Even architectural features such as the location of a staircase can have an influence upon the way we choose our friends. Hogg and Vaughan (1995) have highlighted several reasons why this should be the case:

- *Familiarity* If we are physically close to someone, we are likely to see him or her often. This leads to feeling comfortable with him or her and then to familiarity. This has even been extended to strangers. Jorgensen and Cervone (1978) found that the more we see them, the more we like them.
- *Availability* When it requires little effort on our part to interact with someone the social cost to us is low. It requires much more effort to keep in touch with someone who has moved away.

- *Expectation of continued interaction* If we expect that we are going to have to interact with someone over an extended period we make an effort to like him or her. For instance, if people move in next door, we try to get on with them. We can predict that it will be uncomfortable not to.

Similarity

Newcombe (1961) offered free board and lodging to students who were prepared to participate in his study, giving details of their attitudes and values and filling in numerous questionnaires over the course of the first semester at university. Attraction between students was measured as well as changes in attitudes. During the first few weeks the propinquity factor was important. As time went on, though, similarities in attitudes before the term began became more closely related to degree of attraction.

Byrne (1971) went as far as to formulate a **law of attraction**. This stated that there was a linear relationship between the degree of attraction and the proportion of attitudes in common (Clore and Byrne, 1974). In other words, the more attitudes individuals share, the more likely they are to be attracted to one another. However, Byrne's studies were conducted in a laboratory setting and based upon hypothetical descriptions of people. This gives them less 'ecological validity' – they were less closely related to reality – than Newcombe's study or that of Kandel (1978). Kandel conducted an extensive study with over 1800 male and female adolescents aged 13 to 18. Each student's attitudes and values were measured by means of questionnaires and compared with the attitudes and values of his or her best friend. She obtained strong confirmation that similarity was an important factor.

The process seems to work both ways. Not only are we attracted to those who share our attitudes and values, but we are repelled by those with opposing attitudes and values. Those with different attitudes and values challenge beliefs and threaten our self-concepts. However, the evidence shows that the similarity–attraction process is more likely to occur than dissimilarity–repulsion (Byrne *et al.*, 1986; Dane and Harshaw, 1991).

Sometimes, though, we do *not* dislike those with dissimilar attitudes and values. We may even *prefer* them to have such values and attitudes, especially when a person has been stigmatised (Novak and Lerner, 1968) or is perceived to be of a lower status (Karuza and

Brickman, 1978). This happens because too much similarity to an otherwise undesirable person threatens our own self image.

Complementarity of Needs

Winch *et al.* (1954) have claimed that people choose relationships so that their basic needs may be mutually gratified. This is the theory of **need complementarity**. The evidence for this is ambiguous. Kerckhoff and Davis (1962) have suggested that it only operates in the long term. Similarity of values is more important in the initial stages of a relationship; need complementarity comes later. Brehm (1992) has suggested that it only relates to certain dimensions of behaviour such as dominance and submissiveness. For instance, a dominant person will tend to be attracted to a submissive one and vice versa. Lipetz *et al.* (1970) did find, however, that complementarity was related to marital satisfaction. This seems to support the notion that it is a long term thing, rather than relating to initial attractiveness.

Pleasantness

It seems to be self-evident that we like people who are likeable. Positive traits we find more attractive than negative ones. However, in evaluating the traits we observe in other people as positive or negative we are concerned to consider what these traits mean for us (Clore and Kerber, 1978). When we say that someone is 'kind', we are implying that we are likely to be on the receiving end of that 'kindness'. The yardstick of that evaluation is the way it affects us. On the negative side, 'dishonesty' in another person is likely to be assessed according to how likely it is that that person will cheat *us*.

Physical Attractiveness

Beauty is clearly in the eye of the beholder, or perhaps is dictated by the demands of fashion. Cunningham (1986) has put an interesting sociobiological slant on this personal or ephemeral view of physical attractiveness (sociobiology relates to the biological basis for behaviour, particularly the need to pass our genes on to succeeding generations). American men found 'cute' faces attractive. 'Cute' equates to 'childlike' (eyes large and set well apart, small nose and chin). 'Childlike' implies youthfulness which in turn has implications for the individual's potential to produce offspring.

Physical attractiveness is closely related to the first impressions we have of someone we meet. We will make an immediate evaluation of that person on the basis of their physical attractiveness. Attractive individuals are less likely to be adjudged maladjusted or disturbed, more likely to be offered a job at interview, and likely to have their written applications more positively evaluated than those who are seen as less physically attractive (Cash *et al.*, 1977; Dion *et al.*, 1972; Dipboye *et al.*, 1977). Landy and Sigall (1974) conducted an experiment to test this last point. Male students were asked to grade two essays of different quality written by female students. An independent assessment had previously been given of the essays by someone who had no knowledge of the authors. A good essay was presented to the students together with a photograph of an attractive woman, or with a control photograph of a relatively unattractive woman. In a similar procedure the poor essay was paired with photographs of attractive and less-attractive women as well as with control photographs. The more attractive woman had her essay more highly assessed, both in the case of the good as well as the poor essay.

This preference given to physically attractive people carries over into many spheres. Dion *et al.* (1972) demonstrated that physically attractive people are seen as happier, more successful and more likely to get married than less-attractive people. It even extends into the courts. Sigall and Ostrove (1975) found that jurors take an easier view of attractive women defendants. In a study of criminal trials in Pennsylvania, attractive male defendants received lighter sentences and were twice as likely to avoid imprisonment as less-attractive people (Stewart 1980).

Reciprocity

What has been termed the **reciprocity principle** applies in attraction. We like those who like us, and dislike those who dislike us. Dittes and Kelley (1956) showed as a result of an experiment conducted with students that members of a discussion group were more attracted to the group if the group apparently liked them. Self-esteem seems to be a crucial factor in this reciprocation of attraction. Where someone has a high self-esteem, he or she is less influenced by others liking or disliking them. Where people have low self-esteem whether someone else likes them or not assumes much greater importance. Dittes (1959) found that where the group appeared to like an individual who had low self-esteem, that individual liked the group a lot. Similarly, where the group apparently showed dislike, a low self-esteem individual would take a strong dislike to the group.

Theories of Attraction

Balance Theory

Agreement between people strengthens bonds between them and also involves positive feelings (that is, liking). Disagreement between people who like each other produces tension. This is a state of **imbalance**. This is not a comfortable state and there will be attempts made to restore **balance**. Either one or both the parties concerned will alter their attitudes or their beliefs (their cognitions about whatever or whoever is causing the disagreement) to restore the agreement and so the balance.

If, on the other hand, two people dislike each other when they first meet because there is dissimilarity in their cognitions there will be **non-balance** which neither will have an incentive to change. No balance exists to be restored, so that there is no feeling of discomfort. Heider (1958), who formulated balance theory, proposed that there were two possible relationships between people; a **unit relationship**, (belonging together, being members of a group or having something in common) and a **liking relationship**. Both come into play in relations between people. Members of a group (for example members of a Conservative Club) will assume that other members share many of their beliefs, attitudes and opinions. A liking relationship will be likely to exist between members so long as nothing changes this assumption (Spears and Manstead, 1990). Balance will exist. Discovery of a major source of difference in beliefs produces imbalance. If X believes that taxes should be raised to pay for school improvements, while Y believes in reducing public spending to pay for tax cuts, this will produce a negative affect in X and Y which may be restored to balance by either of them, or both altering their view. Liking will be difficult while there is imbalance. This is discussed further in Chapter 5.

Balance theory is in essence a cognitive theory, based on the notion that there is pressure to achieve and to maintain cognitive consistency.

Reinforcement/affect Theory

Put very simply, we like people who reward us; we dislike those who punish us. Byrne and Clore (1970) use a learning theory model to explain interpersonal attraction. Assuming that most stimuli are either rewarding or punishing, we like those we associate with rewarding stimuli; dislike those associated with punishment. The more positive or negative affect we experience, the greater the feelings of liking or disliking. If neutral stimuli are associated with positive or negative affect, similar feelings result.

How does this work in practice? Someone is kind to us. This is a positive, rewarding experience (that is, positive affect), and so we evaluate that person positively (that is, we like him or her). We also tend to like people and objects which we associate with the rewarding situation. Not only are we well-disposed to the person who has been kind to us, but we like the place where the kindness happened and those other people who happened to be there at the time. There is a contagion in liking or disliking.

Social Exchange Theory

The **social exchange** theory of Clark and Mills (Clark and Mills, 1979; Mills and Clark, 1982) and the **interdependence** theory of Thibaut and Kelley (Kelley and Thibaut, 1978; Thibaut and Kelley, 1959) take reinforcement theory further. Each person in a relationship associates certain costs and certain benefits with that relationship. Attraction is a two-way process and the behaviour and the perceptions of both individuals must be taken together. In different kinds of relationships, costs and benefits are defined differently. We treat relationships with strangers or business associates differently. A strict **minimax** strategy may be adopted. Reciprocity is important. We aim to minimise costs and maximise benefits. There needs to be a balance between what a person gives to a relationship and what he or she gets from it. This is an **exchange relationship**. In **communal relationships**, on the other hand, it is a bit more flexible. With family members and close friends we do not concern ourselves quite as much with balancing every input and outcome. Costs and benefits still come into the equation, though. We help a friend in trouble without expecting anything in return. However, if in the longer term our friend only contacts us when he or she needs help and ignores us the rest of the time, the quality of the relationship will deteriorate and eventually our appraisal of it will alter.

Clark (1984) illustrated the distinction between exchange and communal relationships with an ingenious experiment. This is described in Box 3.1:

BOX 3.1 Clark's Experiment with Record-keeping in Relationships

Participants were pairs of students, either two friends or two strangers. The task they were set was as follows:

In a 15 × 26 matrix of numbers, the two participants had to search for specified sequences of numbers. They had to take turns looking for a sequence then circling it in ink when they found it. There was a choice of pens, one with red ink and one with black. They were promised a joint reward for the task which they could divide as they wished. The dependent variable was the choice of pen. The independent variable was the kind of pair of participants, friends or strangers.

In an exchange relationship, it was argued, the two participants would need to keep a tally of each other's contribution so as to be able to divide the reward according to each's relative contribution. So different coloured pens would be chosen. In a communal relationship, the friends would be more likely to use the same pen. That was how it turned out. The pairs of strangers chose different pens in significantly more cases; the pairs of friends chose the same pen significantly more often.

This experiment recognised the fact that costs and benefits may be defined differently in different relationships. The distinction Clark made was between *exchange* and *communal* relationships as described above.

The interdependence theory of Thibaut and Kelley (1959; 1978) is similar to social exchange theory but includes more detail. Indeed, it also has sometimes been referred to as social exchange. An important further concept is **comparison level**. This is the common standard against which all relationships may be judged. Rewards are compared with what the individuals concerned have come to expect. This is where social cognition comes in. Everyone has stored schemata relating to what is to be expected from a relationship. This is based upon past experience and represents the measure of comparison for any present relationship. Only if the gains to be had exceed the comparison level will the relationship be judged to be satisfactory. As with all schemata, this comparison level is not static but can change with experience and age; as we get older we tend to demand more from a relationship. Comparison level is also situation-specific. Expectations, based upon experience, will vary according to the circumstances. A similar evaluation is made of the costs involved in the relationship, again against a comparison level of costs. Only if the rewards outweigh the costs is the relationship likely to continue.

A further element which enters into the calculations in interdependence theory is that there is also evaluation (conducted in the same way) of the alternatives. Jogging along nicely in a relationship with a friend, the costs and rewards are pretty well in balance. Then we meet an exciting new stranger. The potential rewards of this new relationship are greater; the costs are less. In all probability we might abandon our present relationship for the new one. However, if our present relationship is an excellent one, with rewards that greatly exceed the costs, then we would be likely to be in much more of a quandary.

An Evaluation of Social Exchange   How useful is social exchange? Clearly, it is a very subjective process involving much speculation. It is also hard to maintain the notion that social relationships are based solely upon cost/benefit analysis on a personal level. The influence of the broader community in which we live also counts for something, though it might be argued that this is part of the costs and the benefits. We may want to develop a relationship with someone of a different ethnic background in a racially intolerant community; the intolerance of the community might be said to impose additional costs which might sway the balance.

Reinforcement theory bases itself solely upon learning theory, while social exchange or interdependence theory brings in an element of social cognition.

Equity Theory

Equity theory modifies social exchange, stressing the importance of perceived fairness in what is going on between people. It is summarised by Walster *et al.* (1978) in terms of the following:

- Maximisation of reward and minimisation of cost (the **minimax principle**).
- There is more than one way in which rewards can be shared out, but there must be agreement on a fair system.
- An inequitable relationship produces distress; the more inequitable the more distress it causes.
- Someone who is in an inequitable relationship will try to restore it to equity. The losing partner will put in as much effort as seems necessary to restore equity. This will continue so long as there is a chance of restoring equity.

Adams (1965) dealt with two main situations in relation to equity:

1. A mutual exchange of resources.
2. The distribution of limited resources.

According to Adams, equity exists between two individuals A and B, when A's outcomes plus A's inputs equal B's outcomes plus B's inputs. The ratio of inputs to outcomes is first estimated. Then a comparison is made of the ratio between inputs and outcomes for the other person. If these ratios are equal, people feel they are being treated fairly (equitably). This **rule of distributive justice** was originally propounded by Homans (1961). If there appears to be inequity we are motivated to do something about it. There are two possible ways of going about this:

1. Alter the inputs and/or the outcomes.
2. Alter our *perceptions* of the inputs and outcomes, so that it no longer *appears* that the relationship is inequitable.

Adams claimed that when neither of the above methods works, the relationship is likely to end. In practice, society operates on the basis of **norms**. These include:

- An *equity norm* – the rule of distributive justice, for instance (see above).
- A *social welfare norm* – a rule which maintains that resources should be distributed according to people's need.
- An *equalitarian norm* – a rule that everyone gets an equal share.

Adams claimed that people will always prefer the equity norm when allocating resources, but more recent research by Deutsch (1975) and Mikula (1980) has modified this. It seems that the circumstances and the situation have a bearing on the norm chosen. Various points have been made:

- Lamm and Kayser (1978) suggest that a *friend*'s inputs into a relationship are differently evaluated from those of a stranger. Where a friend is concerned we tend to take into account not only the resources which we perceive that friend as able to contribute, but also the effort which goes into that contribution. With a stranger, on the other hand, it is just ability which matters.
- Gender makes a difference too; women are likely to allocate resources on an equalitarian norm, men tend to use an equity norm (Kahn *et al.*, 1980; Major and Adams, 1983; Major and Deaux, 1982).
- Kahn makes the point that the traditional role of women is that of maintaining group harmony. This may best be achieved by adopting equalitarian norms in allocating resources.

Self-assessment Questions

1. Why do people need to affiliate with others? List three advantages which may stem from affiliation.
2. Make a list of factors which affect our choice of those with whom we form relationships. Which seems to you to be the most important and why?
3. Social exchange and interdependence theories go some way towards explaining why we choose to form a relationship with one person rather than another. Do these theories seem to you to be convincing?
4. *Equity* is claimed to be an important basis for forming and maintaining a relationship. How do you seen Adams' equity theory operating in practice? Illustrate with an example.

SECTION II   FRIENDSHIP, LOVE AND MARRIAGE

Friendship

What do we expect from a friend? Can we say that there is some behaviour which is incompatible with friendship? Argyle and

Henderson (1985) have attempted to answer these questions by setting out four criteria for a friendship rule:

1. People should generally agree that the behaviour specified in the rule is important for friendship.
2. The rule should be applied differently to former friends as compared to current friends.
3. Failure to adhere to the rule should often be cited as a reason for the breakup of a friendship.
4. The rule should differentiate behaviour between close friends and not-so-close friends.

They then proceeded to question students in England, Italy, Japan and Hong Kong about friendship, and attempted to apply the above criteria to the responses they gave. They were able to identify six rules which met the above criteria completely, together with three more which did not meet criterion (4) though they met the others. These are listed below:

1. Share news of success with a friend;
2. Show emotional support;
3. Volunteer help in time of need;
4. Strive to make a friend happy when in each other's company;
5. Trust and confide in one another;
6. Stand up for a friend in his or her absence;
7. Repay debts and favours;
8. Be tolerant of other friends;
9. Do not nag a friend.

Development of Friendships

Hays (1985) has shown that when acquaintances begin to develop into friends, there is a great deal of interaction to begin with. Then this tends to ease off as the two individuals concerned begin to concentrate more on other things. But the *amount* of interaction is balanced by the increase in its quality. It becomes more intimate.

There is a difference in emphasis between male–male friendships and female–female friendships. Because females tend to be more verbally-oriented, communication plays a considerable part as well as self-disclosure. Confidences are more often exchanged. Males on the other hand are more activity-oriented so that friendships develop out of shared activities and interests. An interesting study by Derlega *et al.* (1989) is described in Box 3.2. This study highlighted gender differences in the ways in which friendship was expressed.

BOX 3.2
Gender Differences in the Expression of Friendship (Derlega *et al.*, 1989)

Participants (dating partners, mixed-sex pairs of friends, male friends and female friends) were asked to role-play meeting and greeting their friendship partners at an airport where one of them was coming back from a trip. Greetings were photographed and scored for levels of intimacy and touching. Results showed male–male pairs using minimal touching, mixed pairs of friends and female friends reached a higher level of intimacy and touching. Seven mixed pairs and eight female pairs reached the most intimate levels of touching. But of the dating couples, all reached the most intimate level engaging in some combination of hugging and kissing.

There are also other individual differences which distinguish friendship patterns. Some individuals (both male and female) have a high need for intimacy and are more likely to engage in self-disclosure. Others who have a high dominance-need tend to affiliate in larger groups rather than forming friendships with a single other individual (McAdams *et al.*, 1984).

Love

There seems to be general agreement that love is different from liking. Intuitively, we feel that there is a qualitative difference between liking someone and loving him or her. It is more than simply a matter of degree. Rubin (1973) distinguished 'liking' and 'loving' and developed scales to measure each separately. Hatfield and Walster (1981) went further and separated **passionate love** from **companionate love**. Their definitions are as follows:

> Passionate love is an intensely emotional state and a confusion of feelings: tenderness, sexuality, elation and pain, anxiety and relief, altruism and jealousy. Companionate love, on the other hand, is a less intense emotion, combining feelings of friendly affection and

deep attachment. It is characterised by friendship, understanding and concern for the welfare of the other. (Hatfield, 1987, p. 676)

Most people would accept that there are other people with whom we certainly cannot say we are 'in love', but with whom we enjoy sharing time and whom we find it pleasant and comforting to be with. Argyle and Henderson (1985) have claimed that passionate love is a first stage. Couples who have been together a long time have said that the first passionate love evolves over time into something at once deeper and less violently emotional; a relationship characterised more by attachment and affection than by sexual excitement. This is illustrated in a longitudinal study by Simpson *et al.* (1986) described in Box 3.3.

BOX 3.3
Simpson *et al.*'s Study of Love

Participants in this study were asked: 'If a man (woman) had all the qualities you desired, would you marry this person, even if you were not in love with him (her)?' There were three samples taken at intervals between the 1960s and the 1980s. There were more people in the earlier samples who said they would be willing to marry without falling in love, with just under 80 per cent of women willing to marry without love in 1967 as compared to less than 20 per cent in 1984. For men, the proportions were much lower in 1967 (less than 40 per cent), and much more nearly the similar to the women's sample in 1976 and 1984. Perhaps the security offered to women by marriage was a more important factor in 1967. By 1984, they felt themselves to be more independent economically, so that the romantic side of marriage assumed greater importance.

Falling in Love

Can we say that there is a state of 'being in love?' Milardo *et al.* (1983) suggest that a person *can* fall in love. It really is comparable to some kind of accident over which we have little or no control. The lover becomes the total focus of a person's life. Other friends are excluded. It is very intensely emotional. There is a very strong desire on the part of both individuals to spend as much time as possible in each other's company. However, there is some evidence that we need to have been brought up in a culture which believes in this kind of romantic love, where young people are taught that it exists both in fiction and in real life. Perhaps Romeo and Juliet have something to answer for! If we did not see people 'in love' in films, TV and plays or read about it in fiction, we should not expect it to happen to us. Furthermore, the more a person thinks about love the more likely they are to 'fall in love', and if you really do believe in 'love at first sight' there is a much greater chance that it will happen to us (Tesser and Paulhus, 1976; Averill and Boothroyd, 1977).

Three-factor Theory of Love

Hatfield and Walster (1981) proposed that there are three factors responsible for the experience of 'love'.

- Cultural exposure – an individual needs to have been exposed from an early age to the idea of love and being in love.
- Physiological arousal – being sexually aroused in a physiological sense at a particular time.
- There needs to be an appropriate love object present – an attractive (to you, at least) person (usually) of the opposite sex and of similar age.

FIGURE 3.1
Three-factor Theory of Love

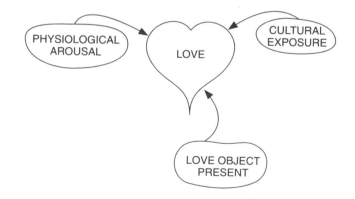

Source: Based on Hatfield and Walster (1981).

Again we return to the cognitive explanation of emotion put forward by Schachter and Singer (1962). Cognitively we need to find an explanation for the physiological changes we experience. The label we attach to the feelings experienced when the three factors above are present is 'love'. Figure 3.1 illustrates this three-factor theory of love.

This is an interesting theory, but the evidence for an external labelling of internal feelings of this kind is not conclusive. While the evidence of Schachter and Singer's study clearly supports the idea, Marshall and Zimbardo (1979) are not so sure. External labelling seems to be just one factor in what is quite a complex process.

You might equally well explain it using the reinforcement/affect theory mentioned earlier. The arousal which is experienced in the 'love object's' presence is associated with that person. This positive emotional feeling is reinforcing. In effect we learn to be in love.

Attachment Theory of Love

Hazan and Shaver (1987, 1990) Shaver and Hazan (1987, 1988) used the **attachment theory** first propounded by Bowlby (1969, 1973, 1980) to explain the various types of love. This has its roots in the evolutionary need to develop an attachment mechanism to keep infants secure in the face of danger. This goes back to studies of imprinting in precocial birds by Lorenz (1937) and others. Box 3.4 shows Hazan and Shaver's attachment theory of love:

BOX 3.4
Hassan and Shaver's Attachment Theory of Love

The researchers used with adults the three main styles of attachment identified by Ainsworth *et al.* (1978) in respect of infants – secure, avoidant, and ambivalent. They argued that love was a form of attachment. A person's adult romantic attachments should therefore have some relationship to other attachment experiences and they characterised them as follows:

Secure attachment: I find it relatively easy to get close to others and am comfortable depending on them and having them depend on me. I don't often worry about being abandoned or someone getting to close to me.
Avoidant: I am somewhat uncomfortable being close to others; I find it difficult to trust them completely, difficult to allow myself to

depend on them. I am nervous when anyone gets too close, and often love partners want me to be more intimate than I feel comfortable being.

Anxious/ambivalent: I find that others are reluctant to get as close as I would like. I often worry that my partner doesn't really love me or want to stay with me. I want to merge completely with another person, and this desire sometimes scares people away.

(Hazan and Shaver, 1987, pp. 511–24)

Hazan and Shaver obtained extensive information from more than 1200 people's romantic experiences and reactions. The reported histories of their relationships with their parents were related to their different adult attachment styles.

More particularly in the context of love:

- **Secure** lovers believed that their relationships were going to have their ups and downs; the extremely intense feelings which accompanied the beginning of the relationship (the falling in love part) can reappear. Second honeymoons are quite on the cards. Indeed, in some relationships romantic love does not fade at all. Their romantic relationships were happy, with great friendship and trust. There was no fear of becoming close to someone else.
- **Avoidant** lovers tended to believe that the fictional kind of romantic love was only fictional and did not exist in real life. People rarely found real love. The relationships of avoidant lovers tended to include high levels of jealousy and low levels of acceptance.
- **Anxious/ambivalent** lovers agreed that real love was rare. However they did believe that to 'fall in love' was possible – indeed easy – and they had started to fall in love quite often. Their relationships tended to go to extremes; excessive preoccupation with sexual attraction, desire for union and love at first sight.

In common with most other social experiences, cognition plays a considerable part in love. In the first place, experience sets the culture within which we relate to other people. Our childhood experiences of attachment to other people establish patterns of cognition which, while they may be modified by experience at any time in life, nevertheless colour our perceptions of what love is.

We have tended to ignore the gender of lovers in this discussion. While heterosexual love has been the major focus (the research is very much greater here), love experiences do not appear to be very different for people with different sexual orientations. Hazan and Shaver did not find any differences between heterosexual and homosexual individuals.

Sternberg's Triangular Theory of Love

Sternberg (1986) saw love as a triangle with three components, intimacy, passion and commitment. *Intimacy* relates to the feelings of bonding and attachment just mentioned – the desire to be close to someone else; *passion* relates to the sexual and romantic aspects of a relationship and *commitment* has two aspects – a decision to unite with someone else and commitment to remain with that person. In different individuals, these three components are present in different strengths and this results in different kinds of love. *Liking* involves a strong dose of intimacy but little passion or commitment; *infatuation* involves high levels of passion but not so much commitment or intimacy; *empty love* is mostly commitment with little passion or intimacy; *romantic love* is strong on passion and intimacy but there is little commitment. In the centre of the triangle Sternberg puts *consummate love*. Figure 3.2 illustrates this theory.

FIGURE 3.2
Sternberg's Triangular Theory of Love

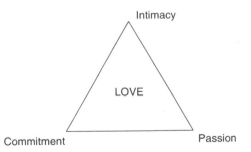

Source: Based on Sternberg (1986).

Mate Selection

Economic advantage has been considered to be of overwhelming importance in choosing a mate. It used to be said, 'You do not marry for money, but you marry where money is.' In the recently televised adaptation of Jane Austen's *Pride and Prejudice*, Mrs Bennett's preoccupation was that her daughters should marry 'well'. Considerations were entirely those of wealth and expectations. However, the drama made plain that this preoccupation did not coincide well with that of the daughters themselves. Personal characteristics were seen as more important. A series of studies going back to the 1940s have consistently highlighted such traits as dependability, emotional stability, pleasing disposition and mutual attraction (Hill, 1945; McGinnis, 1959; Hudson and Henze, 1969; Silva, 1990). Buss and Barnes (1986) conducted a study in which the participants were married people aged from 18 to 40. The following 10 characteristics were listed as being most important:

- good companionship;
- considerateness;
- honesty;
- affection;
- dependability;
- intelligence;
- kindness;
- being understanding;
- loyalty; and
- being interesting to talk to.

On the other hand, the respondents valued least highly the following characteristics:

- dominance;
- agnosticism;
- being a night owl; or
- being an early riser.

Buss (1984) has stressed the importance of similarity on mate selection. The ethological concept of **assortative mating** seems to apply as much to the choosing of a mate by humans as to animals. We tend to choose a mate who has similar characteristics or who engages in similar forms of behaviour. Lesnik-Oberstein and Cohen (1984) found that married couples tended to share similar characteristics, for example susceptibility to boredom, a desire to seek out new experiences or impulsivity. Buss found similarities in choice of activities, willingness to display intimacy and tolerance of quarrelsomeness. It has to be borne in mind, of course, that psychologists are tending to question couples about these things after they have been together for some time, so that the ones who do not share these characteristics may no longer be together to be questioned!

Development of Love

A close and intimate relationship does not just happen overnight, but develops fairly slowly and through a number of stages. Kelley *et al.* (1983) have identified some of them and these are detailed in Box 3.5.

BOX 3.5
Kelley *et al.*'s Stages of Love

Stage 1   Acquaintanceship. Two people get to know each other and begin to interact. In the case of many contacts we make, it never gets any further than this. We meet someone casually at a party, get on all right but there it ends.

Stage 2   Discovery. Increasing degrees of interdependence emerge at this stage and both partners become more willing to disclose information about themselves. A fair amount of energy is expended on the relationship at this stage. The activities of each of them as individuals are brought together and coordinated and they each look forward to future rewarding interactions. The attractiveness of each partner is accentuated in the eyes of the other, and other people are correspondingly downgraded in attractiveness. This is **cognitive dissonance** in action (see Chapter 5). When we have made our choice in anything, that choice assumes greater attractiveness; all other alternatives become less-attractive.

Stage 3   Build-up. The course of true love does not always run smoothly. Circumstances and problems unfold at this stage which may increase tension. The idealisation which has occurred in stage 2 comes up against the reality of the partner's less than ideal characteristics. Sacrifices may also be needed in order to respond to the needs of the partner and this produces further strains (Brehm, 1988; Holmes, 1989).

Metts (1989) has noted that patterns of deception change too at about this time. In the early stages of a relationship we tend to tell little white lies (or sometimes even bigger ones!) to protect our self-concept. At the build-up stage deception may be used to protect the relationship rather than ourselves. If we receive a Valentine card from someone other than our partner we might say nothing about it because it might cause problems for the relationship.

Jealousy also grows as commitment grows. Research has suggested that jealousy arises out of two factors:

1. A desire for exclusivity in the relationship.
2. Feelings of inadequacy.

However, causes of jealousy are different in men and women; in men it is related to self-esteem. A man's partner is a source of self-esteem. His manhood depends to some degree upon maintaining a relationship with her and also, if he holds fairly traditional views about gender roles, she is part of his territory on to which someone else may be encroaching. Women on the other hand, believing that the relationship holds more rewards for them than any available alternative, are jealous in protecting it. For men it is a matter of status; for women it is the nature of the relationship itself which is at stake. This determines the ways in which jealousy shows itself according to a study by Shettel-Neuber *et al.* (1978); men become angry and are likely to engage in activities which could endanger the relationship; women on the other hand are likely to become depressed and also to try to improve the relationship.

Stage 4 Commitment. At this stage it begins to become evident that the advantages of the relationship outweigh the disadvantages, and commitment to it develops. Even in the case of arranged marriages which have started with a formal agreement, emotional involvement and love can follow. The important thing, according to research by Blais *et al.* (1990) is the motivation behind the commitment at this stage. Where motivations to remain committed are intrinsic and self-determined, people take a positive view of behaviour related to maintaining the relationship and because their view of the relationship and behaviour related to it is positive they remain happy with it. Each partner's perceptions of the relationship are likely to affect the other's. Blais and his colleagues found, however, that this was true of women more than men, so that it seems that women have a greater role to play in the development of a relationship than men.

Rempel *et al.* (1985) identified increasing trust as one of the crucial ways in which behaviour and feelings change as a relationship develops. Trust involves three separate ways in which one partner in a relationship views his or her partner:

1. *Predictability* Each partner can predict more easily what the other will do.
2. *Dependability* Past evidence and experience lead each partner to develop assumptions about the disposition and characteristics of the other, which lead him or her to be able to depend upon him or her.

3. *Faith* This involves each partner in looking ahead to outcomes which are becoming more certain.

Break-up of Relationships

The fairy story version of relationships involves the couple 'living happily ever after'. However, it frequently does not work out like this. Hill *et al.*'s (1976) longtitudinal study followed 231 couples in Boston over two years. After that time, 103 had broken up, 43 were married, 9 were engaged, 65 others were still courting and the remaining 11 could not be contacted. Going back to an initial questionnaire given to the couples at the beginning of the study, it emerged that those who felt closer in 1972 were more likely to be together in 1974. Also, as it has been mentioned earlier, women appeared to be more influential than men in maintaining the relationship, and their feelings were a more sensitive index than men's of the health of the relationship. Similarities were an important factor in determining whether a couple stayed together. Figure 3.3 shows correlation coefficients on age, education, verbal test score, numerical test score, attractiveness and views on sex roles between partners. Those who stayed together were clearly more highly-correlated on these measures than those who did not.

Another factor is the man's need for power. Men who showed a high need for power in the first questionnaire were much less likely still to be in the relationship after two years. 50 per cent of these relationships had broken up by 1974 compared to 15 per cent of the relationships in which the man had a low need for power. As far as women's need for power was concerned, there was no relationship between this measure and the success or failure of the relationship.

Timing of Relationship Break-ups

As is so often the case in social psychological studies, a high proportion of the couples studied were college students. Intensive interviews conducted as part of the second stage in the study (after two years) provided insights into when break-ups were likely to occur. Relationships were most likely to break-up at the beginning of the autumn term and at the ends of the autumn and spring terms. It seemed that the partner who was less committed to the relationship tended to take advantage of natural break points in the year to

FIGURE 3.3
Similarity and Relationship Break-up

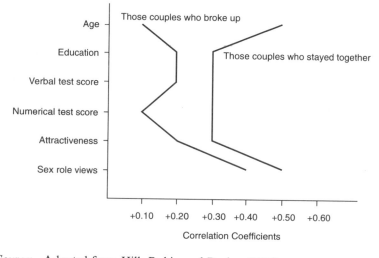

Source: Adapted from Hill, Rubin and Peplau (1976).

end it. By contrast, when the more committed partner chose to end the relationship, the break-up usually came in the middle of the year.

Most break-ups seem to come from a decision by one partner or the other to end it. This was the case in 85 per cent of both the women and the men. Both men and women were more likely to say that it was they who wanted to end it rather than their partner. Thus self-esteem is protected. Hill *et al.*'s data also support the view that it was more likely to be the woman who decided to break it up. What is more, when it was the man who decided to end it the couple often remained 'good friends'. When it was the woman who broke it off this was much less likely to happen.

Role-complementarity and Break-up

It is very important for the maintenance of a relationship, either inside or outside marriage, that there should be **complementarity of roles**. Whenever there is a change in the roles within a relationship there needs to be re-negotiation. Suppose a man is made redundant and begins to work from home, the wife who has had control within the home, perhaps for a long time, now has to share this control. Unless there is careful re-negotiation, tensions will build up until a break-up becomes possible. Even without such dramatic changes as redundancy or retirement, role changes may gradually occur. Children growing up and leaving home, for instance, will alter the wife's role of mother and care-giver to them, perhaps. In any case there is a redefinition of the role of women taking place in the second half of the twentieth century. The role strain which has developed because of this is not unrelated to the increase in marriage break-ups.

Equity and Break-up

Equity theory has been discussed earlier (p. 68). It suggests that people have a notion of what they deserve from a relationship. This will be based at least in part on comparisons with what they see their partners getting from the relationship. When one partner feels that the relationship is out of balance, he or she will try to restore the balance, either actually or psychologically, changing inputs or outcomes or else perceptions of input and outcomes. Dissatisfaction will arise whenever the relationship appears to be out of balance; this will apply not only to the individual who appears to be under-benefitting, but also to the partner who sees himself or herself as gaining too much. Sprecher (1986) has reported feelings which include hurt and resentment on the part of men; sadness and frustration on the part of women. When men feel they have under-benefitted they feel anger; when they overbenefit, guilt. Women become depressed when they see themselves as underbenefitting; angry when they are over benefitting. When the imbalance becomes too great equity theory would predict break-up. Berscheid and Walster (1978) tested this prediction the details of which are shown in Box 3.6.

BOX 3.6
Equity and Relationship Break-up (Berscheid and Walster, 1978)

511 men and women at the University of Wisconsin were interviewed about their relationships. Initially they were asked to evaluate their relationships by assessing the contributions and benefits of each partner. Four estimates were made:

1. All the contributions each partner considered he or she made to the relationship, rated on a scale +4 to −4. This should include personality, emotional support, help in decision-making and the rest.
2. Then each partner was asked to rate his or her partner's contributions in the same way.
3. Similarly, benefits received from the relationship were rated such as love, excitement, security or having a good time.
4. The partner's benefits were finally rated in the same way.

The investigators were thus able to determine how equitable the relationship was perceived to be. Then three months later, couples were interviewed again and asked whether they were still going out with the same partner and how long they expected the relationship to last. Those whose relationships were equitable at the first session were both more likely to be going out with the same individual, but also more likely to predict that the relationship would last.

Duck's Model of Relationship Break-up

Duck (1988, 1992) has produced a detailed **relationship dissolution model**. There are four phases, each of which incorporates a threshold. When this threshold is reached, certain behaviours are predicted to follow. Figure 3.4 illustrates this model.

Post-Break-up Loneliness/Bereavement

With divorce becoming so common that it is no longer considered to be deviant, the consequences of separation and divorce in psychological terms have to be considered. Loneliness is one of these consequences, not only after the separation and divorce but during the break-up. Williams and Solano (1983) have suggested that it is the *quality* of relationships which is a factor in feelings of loneliness, not just the presence or absence of them. There was no difference in their study between the *number* of friends which lonely and non-lonely people had, but there was a difference in the intimacy of their relationships. Maxwell and Coeburgh (1986) have identified four predictors of feelings of loneliness:

1. Closeness – how close individuals were to the closest person in their lives.
2. How many close friends they had.
3. Degree of satisfaction with their relationships.

FIGURE 3.4
Duck's Relationship Dissolution Model

PHASE	THRESHOLD	BEHAVIOUR
Intra-psychic Phase Brooding with little outward show Needling partner Seeking third party to voice concern	Partner's behaviour unbearable	Assessment of partner's behaviour Assess negative features Assess positive features Assess withdrawal costs
Dyadic Phase Justify withdrawing What can be done? Attributing responsibility	Shall I withdraw?	Confrontation or avoidance dilemma Negotiate Repair and reconciliation Assess withdrawal costs
Social Phase Negotiate with friends for social support and reassurance of rightness	Decision to withdraw	Negotiate post-withdrawal state with partner Discussion among friends Create face-saving/blame placing stories
Grave-dressing Phase Division of property Access to children Protection of reputation for reliability Socially acceptable version of the life and death of the relationship.	Withdrawal inevitable	Activity to do with getting over it Retrospection: post mortems Publish own version of break-up

Source: Adapted from Duck (1988).

"IT'S REALLY HOMEWORK — I NEED TO PREPARE MYSELF FOR THE PUNCH-UP IN THE PLAYGROUND TOMORROW."

Conflict and Cooperation

At the end of this chapter you should be able to:

1. Identify what is meant by **group identity** and highlight the distinction between **out-groups** and **in-groups**.
2. Describe what is meant by **social identity** and appreciate the effect social identity has on the way in which we interact with other people.
3. Describe and evaluate some of the theories relating to aggressive behaviour, including psychoanalytic theories and learning theories.
4. Identify factors which may cause people to be aggressive including environmental and situational factors.
5. Evaluate the evidence linking violence on television and aggressive behaviour.
6. Describe and evaluate some theories and models which account for altruism and prosocial behaviour, including **empathy–altruism models** and **arousal–cost reward models**.
7. Describe Latané and Darley's research into bystander behaviour and identify some of the factors which may inhibit people from helping.

SECTION I INTER-GROUP RELATIONS

Margaret Thatcher had a habit of enquiring concerning any individual whose name cropped up, 'Is he/she one of us?' Any group to which an individual belongs can be referred to as an **in-group**; a group to which an individual does not belong is an **out-group**. In-groups and out-groups are defined entirely in terms of the individual's membership. Margaret Thatcher's 'one of us' referred to the in-group to which she belonged, a group of people who shared her political analysis and attitudes. All the rest constituted an out-group. This again is part of social cognition. Experiences have been transformed into mental representations which in turn play a part in determining behaviour. Margaret Thatcher's experience of the Miner's Union coming close to unseating a Conservative government were transformed into representations of the miners as subversive and hostile which in turn coloured her behaviour in relation to them.

Social Identity

Categorisation leads to assumptions of similarity among those who are categorised together. For Mrs Thatcher, therefore, all union members, were alike; all non-union people were also alike. The differences which exist between members of a group are minimised; the differences between groups are accentuated (Brewer and Kramer, 1985; Wilder, 1986). Members of a group, viewed from outside, are relatively homogeneous. But, from within the group, the same homogeneity does not exist. It depends also upon how well acquainted we are with group members. Those we know very well we will tend to discriminate between and categorise on finer criteria than when we are considering members of a group we know less well.

When all are members of the same group some additional criteria, other than group membership, is needed to discriminate between people. This does not apply when we are judging members of another group. Group membership itself is an important discriminator. The out-group will be stereotyped and this stereotypical information extends our relatively meagre knowledge of the members of the group. We have assumed a **social identity** and this is the standpoint from which we view other people.

Activation of Group Identity

The presence of members of an out-group serves to trigger in-group social identity. Perdue *et al.* (1990) demonstrated that activation of group social identity is a spontaneous cognitive process. Their study is detailed in Box 4.1

This is another manifestation of **social identity theory**, outlined by Tajfel (1978, 1982) and Tajfel and Turner (1986). The groups to which we belong are a part of our self-concept. An individual is motivated to maintain or enhance self-esteem, and the discrimina-

> **BOX 4.1**
> **Activation of Group Identity. An Experiment by Perdue *et al.*
> (1990)**
>
> The experimenters flashed adjectives on a computer screen and asked
> participants to say whether they could be used to describe a person
> (any person). There were three categories of adjectives:
>
> 1. positive adjectives which could be applied to people. (e.g. good,
>   kind, trustworthy);
> 2. negative adjectives which could be applied to people (e.g. bad,
>   cruel, untrustworthy);
> 3. control adjectives such as draughty or brick which were not usually
>   applied to people.
>
> Before each adjective was presented, a 'prime' appeared on the screen.
> This is something presented so rapidly that the participant does not
> have time to process its meaning consciously. Even though no con-
> scious cognitive processing occurs, the prime has the effect of sponta-
> neously increasing the cognitive accessibility of related concepts for a
> brief period. This effect has been verified by Fowler *et al.* (1981). Three
> such 'primes' were used in this case, we, they, and XXX. Perdue and
> his colleagues found that participants took significantly less time to
> decide that positive traits were applicable, and more time to decide
> that negative traits applied when primed with 'we' than when primed
> with 'they' or 'XXX'. Even such very general references to social
> identity as 'we' were enough to trigger positive associations in memory
> so that it was easier to decide that positive adjectives applied. To be
> reminded of our group social identity gives us a positivity bias, which
> enables us to discriminate in favour of our own group.

tion mentioned above in favour of his or her own group helps this
maintenance or enhancement. As van Knippenberg and Ellemers
(1990) have put it, if the status of group X is higher than that of
group Y, then as a member of X an individual will share in that
status.

Ethnocentrism

Sumner (1906) described how out-groups are evaluated from the
standpoint of an in-group. Our own group is the centre of everything, and all others are rated by reference to it:

Each group nourishes its own pride and vanity, boasts itself superior, exalts its own divinities and looks with contempt upon outsiders. Each group thinks its own folkways are the only right ones, and if it observes that other groups have their own folkways these excite its scorn. (Sumner, 1906, p. 13)

This was termed **ethnocentrism**. Sherif (1962, 1966) believed that the origins of ethnocentrism lie in the nature of inter-group relations. Where groups compete for scarce resources there is conflict and ethnocentrism arises. Three field experiments were conducted using as participants young boys in summer camps.

Summer camps are a very usual phenomenon in the USA, and Sherif and his colleagues used this institution to conduct experiments. There were three separate experiments in group conflict, each lasting about three weeks. The third in 1954 became known as the 'Robbers' Cave' experiment after the location in Oklahoma where it took place. This is detailed in Box 4.2.

BOX 4.2
Sherif *et al.*'s 'Robbers Cave' experiment

Twenty-two boys took part, carefully selected so that no initial prejudices were likely. Three bases were chosen for selection:

1. They had no prior acquaintance with one another. They came from different schools and neighbourhoods.
2. The boys were healthy and well-adjusted, with no neurotic tendencies, members of stable families, and with both parents living at home. They had no record of past disturbances in behaviour. Minority group members were not included.
3. They came from stable white Protestant families of the middle socio-economic level. They showed the normal range of individual differences but were matched as far as possible for size and skills when the groups were formed.

Stage one – spontaneous personal choices

All the boys were housed at first in one large bunk-house. Activities were camp-wide, and full opportunities were given for friendships to be formed. They were asked who their best friends were. Then they were divided into two cabins; about two-thirds of best friends were separated and allocated places in different cabins. This stage was omitted in the 1954 'Robbers' Cave' experiment on the grounds that the previous two experiments had provided sufficient information about friendships formed on the basis of pure personal preference.

Stage two – group formation

At this stage activities were on a cabin basis. Within each cabin they were independent, and included camping-out, cooking, improving swimming places, transporting canoes over rough terrain to water and playing various games. Different individuals assumed different responsibilities and displayed different skills. In the 1954 experiment the groups were named 'Rattlers' and 'Eagles'. They became cohesive groups with low-ranking and high-ranking members. Each group developed its own jargon, special jokes and special ways of performing tasks. This stage lasted one week.

Stage three – intergroup conflict

In the 1954 study the groups were not even aware of each other's existence until just before this stage began. A tournament of games was arranged apparently at the boys' own request, soon after they became aware of each other's existence. There was friendly rivalry to begin with, then animosity. Members of each group began to call members of the other 'sneaks', 'cheats' and 'stinkers'. The 'Eagles' burnt a banner left behind by the 'Rattlers'. Next morning the 'Rattlers' seized the 'Eagles' flag, and there were scuffles. Each group had negative feelings towards all members of the other group. Within each group, solidarity, cooperativeness and morale increased, but this did not extend to members of the other group.

Stage four – intergroup cooperation

In an earlier experiment (Sherif, 1951), the introduction of a common enemy was found to be a means of reducing conflict. Common goals seemed to afford a means to promote cooperation. The first opportunity for this arose when there was an (arranged) breakdown in the water supply. First, each group explored the pipeline separately to find the cause of the problem and then they came together and jointly located the source of the difficulty. Second, an opportunity came to see a film which both groups had high on their list of preferences. They were told that the camp could not afford it, but the groups got together and worked out how they could jointly raise the money and finally enjoyed the film together. The third opportunity arose when the groups were due to go on an outing to a lake some distance away. The lorry which was to have transported the food refused to start (this too was arranged). The boys got a rope and all pulled together to get it to start.

Finally, when the time came to go home the boys were given the choice of travelling on separate buses or on the same bus and they opted for the latter. A stop was made for refreshments on the way home and one group had five dollars which they had won as a prize. They chose to spend it on the whole group, inviting their former rivals to be their guests for a malted milk.

Ethical Issues Raised by Sherif's Experiments

Sherif's experiments raise a number of ethical issues which have already been fully explored in Chapter 1, Section III. In particular:

- There are ethical issues which arise from the very fact that questionable attitudes were deliberately induced in the children.
- There was certainly a problem of informed consent. Where children are concerned, parents should have been fully informed of the true purposes of the study before the experiment took place. It seems unlikely that a cross-section of middle-class parents would have given their consent to prejudice deliberately being induced in their children.
- The children had no inkling as to what the whole thing was about. They were manipulated.
- There is no evidence that any of these children could have withdrawn from the experiment at any time during it.
- There is no doubt at all that pain and stress was caused at various stages in the experiment.

The experiment was justified by the experimenters in that a great deal of insight was gained into the way in which inter-group tensions arise and that it all ended happily. There did not appear to have been any permanent damage done. However, there clearly were risks which it is hard to justify.

Ultimate Attribution Bias

Pettigrew (1979) refers to **ultimate attribution bias**. In-group members attribute their own desirable behaviour to internal stable factors, while the out-group's desirable behaviour is attributed to factors within the immediate situation. Where undesirable behaviour is at issue, the opposite occurs; a group's own undesirable behaviour is attributed to the situation while the other group's undesirable behaviour is the result of disposition.

Social Representations

A group will also construct and transmit to its members explanations of what are complex and unfamiliar ideas in much more familiar and straightforward terms. What starts out as being a specialist and technical explanation of some phenomenon is given public attention, and by a process of simplification, distortion and ritualisation becomes a 'common-sense explanation' which is then accepted as orthodoxy. The process is illustrated in Figure 4.1.

The original **theory of social representations** was formulated by Moscovici (Farr and Moscovici, 1984; Moscovici, 1988). Let us take an example of the way in which social representations operate. Moscovici explored the way in which the technical and scientific ideas about psychoanalysis have become simplified and familiar, from being complex and unfamiliar. People are commonly referred to as having a 'complex', suffering from 'repression' or being 'neurotic', in very much the same way as you might describe someone's condition, 'He's got 'flu' or 'She's broken her leg'. The original set of ideas put forward as theory by Freud and others have become simplified, distorted and familiar.

Similarly, social representations may distort and simplify perceived events or phenomena. There arises a kind of 'group think' about something which happens. This is discussed in Chapter 6. For instance, Reicher (1984) conducted an analysis of the causes of the riots which took place in the St Paul's district of Bristol in the Spring

---

FIGURE 4.1
Theory of Social Representation

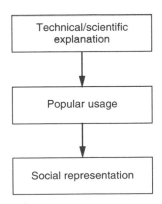

Source: Based on Moscovici (1984, 1988).

of 1980. St Paul's is the main residential area of the black community in Bristol, a relatively deprived inner-city area, but one with a
certain cohesion as a community. The conclusion that Reicher came
to relating to the rioting which took place was that the community
saw themselves as a cohesive in-group, threatened by outside forces
(the police raid on a social centre for the community, the Black and
White café). The police and their cars were the only real target. The
common view taken of the riots was that they were 'race riots' or
else that they were the response of a deprived group to 'government
cuts'. Litton and Potter (1985) have contrasted the popular concep-
tion of the cause of the rioting – the social representation of it – with
Reicher's analysis.

In a similar way we could contrast the 'social representation' of
electricity as a source of heat or light emanating from a socket, with
the technical/scientific description of electricity in terms of electrons
moving within conductive material.

Relative Deprivation

Berkowitz (1962, 1972) argued that subjective rather than objective
frustration was the source of hostility and aggression. Deprivation is
never absolute, but relative. Deprivation and frustration only become apparent when there is some standard against which to
measure it. Primitive peoples living in what would be to us extreme
deprivation do not *feel* deprived until they have an external standard
to measure their situation against. **Relative deprivation** occurs when
a person's own experiences are compared with his or her expectations. Davies (1969) produced his J-curve hypothesis of relative
deprivation, in which people's past and current attainments determine their future expectations. Where attainments suddenly fall
short of expectations there is acute relative deprivation. Figure 4.2
illustrates this J-curve.

What seems to happen is that when there is a long period of rising
prosperity expectations rise. Then, when there is a sharp drop in
fortunes, people's expectations continue to rise while their fortunes
do not. This leads to circumstances where collective violence is more
likely to occur. Davies cites various examples:

- The French revolution.
- The Russian revolution.
- The American Civil War.

- The rise of Nazism in Germany.
- The growth of Black Power in the USA in the 1960s.

However, the theory does not seem entirely to fit the facts. It is hard to claim that French or Russian peasants had rising expectations. They were simply downtrodden to the point where they had little more to lose. It is perhaps more appropriate in the case of the American Civil War, where cotton plantation owners in the South felt their way of life threatened by an anti-slavery movement based mainly in the North, and saw secession from the Union as a way of maintaining their prosperity. The rise of Nazism in Germany followed a period of extreme unemployment and hyper-inflation resulting from reparations exacted by the Allies after World War I. It is hard to say that there were rising expectations unless we go back to the prewar period. Finally the Black Power movement was the *result* of discrimination and prejudice; there was hardly much sign of rising expectations among the blacks who were discriminated against. Moreover, systematic tests of Davies' predictions such as that of Taylor (1982) did not show that expectations were

FIGURE 4.2
J-curve of Relative Deprivation

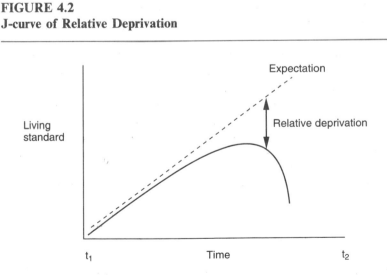

Source: Adapted from Davies (1969).

constructed from immediate past experience or that dissatisfaction was based upon a mismatch between people's actual situations and what they had confidently anticipated.

Berkowitz's (1972) view is that aggressive behaviour results from an array of aversive events of which frustration is one, and which might include such things as a long hot summer. There might also be perceived relative deprivation, poor housing and overcrowding, hot weather with little relief from air conditioning or green vegetation in the hot city streets, aggressive stimuli such as violence from armed police which leads to individual acts of violence and thence to collective rioting. Runciman (1966) distinguished two forms of relative deprivation:

- *Egoistic relative deprivation*: this is where an individual feels deprived relative to other similar individuals.
- *Fraternalistic relative deprivation*: this is where individuals make comparisons with members of other groups or individuals dissimilar to themselves.

Walker and Mann (1987) made a study of unemployed workers. Where there was fraternalistic relative deprivation there were likely to be militant protest, demonstrations and damage to property. We could cite the poll-tax riots in the late 1980s, where individuals collectively felt that they were carrying an unfair share of the burden of the cost of local government *in comparison with* people who were clearly much better off than they were. Where individuals felt themselves to be egoistically relatively deprived, symptoms of stress were reported such as headaches and sleeplessness rather than militancy. In French Canada, for instance, there was extreme dissatisfaction on an individual level between salaries of French as compared to English-speaking Canadians. There was fraternalistic deprivation which resulted in militancy (Guimond and Dubé-Sinard, 1983). Inter-group comparisons which lead to conflict and militancy seem to be most common between dissimilar groups.

Realistic Conflict Theory

Out of these experiments arose **realistic conflict theory** (Sherif, 1966) (depicted in Figure 4.3).

FIGURE 4.3
Realistic Conflict Theory

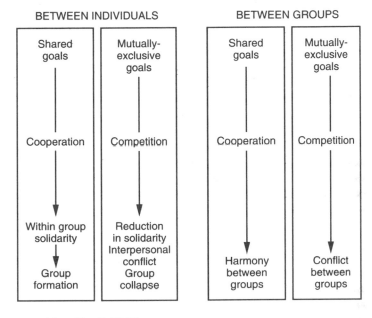

Source: After Sherif (1966).

Sherif argued that:

- Where individuals share goals which require them to be interdependent in order to achieve them, then they will tend to cooperate and form a group.
- Where individuals' goals are mutually exclusive (as, for instance, in a competitive game), the inter-individual competition prevents a group from forming and may result in an existing group collapsing.
- Where groups have mutually exclusive goals (where, for instance, one football team competes with another), realistic inter-group conflict is likely to be the result with ethnocentrism, prejudice and discrimination the likely outcome.

- Where the achievement of shared goals demands inter-group interdependence, conflict will be reduced and there will be increased harmony.

Naturalistic experiments reported by Fisher (1990) have supported realistic conflict theory, as have experiments conducted earlier by Blake and Mouton (1961). A series of 30 studies were conducted across the USA involving more than 1000 business people on management training programmes. There is also support cross-culturally for Sherif's conclusions from Diab (1970) in the Lebanon, and from Andreeva (1984) in the Soviet Union. However, Tyerman and Spencer (1983) in Britain attempted a replication in Britain involving Boy Scout patrols as participants. Competition between patrols did not produce as much hostility as Sherif's model would have predicted, and it proved easy to foster inter-group cooperation even where there was no superordinate goal. Tyerman and Spencer's explanation for this lies in the ethos of the Scout movement which provides its own superordinate goals.

The focus in realistic conflict theory lies in the relationship between the cooperative or competitive nature of human behaviour and people's goals. This has been explored in a very abstract way using games devised for two or more people to play. The problem, though with this has been with its ecological validity – that is to say, the extent to which it reflects what happens in 'real life': We shall describe the most frequently used of these games, Prisoner's Dilemma (PD).

The Prisoner's Dilemma (PD)

This is based upon an anecdotal 'real life' situation where two prisoners found themselves being questioned by detectives. They are clearly guilty, but the detectives only have enough evidence to convict them on a lesser offence. The confession of one of them would tip the balance, so they are questioned separately and persuaded to confess by offers of more lenient sentences. If one confesses, then he or she will get immunity; the other will be convicted of a more serious offence. If neither confesses they will both get light sentences. The dilemma facing them can be illustrated in terms of a matrix (Figure 4.4).

FIGURE 4.4
Prisoner's Dilemma Pay-off Matrix

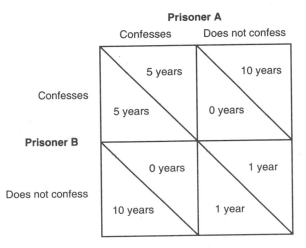

Source: Based on Luce and Raiffa (1957).

When the game is played out in a laboratory situation, participants have two choices:

1. To confess (C); or
2. To inform on the other (that is to defect – D).

Experimenters in the hundreds of experiments which have been carried out using PD have focused on:

- Strategies employed;
- The rewards on offer;
- Opportunities to communicate;
- Encouragement of cooperation.

Experimenters have tried to identify those factors which might make players more cooperative and less competitive.

Strategies Employed

It frequently happens in the laboratory that one of the players is a stooge, a confederate of the experimenters, who plays a pre-determined game. This might be:

- 100 per cent competition (D). This has the effect of forcing the participant to compete in self-defence.
- 100 per cent cooperation (C) This produces more cooperation from the participant.
- Tit for Tat (that is, whatever the participant does, the stooge does the same). This rewards the participant for cooperation and punishes defection. Cooperation rates consequently rise.

Rewards on Offer

Where the game is played in a laboratory the actual pay-offs are often merely in the form of points. These have no significance other than in the game; or else the points represent minimal amounts of money (for example 1 point = 1 penny). With only these negligible rewards, any incentive to cooperate may be effectively taken away. McClintock and McNeel (1966) found that there was more cooperation where there were greater real rewards (that is, actual money).

Opportunities to Communicate

The lack of opportunity to communicate may reduce cooperation between players. This may be for no other reason than to maintain the simulation of prisoners being separately interrogated. It is reasonable to assume that greater opportunity to communicate will lead to greater cooperation. Scodel *et al.* (1959) gave participants a discussion period midway through the game and found greater cooperation. Voissem and Sistrunk (1971) allowed some participants to pass notes in a standard form, expressing their intentions and\or expectations before each trial of a 100 trial PD game, and found that cooperation progressively increased as compared to other participants who were not allowed to communicate at all. Where partial communication was allowed there were intermediate levels of communication.

Encouragement of Cooperation

Deutsch (1958) established *cooperative, individualistic* and *competitive* conditions for participants:

- *Cooperative condition:* participants were encouraged to feel concerned about how well the other player was doing.
- *Individualistic condition:* participants were told that they should be concerned only about their own outcomes.
- *Competitive condition:* participants were told to make as much money for themselves as they could, and to do better than any other player.

Under each condition, participants were made to feel that the other player had the same goals. In each condition participants were sometimes allowed to exchange notes beforehand and sometimes not. There was an increase in cooperation in each condition when communication was allowed by the exchange of nots beforehand. The individualistic condition showed the greatest increase, from 35.9 per cent to 70.6 per cent. The cooperative condition showed an increase from 89.1 to 96.9 per cent. In the competitive condition the increase was from 12.5 per cent to 29.2 per cent.

The Commons Dilemma

Hardin (1968) has described the 'tragedy of the commons'. When villagers used the common pasture of the village to graze their animals, provided that there was moderation the common supported the animals grazed on it and replenished itself. But supposing an individual villager decided to double the number of the animals grazed to increase profits, this might not *by itself* affect the outcome. But when others, lured by the first villager's rewards, decided to do the same, the common can no longer replenish itself and is destroyed.

This represents a paradigm for much of the problems of environmental conservation. Canadians, worried about the depletion of fish stocks implement a voluntary restriction on catches, and even lay up some of their vessels. But when Spanish trawlers invade their waters, catching even immature fish, there is conflict and the stocks are depleted. However, there do seem to be circumstances where the common good is supported through voluntary cooperation. Brewer suggests that this is likely to happen when individuals identify closely with the common good, that is, where they derive their social identity from it. For instance, where villagers identify closely with the village, self-interest becomes subordinate to the common good. (Brewer and Kramer, 1986; Brewer and Schneider, 1990; Kramer and Brewer, 1984, 1986).

Self-assessment Questions

1. What are meant by the concepts of *in-group* and *out-group?* Illustrate these concepts by using examples.
2. What is meant by *social identity?* What effect can this have upon the cognitions of individuals.
3. Moscovici has developed a theory of *social representation.* Describe how this may result in a sort of 'group think' which may colour the perception which individual members of a group may have of events.
4. Explain how 'games' such as Prisoner's Dilemma may assist explanation of competitive or cooperative behaviour. What is the limitation of such games?

SECTION II   AGGRESSION

Introduction

It is as well at the outset to make clear what is meant by aggressive behaviour. For the purposes of this book it is defined as behaviour which is *intended* to cause harm to another living organism. Intention is important. Where a person is knocked down by a car because he or she steps off the pavement, there is no aggression; but if the car mounts the pavement in order to knock a person down, then that *is* aggressive. The idea of a living organism is also crucial. If we fly into a temper and kick the cat, that is aggression; but if in our temper we slam the door so hard that the glass in it shatters, that is not aggressive behaviour. We did have not intend to harm another living organism.

Explanations of aggressive behaviour fall roughly into three categories:

1. Biological explanations;
2. Bio-social explanations;
3. Social psychological explanations.

Biological Explanations

Again there are three categories of explanation:

1. Those which are based upon the psychoanalytic theory of Freud and his successors.
2. Those which are based upon ethology (the study of animals in their natural environment).
3. Those which have their basis in sociobiology (the study of the biological basis for social behaviour).

Psychoanalytic Theories of Aggression

Freud (1930) proposed that there were two opposed instinctive forces at work in humans, *eros* and *thanatos*, the former a life instinct, the latter a death instinct; self-preservation as opposed to self-destruction. In humans aggression was related to the second of these forces, self-destruction, and this instinct is directed outwards towards others, to cause harm to them. The important point is that aggression is for humans a natural and instinctive urge which has to find expression, either prosocially through activity, or antisocially through causing harm to others. A young man may give vent to his aggression by a hard game of rugby football. A vigorous debate may allow aggression to be expressed verbally, but within what is socially accepted. Alternatively, there may be verbal insults or fighting aimed at harming someone else. This urge is considered to be innate, inevitable and needing to be tamed.

Ethololologically-based Theories of Aggression

Ethologists study the normal behaviour of animals. It is suggested that there is a build up of energy which finds expression in **fixed action patterns** (Crook, 1973). The release of this energy is dependent on the presence of a *trigger*, which Hess (1962) has called a **releaser**. The threatening behaviour of another animal (bared teeth, for instance) may act as the trigger, or the invasion of territory. These mechanisms have a function to preserve the species as well as the individual according to Lorenz (1966). The protection and preservation of territory allows each animal to have the resources it needs to survive. There is also a purpose served in sexual selection. Within a species, aggression allows the stronger members of a species to mate and so to produce stronger offspring. The losers in such contests signal appeasement so that injury or death rarely occurs in these conflicts. The problem with humans is that such appeasement gestures have not been developed (there was no need in a harmless omnivorous creature) so that they deploy the killing power of weapons to cause death and destruction.

Sociobiology

Wilson (1975) defined sociobiology as the study of the biological bases of social behaviour. He has extended the Darwinian theories of evolution. Aggression (or indeed any behaviour which survives) must be **adaptive**. This means it must make it more likely that an individual member of a species exhibiting that behaviour will reproduce and so pass on its genes. Neo-Darwinists, as they have been called, are not so much concerned with the species as with the genes which determine an individual's patterns of behaviour. Such genetically-based behaviour will continue if it serves to increase the genetic **fitness** (that is, reproductive success) of the individual or of close relatives who carry the genes for that behaviour' (Cunningham, 1981, p. 71).

Aggression may enable an individual to acquire or to preserve more resources or to defend and protect relatives all of which make it more likely that the individual (or its close relatives) will be able to pass on its genes and so perpetuate the behaviour they determine. We are not talking about the preservation of the species, but the success of individuals or groups within that species. It has to be remembered that aggression also carries a potential cost, severe injury or death, which may prevent its aims being realised so that gains have to be balanced against costs. The development of aggression is bound to be selective (Krebs and Miller, 1985).

The assumptions of all the biologically-based explanations of aggression centre upon it being instinctive and innate. It is a basic part of the condition of all animals including humans.

Biosocial Explanations

These explanations include the **frustration/aggression** hypothesis, and also Zillman's **excitation/transfer** theory.

Frustration/Aggression Hypothesis

Dollard *et al.* (1939) proposed that aggression was always caused by some frustrating event or situation. On the other hand, frustration does not inevitably lead to aggression. This theory was welcomed as not involving the kind of psychoanalytic 'mumbo-jumbo', prevalent at the time. Frustration was defined as anything which interfered with the realisation of a goal. When someone expects to be able to buy an electric light bulb from a shop, but finds it closed, that is frustrating even when there is a supermarket half a mile away. Frustration may come from the difficulty of the task itself or from interference from someone else.

While there is evidence that aggressive behaviour may sometimes have its roots in frustration (Azrin *et al.*, 1966; Rule and Percival 1971) the link is by no means as strong as Dollard had suggested. Buss (1961, 1967) suggested that the link only existed when the aggression had instrumental value (that is, when aggression might help to get over the frustration). The amount of the frustration is important too. Mild frustration does not seem to result in aggressive behaviour. Harris (1974) carried out some field studies, cutting in on people who were queuing for the theatre or in a store. When she cut in on someone who was second in line, she was often met with verbal abuse, while someone who was twelfth in line responded much less aggressively. Interference when you are close to your goal is more frustrating than when you are further away.

Berkowitz (1965) has suggested that frustration creates a readiness for aggressive action. Frustration creates anger which may or may not be translated into aggression. There is an interaction between the cognitive and emotional states engendered and the environmental cues. In the example above, we feel cross that someone has cut in on us and we react to the whole situation.

Excitation/Transfer Theory

Zillman has developed an excitation/transfer model of aggression (Zillman, 1979, 1988). This attempts to link the effective and the environmental elements. Zillman's model suggests that there are three factors which determine whether aggression is expressed in action:

1. Learned aggressive behaviour;
2. Arousal or excitation from another source;
3. The individual's interpretation of the aroused state.

Excitation might occur from a wide variety of sources. We might just have played a stimulating game of squash which we won in a close-fought contest. We might just have had a row with someone at work and there is residual excitation or arousal. If someone then cuts in on us at a traffic intersection, we are much more likely to react with 'road rage' than we would if we were not aroused. Figure 4.5 illustrates the excitation/transfer theory.

Social Psychological Explanations

Learning to be Aggressive

Bandura (1973, 1977) has suggested that aggressive behaviour is largely learned. Both prosocial and antisocial behaviour may be learned, though there is certainly some biological component. The experiences through which it is learned can be either first-hand or vicarious. Socialisation into aggressive behaviour may be through straightforward conditioning processes or else through observational learning. These ideas have been discussed more fully in Chapter 1.

Direct Experience

Behaviour is established and maintained through rewards and punishments. Suppose a child wants a toy which his sister is playing with; he attacks her and seizes the toy. When no one intervenes to stop him he has been rewarded for his aggression; he has the toy. Conversely, when an adult intervenes with harsh words every time he tries to gain his way through aggressive behaviour, socialisation will reduce natural aggressive tendencies.

The range of possible reinforcements for aggressive behaviour is very large. It might be social status or social approval (Geen and

FIGURE 4.5
Zillman's Excitation/Transfer of Aggression

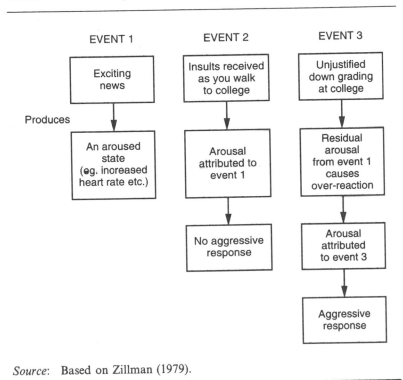

Source: Based on Zillman (1979).

Stonner, 1971; Gentry, 1970). Money is a reinforcer for adults; sweets for children (Buss, 1971; Gaebelein, 1973; Walters and Brown, 1963). In cases of extreme provocation it may be reinforcing to watch a victim suffer (Baron, 1974; Feshbach *et al.*, 1967). It has been suggested as a reason why serial killers commit their crimes.

Observational Learning or Modelling

Bandura and his colleagues conducted a series of experiments into the ways in which aggressive behaviour is learned through observation and modelling. These are described in Box 4.3.

BOX 4.3
Experiments on Observational Learning (Bandura, 1973, 1977)

A child of nursery-school age was brought into a room and introduced to making pictures using potato prints and colourful stickers. After a short time another adult came into the room and was shown a corner where there was a mallet, a large inflatable 'Bobo' doll, as well as some other toys. The experimenter set up two conditions:

- A non-aggressive condition where the second adult plays quietly for ten minutes.
- An aggressive condition where the second adult attacks the Bobo doll, hitting it kicking it, pounding its nose and yelling aggressive comments.

Then the child was taken into another room where there was the child's favourite toy as well as a Bobo doll and some other toys, aggressive and non-aggressive. The child was forbidden to play with the favourite toy, but could play with anything else in the room. Bandura and his colleagues were interested to see how the adult's behaviour in the first stage of the experiment affected the child's choice of playthings. Children who had watched the aggressive model were found to choose more aggressive playthings and to play with them more aggressively than those who had watched the adult playing non-aggressively, or indeed than the control group who had had no initial session. It has to be remembered that the Bobo doll is inanimate so that strictly it falls outside our definition of aggression, but there does seem to be a link between aggressive behaviour in a play situation and in other contexts. Among adults, most people know how to be aggressive but there is evidence that the presence of an aggressive model serves to remove some of the inhibitions which prevent people from behaving aggressively.

Factors Influencing Aggression

Among those factors which have been found to influence aggressive behaviour are:

- Personal factors including individual differences;
- Environmental factors such as hot weather or poor air quality;
- Situational variables such as the presence of weapons or of provocation of some kind.

It is not easy to separate such factors and there is bound to be interaction between them. However, it is worthwhile to discuss each factor on its own so long as it is borne in mind they are never going to be discrete.

Individual Differences

The idea of an 'aggressive personality' is quite an attractive one. If it were possible to measure the aggressiveness of people's personalities we might be able to determine how likely it was that a violent offender might re-offend. Age, gender, culture and personal experiences combine to make some people more likely to behave violently than others.

Type A Personality

There is evidence that there exists a pattern of behaviour which has been described as a **type A personality** (Matthews, 1982). Those who exhibit this pattern of behaviour have been found amongst other things to be more prone to coronary heart disease. They are hyperactive and very competitive in their interactions with other people. They are also more aggressive towards those who are perceived as competing with them on an important task (Carver and Glass, 1978). Dembroski and McDougall (1978) found that such individuals were happier to work alone than with others so that they could be in control of the situation and not have to endure the incompetence of others. Within an organisation, Baron (1989) found that type A personalities were more frequently in conflict with their subordinates and with their peers, though not with their superiors. In this they appear to have something in common with the authoritarian personality described by Adorno *et al.* (1950) (see p. 233). Strube *et al.* (1984) found that type A personalities were more prone to engage in child abuse than other personality types. There are also suggestions that the aggressive tendencies of type A personalities are inherited (Rushton *et al.* 1986). Twin studies have been used to support these conclusions. Identical (monozygotic) twins have the same genetic make up, while fraternal (dizygotic) twins are no more alike genetically than other brothers or sisters. It is possible to compare pairs of monozygotic with pairs of dizygotic twins. If monozygotic twins are more closely alike in levels of aggression (in this case) it is possible to conclude that inheritance plays a part.

There is a fuller discussion of the use of twin studies in Birch and Hayward (1994), *Individual Differences*, in this series.

Gender and Socialisation

Maccoby and Jacklin (1974) in their extensive review of the literature on gender differences suggested that females are less aggressive than males. Later research by Eagly and Steffen (1986) casts some doubt on this. While men do seem to be more aggressive, the differences are small and not always consistent. When the issue is solely physical aggression it is undoubtedly true that men are more aggressive, but when psychological or verbal aggression are added into the equation gender differences are not clear cut at all. However, there are substantial differences in the ways in which men and women view aggressive behaviour. Women are much more guilty and anxious about behaving aggressively, more concerned about the harm they may be causing to their victims and worried about possible danger to themselves.

Dodge and Crick (1990) reviewed the literature on aggression in children and came to the conclusion that individual differences in aggression may reflect differences in the ability to process information about social situations. There were three specific areas of difference:

1. Differences in ability to interpret social cues and the meaning of other people's behaviour.
2. Difference in ability to generate alternative possible responses in social situations.
3. Differences in ability to decide which response to adopt.

Aggressive children and adolescents appear to Dodge and Crick to have what they refer to as a **hostile attributional bias**. That is to say, they are more likely than non-aggressive children to attribute hostile intent to others' actions.

Environmental Factors

Environmental factors to be discussed include noise, air-quality and heat.

Noise

Donnerstein and Wilson (1976) found that there was evidence of a greater tendency towards aggression in conditions of high noise levels. It has to be borne in mind that their experiment was laboratory-based and involved participants being prepared to deliver higher levels of shock to a partner in high-noise conditions than in low noise or no noise at all. Noise itself did not provoke violence, but lowered the threshold when an instigation to violence was present. However, this kind of study may not be very valid ecologically. How often in 'real life' do you deliver shocks to other people?

Air Quality

In an archival study, Rotton and Frey (1985) matched reports of family disturbances with levels of ozone in the atmosphere and revealed a correlation between weather conditions and violent crime. Days when the temperature was high and the winds were low (when air quality was at its worst) tended to preceded violent episodes

Heat

When there have been civil disturbances, media reports have emphasised the 'long hot summer' effect. In fact the US Riot Commission (1968) cited hot weather as a cause of riots. In fact the relationship between high temperatures and aggressive behaviour is not quite as simple as that. Research has found that while it is true the heat increases the tendency towards aggression, it is not a linear relationship (Baron, 1977). It appears that aggressive tendencies are mediated by the amount of discomfort people feel and that the relationship between discomfort and aggression is curvilinear. The highest levels of aggression are found when discomfort is at an intermediate level, with lower tendencies towards aggression both when there is little discomfort and when it is very high. Figure 4.6 illustrates Baron's conclusions.

Other research has corroborated Baron's findings. Palmarek and Rule (1979) in a laboratory study used two conditions of ambient temperature, one of high temperature (96° Fahrenheit) and one of comfortable temperature (73° Fahrenheit). In the course of the tasks which participants were asked to perform, various levels of insult

FIGURE 4.6
Discomfort and Aggression

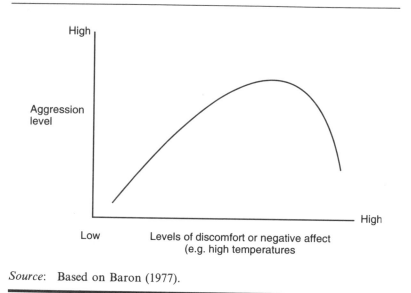

Source: Based on Baron (1977).

were used against them. Greater aggression occurred when there was moderate arousal, caused either by the excessive heat or by the insults. But when there was no such arousal or when there was extreme arousal as a result of *both* insults *and* heat, there was less aggression. However, Anderson and Anderson (1984) have suggested that these findings were the result of the experimental procedures. Participants may have guessed what the experiment was about and consciously tried to resist being aggressive. Laboratory studies such as those of Baron and of Palmarek and Rule are bound to be artificial and therefore less ecologically valid than field studies might be. However, Baron and Ransberger (1978) found support for the curvilinear relationship in an archival study. Instances were collated of communal violence in the United States and matched with records of temperatures on the days when the violence occurred. As it got hotter, riots became more likely, but only up to a point. It seems it sometimes gets too hot even for causing trouble!

However, Anderson has more recently (1989) reviewed a wide range both of field and laboratory studies in this area and has drawn the following conclusions:

Temperature effects are direct: they operate at the individual level. Temperature effects are important; they influence the most antisocial behaviours imaginable.   (Anderson 1989, p. 94)

Influence of the Situation

Arousal

Zillman's excitation/transfer model which has been discussed earlier illustrates the importance of an aroused state in relation to aggression. This may come from a direct verbal or physical attack, from an emotional state caused by some other source, or from expenditure of energy and stimulation (anything from watching an exciting sporting contest to a couple of hours spent Scottish dancing).

Provocation and Aggression

Much more obviously than in Zillman's model, aggression is likely to result from provocation of some kind. Someone makes a direct verbal or physical attack and we retaliate. There is a much stronger link between aggression and provocation than between frustration and aggression. Geen (1968) demonstrated that this was the case in an experiment. Participants were frustrated in attempts to complete a jig-saw puzzle, or else were allowed to complete the task unhindered. In this second condition, after the task was completed, a confederate of the experimenter's insulted both the participant's intelligence and motivation. The aggressive behaviour which ensued was far stronger than in the frustration condition.

The perception a person has of another's intention in attacking has an effect on retaliatory action. If we believe that someone has *intentionally* tried to harm us, then we are much more likely to retaliate. In addition, Lysak *et al.* (1989) showed that the avoidability of harm which is caused is also important. Where we perceive that another person could have foreseen the consequences of his or her actions, then we place blame upon that person and may retaliate even though there was no intent to cause harm. In fact the actual harm caused does not appear to be as important as intent or foreseeability. Where there is advance knowledge of some mitigating circumstance this can reduce the likelihood of retaliation.

Instigation from Third Parties

It happens not infrequently that witnesses or bystanders become involved in confrontations between people. Borden (1975) suggested that even inactive bystanders may influence events. The presence of a male observer may be the cause of a higher level of aggressive behaviour than if the observer were female. Society norms implicitly suggest that women are less likely to approve of violence than men are. Milgram's experiments, which will be fully discussed in Chapter 6, showed that external pressure was influential in persuading individuals to administer apparently massive shocks to others (Milgram, 1963, 1965, 1974). If the bystanders perceive that their urgings are having an effect, they will urge even more aggression; while if the individual being attacked refuses to retaliate they will give up their instigation (White and Gruber, 1982).

Disinhibition, Deindividuation or Dehumanisation

Disinhibition refers to any reduction in the social forces which restrain us from acting in an aggressive manner. Inhibitions against aggression are part of the socialisation process. In most societies people are brought up to regard aggression and violence as undesirable and to be avoided. Shame and guilt are attached to behaving in an aggressive way. However, several factors may reduce or even eliminate these inhibitions, and these include:

- *Deindividuation* This involves the individual who is perpetrating violence or aggression feeling that he or she is somehow anonymous; that *as individuals* no shame or blame can be attached to them. Examples of this kind of disinhibition include the effects of military service. In the My Lai incident during the Vietnam war, a platoon of soldiers entered a Vietnamese village and slaughtered men women and children indiscriminately. Hersh (1970), commenting on this incident, has suggested that a climate in which it was legitimate to shoot anything which moved had grown up. Soldiers no longer thought of themselves as individuals who were individually responsible for their actions and who might be punished for them, but as anonymous soldiers. The wearing of uniforms serves to promote this feeling of anonymity. In war-crimes trials at the end of the Second World War it was a frequent defence that those on trial were only obeying orders. Middlebrook (1980) has suggested that the hoods worn by Ku Klux Klan members, or the stocking masks which armed robbers wear, serve this same purpose.

- *Dehumanisation* The same effect of anonymity is evident in relation to the victims of violence. Reports of military encounters refer to units of the enemy being 'taken out'. Individual human beings were not perceived as being killed, but units of the enemy fighting force were being eliminated. Cohen (1987) demonstrated the way in which the use of nuclear weapons in war might be made acceptable. Victims were referred to as 'targets' and the wholesale death and destruction which accompanies the use of nuclear weapons is referred to as 'collateral damage', even though this might refer to thousands of human casualties. The references made by Bosnian Serbs in the war in Yugoslavia to 'ethnic cleansing' disguise genocidal acts by sanitising them.

Alcohol and Drugs

The use of drugs and alcohol may have the same disinhibiting effect. It is common to see images of drunks engaged in violence. At the same time it has been suggested that the use of marijuana has the opposite effect of minimising tendencies towards aggression. Taylor and his colleagues conducted a series of laboratory studies to verify this (Myerscough and Taylor, 1985; Shuntich and Taylor, 1972; Taylor, 1986; Taylor and Gammon, 1975; Taylor, Gammon and Capasso, 1976). This was a laboratory experiment where participants had to compete with a partner in a reaction-time trial. During each trial the winner had the chance to administer a shock to the loser at a level of his or her choosing. Different amounts of either alcohol or THC (tetra-hydrocannabinol), the major active ingredient of marijuana, were administered to participants. Levels of aggression were measured by the mean shock settings used by winners against losers. Small amounts of alcohol reduced aggression levels, but those who had had larger amounts were found to be progressively more aggressive. THC, on the other hand, had no effect in small doses,

but decreased aggressive behaviour when larger doses were administered. Figure 4.7 shows the findings of Taylor *et al.* (1976).

FIGURE 4.7
**Aggression and Drugs. A Comparison of the Effects of Alcohol and
THC on Aggression Responses**

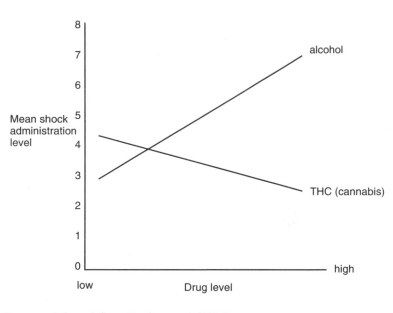

Source: Adapted from Taylor *et al.* (1976).

Anger and Aggression

Berkowitz (1983a, 1983b) developed a model of the relationship
between anger and aggression which he termed the **cognitive/neo-
associationistic model**. In this model aversive stimuli of a wide
variety of kinds, ranging from the discomfort of excessive heat or
noise to frustration of one's achievement of a goal, or to the insults
or attacks of another individual, produce negative emotional feelings (dislike). These are not specific but are interpreted in the light of

other cues which may be available. What we *do* about these negative feelings may be either avoidance or attack. Which way it turns out depends, among other things, upon the network of associations which exist in memory between anger and aggression. If in similar circumstances before, feelings of anger have been associated with aggressive behaviour this may have the effect of **priming** (or making more accessible) thoughts about aggression. These images of violence or aggression may be real or they may be fictitious. This is interesting as a cognitive explanation of the linkage between media violence and aggressive behaviour. In a similar way experiences of prosocial behaviour (discussed in the following section) may 'prime' helping. We watch a film of someone coming to the assistance of a person in distress; that event is stored in memory and makes more accessible to us (that is, primes) prosocial behaviour at a later date. It is well to note that this operates in two directions. Thinking about anger/sympathy may prime aggressive/prosocial behaviour; equally, thinking about aggression/helping may prime anger/sympathy. Figure 4.8 illustrates the neo-associationistic model of Berkowitz.

FIGURE 4.8
Berkowitz's Neo-associationistic Model of Aggression

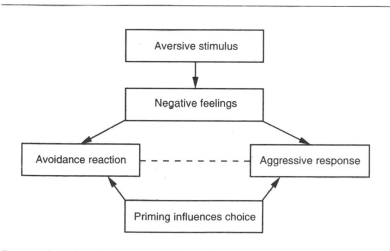

Source: Based on Berkowitz (1983a and b).

Violence on TV

While the influence of violence and aggressive behaviour depicted by the media and in particular on TV has received attention, it has proved more difficult to establish causal links in a *formal laboratory situation*, while there have been many reports of individuals copying violent attacks seen on TV. The two children involved in the murder of James Bulger in Liverpool in 1994 are a particular case. Geen and Donnerstein (1983) have conducted a review of such studies. The following points are made:

- The TV violence to which participants were exposed was often of a fairly mild kind and of short duration.
- The violence to which viewers are exposed is much more extended in time and much less mild. Research in the US has shown that on children's Saturday morning television there is a violent act every two minutes. By the time a child is 16 it will have witnessed more than 13 000 killings on television (Liebert and Schwartzberg, 1977). While there are more constraints in the UK over children's exposure to TV violence (the 9 o'clock watershed for instance), children are exposed to violence consistently and over a prolonged period. The availability of video cassette recordings and of satellite and cable TV has increased this. In addition, news programmes often report violence. During the Gulf War, for instance, there were regular reports of bombs and missiles destroying Iraqi installations. The war in Bosnia and reports of violence and massacres in Rwanda are other instances.

- Violence to which people are exposed has the effect of disinhibiting and sanitising violence.
- Violence and aggression is often portrayed as not being harmful to the victims. Injuries received are underplayed.
- In many instances the aggressor is seen as the 'good guy', and is only rarely portrayed as being punished for his or her violence.

The attempts which have been made to study links between TV violence and aggression have taken several forms

- There have been artificial experiments using material specially produced for the purpose, as in the case of Bandura's Bobo doll experiments (reported earlier). Then there were experiments using actual TV or film material.

● There were also field studies using quasi-experimental designs (naturalistic studies) and actual TV viewing patterns.

Laboratory Studies

Studies (Berkowitz and Alioto, 1973; Geen and Stonner, 1971; Josephson, 1987; Liebert and Schwartzberg, 1977; Turner and Berkowitz, 1972) have identified various factors which modify the link between TV violence and aggressive behaviour including:

● Justification: only where the film justifies the violence it shows is aggressive behaviour likely to follow.
● The initial aggressiveness of the viewer: only where there was a high initial level of aggression was exposure to violence likely to lead to it.
● The link between TV violence and aggression is valid only to the extent to which the viewer identifies with the aggressor in the film.
● Where the aggressor is portrayed as having redeeming features, aggression is more likely to follow.
● Aggression is more likely to occur where there are cues which remind viewers of violent episodes.

Field Studies/Naturalistic Studies

An example of a study conducted in a more natural setting is that of Leyens *et al.* (1975); this is described in Box 4.4.

Conclusions from a number of such studies confirm that there is a relationship between violence on TV and aggressive behaviour. Children who watch more violence on television are more aggressive. Sheehan (1983) correlated children's TV viewing habits and the levels of their aggressive behaviour. Participants in his study were middle-class boys and girls in Australian primary schools aged between five and ten years old. Some age cohorts were tested more than once during the years 1979–81. Aggression was measured by peer ratings of incidents of behaviour by each child which caused physical injury or irritation to another child.

Correlations between the viewing of violent TV programmes and aggression measured in this way were significant among eight to ten-

> **BOX 4.4**
> **A Naturalistic (Quasi-experimental) Study of the Link between Watching Films and Aggression (Leyens *et al.*, 1975)**
>
> The participants were boys who lived in four small dormitories in a boarding school in Belgium. In two of the dormitories aggressive behaviour tended to be high, and in the other two low. A particular week was designated as 'Movie Week' during which the investigators were able to manipulate the amount of violence shown in television films. The television sets the boys ordinarily watched were disconnected and special films shown. In two of the dormitories (one high aggression, one low aggression) films were shown that were saturated with violence. In the other two dormitories (again, one high aggression, one low aggression) only non-violent films were shown. During the week and in the week that followed, each boy's aggressive behaviour was monitored and rated. Physical aggression increased in both the dormitories which had been shown the violent films; but verbal aggression only increased in the aggressive dormitory. In the other there was actually a decrease in verbal aggression.

year-olds but not among the younger children It has to be remembered that correlational data of this kind does not imply cause. It has also to be said that there has been considerable criticism of the methodology of many of these studies. Durkin (1995) makes the following points:

- Many of the studies suffer from' demand characteristics' (see Chapter 1);
- Some of the analogies made with real life violence are less than totally believable;
- There are frequently confounding variables which may have been overlooked;
- Alternative explanations for the findings of some of these studies have not been fully examined.

He says 'The topic is contentious and the widely cited proof of the effects of media violence is at least open to criticism – a point which is overlooked in many orthodox treatments of the topic' (Durkin, 1995, p. 409)

Perhaps we should be cautious in the way in which we interpret these studies, particularly in view of the fact that there may be a political motive behind some of the conclusions which are drawn. It may be easier for governments to blame the media than to tackle the root causes of violence, the social problems of our time – poverty, for instance, deprivation and the growth of inequality between rich and poor.

However, there have been other longitudinal studies done by Eron (1982) and by Huesmann *et al.* (1984) which have shown not only that there is a causal link but that it is bi-directional. Children as young as eight were observed, their aggressiveness assessed, as well as the amount of time they spent watching TV. Then some years later aggressiveness was again assessed together with TV viewing time. Eron came to the conclusion that the amount of time the eight-year-olds spent watching TV is linked to how aggressive that child will be by the time he or she reaches the age of 18 (Eron, 1980).

Reasons for the Link between TV Violence and Aggression

Two sets of explanations for the link have been advanced:

1. *Observational learning or modelling*: as we watch television we are assimilating models of behaviour which can be imitated at a later time. How effective this learning is depends upon such things as,

   - the degree to which children watching violent TV shows really believe that this is what 'real' life is like; and
   - the degree to which the child identifies with the aggressive characters in the film.   (Huesmann *et al.*, 1984)

2. *Cognitive explanations*: these are dependent upon thinking and memory processes rather than associative learning. Where children have frequently watched violence on film, aggressive scenarios become more accessible in memory. TV may become a priming device in Berkowitz's neo-associationistic model (described earlier). Bushman and Geen (1990) extended this to include adults and Berkowitz demonstrated that desensitisation occurred. People who see a great deal of violence become less concerned about the possible harmful consequence of their actions. However, Josephson (1987) has shown that the priming effect may work in the opposite direction also. Violence may prime social norms to *reduce* the extent to which naturally non-aggressive children act out the aggressive themes they see on TV.

Bushman and Geen (1990) found similar effects with adults. Where there was high hostility, viewing even moderate levels of violence increased violent cognitions, but among those whose personality showed low levels of hostility the effect was the opposite; violent cognitions decreased.

Pornography and Aggression

Pornography has been defined as a particular type of erotic material in which sexual and aggressive elements combine to portray force and coercion being used to accomplish the sexual act. Freud (1938) suggested that there was a close link between aggression and sexuality. Later psychoanalysts have maintained the existence of this link. Stoller (1976) has stated:

> Hostility, overt or hidden is what generates and enhances sexual excitement and its absence leads to sexual indifference and boredom. (Stoller, 1976, p. 903)

Kutchinsky (1973) in a study carried out in Denmark measured the frequency of sex offences before and after restrictions were lifted on the sale of pornographic material. Sex crimes were found to have declined markedly after the lifting of restrictions. This gave rise to a theory which suggested that pornography acted as a safety valve. Now that it had become easier to obtain sexual materials, Kronhausen and Kronhausen argued (1964), potential sex offenders get their 'kicks' from such materials and do not have to resort so much to sex crimes. However, this was an initial reaction. Bachy (1976) found that once pornographic materials were readily available the incidence of rape increased rather thaan decreased. These were correlational studies, though, and great caution is necessary before cause is inferred.

A more extensive programme of research, which included experimental work was carried out by Donnerstein (Donnerstein, 1982; Malamuth and Donnerstein, 1982, 1984). They concluded that men who are exposed to pornography will become more aggressive towards women. The important point seems to be that the material to which they are exposed should be pornographic rather than simply erotic (see definition above). Unless anger is involved, erotica have little effect on aggression, while intense provocation or more-arousing erotic material *will* result in increased aggression (Donnerstein *et al.*, 1975; Ramirez *et al.*, 1982). Zillman and Bryant (1982) found that men became more callous in their dealings with women when they were exposed over a long period to such materials.

Control of Aggression

For theorists who believe that aggression is an innate urge (for instance, psychoanalysts who see aggression as the expression of *thanatos* or the death instinct), to eliminate aggression is not possible. The aim must be to channel it into acceptable ways. Sporting events or other competitive activities serve to provide an outlet.

Similarly, ethologists such as Lorenz (1966) do not believe that it could be possible to eliminate aggressive behaviour entirely. If we can identify the cues which trigger aggressive behaviour then it might be possible to control it.

Instrumental learning depends upon the reinforcement of behaviour. If aggressive behaviour is not reinforced, theory suggests it should die away. Brown and Elliot (1965) found that a person who is not rewarded for displays of aggression is less likely to acquire or maintain aggressive behaviours. Punishment of aggression is more problematical. Baron (1977) has suggested that punishment or the threat of it is effective in reducing aggression only in certain conditions:

- It must be predictable. Where a parent or a teacher is attempting to control aggressive behaviour, he or she above all needs to be consistent.
- It must follow the aggression closely. It is not effective for there to be delay as it depends upon the association of the punishment with the behaviour.
- It must be legitimised by the existing social norms.
- Those who administer punishment must be seen as non-aggressive models.

The threat of punishment is even less certain in reducing aggression. Baron suggests that it is effective only when:

- The person threatening is not especially angry.
- The punishment which is threatened is quite severe.

- The aggressor sees it to be very likely that the threat will be carried out.
- The aggressor has not much to gain by his or her aggression.

These very considerable limitations on punishment and the threat of it as a means to reduce aggressive behaviour must mean that it is not a very effective means. Phillips (1980) used archival information to highlight some relevant points. He used records of murders and executions in London between 1858 and 1921. During the weeks immediately following the well-publicised execution of a murderer, the incidence of homicide decreased by about 35 per cent, but about six weeks later returned to what it had been before. While capital punishment may be a deterrent *in the short term*, in the longer run there is little evidence of deterrence.

Social learning theorists are more optimistic. They believe the answer lies in replacing violent and aggressive models with non-aggressive ones. Baron (1971) has found that the influence of a non-aggressive model can neutralise the effect of aggressive models. This suggests that even if it not possible to remove all potentially aggressive models, providing non-aggressive model will be of some help.

Incompatible responses

It has been suggested that as it is difficult to do two things at once, a means of controlling violent responses might be to provide conditions which induce responses that are not compatible with aggressive ones. Baron and Ball (1974) used humorous cartoons, while Rule and Leger (1976) attempted to foster empathy. In both cases, participants in their studies were found to be less aggressive when there was an alternative non-aggressive response available.

Discouragement of Retaliation

It is sometimes possible to defuse retaliation and reduce the chance of aggression in response to attack by explaining why the attack was beyond the aggressor's control; that is, by providing mitigating circumstances. This was most effective if the information was available before the act of aggression and if this was accepted as reasonable (Zillman *et al.*, 1975; Zillman and Cantor, 1976).

Reducing Frustration

If frustration is a major factor in aggression (see above), it ought to be possible to look to ways of controlling frustration in order to reduce aggression. Ransford (1968) found that those blacks in Los Angeles with the most profound feelings of frustration were those who were most liable to resort to violence. If some of the social and economic frustrations can be removed then there is a chance that there will be less violence. It is possible to see the growth in unemployment and in the numbers of disadvantaged people in the UK as linked to the growth of violent crime during the last 15 years.

Catharsis

Catharsis refers to the release of pent-up aggressive energy through other forms of behaviour. It has been suggested that fantasy might provide a means whereby catharsis might occur and aggression might be reduced. However, while it has been found that aggression works to reduce aggressive fantasies, there does not seem to be much evidence that it works the other way round. There is more support for efficacy of **behavioural catharsis** in reducing subsequent aggression. This refers to the opportunity to express aggression at the time the frustration occurs (Konečni, 1975).

Cognitive Means of Aggression Control

It was noted earlier that Berkowitz's **neo-associationistic model** points to a link between the priming effect of experiences, whether direct or by means of film or television, to make the memory of earlier experiences more accessible. When a link is built up between aggression and feelings of anger, aggression becomes more likely. Alternatively, if a cognitive link can be established between non-violent responses and emotional arousal, this may make an aggressive response less likely. Accordingly, the presentation of non-aggressive responses on film or on television may serve to 'prime' non-violent behaviour. Berkowitz (1989) has pointed to measures which:

- reduce aversive stimuli (by, for instance, ensuring adequate food and shelter);

- strengthen social norms against aggression (by rewarding non-aggressive responses and not rewarding aggressive ones, for instance);
- reduce the accessibility of aggressive actions in memory by reducing overall exposure to aggressive models. In this way feelings of anger will not be so likely to 'prime' aggressive action.

Self-assessment Questions

1. Describe some of the different explanations of aggression, including biological, biosocial and social psychological explanations. Is it possible to say that any one approach provides a complete explanation?
2. Is it plausible to say that some individuals are *naturally* more aggressive than others?
3. List some factors which seem to contribute to aggressive behaviour. Is there good evidence for the 'long hot summer' factor?
4. Is there convincing evidence that watching violence on TV may make children more aggressive?
5. Identify some ways in which aggressive behaviour may be reduced. Do you think that Berkowitz's neo-associationistic model might contribute to this?

SECTION III   PROSOCIAL BEHAVIOUR

Wispé (1972) defined prosocial behaviour as behaviour which has social consequences which contribute positively to the psychological or physical well-being of another person. This encompasses a very wide spectrum of behaviour. At this time consideration will be limited to the following:

- Helping behaviour;
- Altruism – that is, giving or sharing with no obvious self-gain;
- Bystander intervention.

Helping Others and Altruism

There are three approaches which have been taken to explain human helping behaviour:

1. Biological approaches.
2. What might be termed biosocial approaches.
3. Social learning approaches.

Biological Explanations

Biologists take the view that that just as there is an innate need in humans to eat or to drink, there is also a need to help others and this has been taken as one explanation for the comparative success of the human species. In particular, sociobiologists have drawn attention to the evolutionary benefits of altruistic behaviour (Krebs and Miller, 1985; Wilson, 1978). As we have seen, sociobiologists approach human (as well as animal) behaviour from the point of view of genetic and evolutionary survival. The basic proposition is that humans, in common with all animals, have one pre-eminent goal which is the survival of the genes. Human beings will be predisposed to help relatives because in so doing they are furthering the survival of the genes which they share with those relatives. Your son, because of his parentage, shares genes with you. If your paramount interest lies in ensuring that your genes are passed on to succeeding generations, you have a vested interest in your son's survival. Not quite as much as in your own, perhaps, but more than an unrelated stranger's. Then again, if I myself have passed the time of life when I can myself reproduce, gene survival may be ensured to an even greater extent if I can ensure my son's survival. Hence there may be circumstances when a person might sacrifice themself for their children.

Reciprocal altruism takes this one stage further. Trivers (1971) has used **reciprocal altruism** as an explanation for 'Good Samaritan' behaviour. A man dives into a river to save another from drowning. The man has a 50:50 chance of drowning. The chances of the rescuer dying in the attempt are perhaps one in 20. If at some future date the roles are reversed, both will have benefited. Each will have traded a 1:2 chance of dying for a 1:10 chance. Within the population as a whole, such reciprocally altruistic behaviour will have enhanced each individual's personal genetic 'fitness'. There is a fuller discussion of altruism, including reciprocal altruism, in *Comparative Psychology* in the same series as this book (Malim *et al.*, 1996).

The main problems with this sociobiological approach to helping behaviour are:

- That there have been no good studies done with human participants which have supported the biological explanation of helping.
- That the extensive research done by social learning theorists into helping behaviour has been ignored.

Learning Approaches to Helping Behaviour

These can be divided into two, those based upon basic learning theory and those which depend upon social learning and modelling. Both of these approaches contend that there is no innate tendency to help others but that this behaviour needs to be learned. Classical conditioning and instrumental learning represent the basic learning theory approach; observational learning and modelling represent the social learning approach. These processes of learning are part of the socialisation process during childhood. Straightforward telling, reinforcement and modelling each have a part to play. Grusec *et al.* (1978) have found that it increases a child's helpfulness just to tell him or her what the right behaviour is. Children learn to expect people to be helpful. But to instruct children to help others is less helpful unless there is evidence that the instructor is practising what he or she preaches.

Reinforcements such as praise also work as Fischer (1963) found. Where children are praised or reinforced with bubblegum for sharing what they had, they learnt to share with other children. Vicarious reinforcement also plays a part. Where children saw another person behaving generously to a third person they tended to imitate.

Modelling Behaviour

There is evidence that people learn to be helpful by observing others helping. Grusec and Skubiski (1970) found that where children won tokens in games and then saw an adult giving away tokens to a needy child, they were more likely to behave generously. Children's attitudes to prosocial behaviour also improved where they watched prosocial behaviour on television (Coates *et al.*, 1976). An experiment described in Box 4.5 illustrates this modelling effect.

BOX 4.5
Modelling Prosocial Behaviour (Bryan and Test, 1967)

Bryan and Test (1967) demonstrated that adult behaviour as well could be influenced by modelling. They set out to test whether the presence of a model would influence the number of motorists who stopped to help a woman who had had a puncture. This was an experiment where there were two conditions

1. In the experimental condition motorists first passed a car by the side of the road whose driver (a woman) was being assisted to change a wheel by a male motorist who had stopped to help her. A short way along the road there was another car with a puncture, again with a woman driver. In this case she was alone and clearly needed help.
2. In the second condition (control) there were only the second car and its woman driver. There was no model.

Results showed that more than 50 per cent more motorists were prepared to stop and help in the experimental condition (that is, where there was a model).

Vicarious Experience

The outcomes, so far as the model is concerned, have been found by Bandura (1973) to make a crucial difference. Where the model is seen to have been reinforced for helping, the model is much more likely to have been effective in influencing behaviour; where the outcomes are negative, models will be much less effective. This was borne out in a experiment conducted by Hornstein (1970). Participants who observed an individual returning a lost wallet and having a good reception were found to be more likely to help on another occasion than those who witnessed someone returning the wallet and having either an indifferent or a hostile reception.

Theories Relating to Helping Behaviour

Attribution Processes

In the section on 'self' in Chapter 2, we discussed Bem's theory of self-attribution (p. 68). In the present context it is suggested that individuals may develop self-attributions of helpfulness. A person may see himself or herself as *helpful* and this self-attribution will serve to focus behaviour onto the helping option where there is a choice of possible behaviours. An old man slips on a loose paving stone and falls. The choices available to us, as passers by, are either to assist or to leave it to someone else. If our self-attributions lead us to see ourselves as helpful persons we will be more likely to take the choice of helping rather than leaving it to someone else. Grusec and Redler (1980) found that such self-attributions of helpfulness provided a stronger reinforcement for helpful behaviour than external reinforcements such as verbal praise. Where they fail to live up to their self-imposed standards of helpfulness, Perry *et al.* (1980) found that children experience bad feelings.

Just World Hypothesis

According to the **just world hypothesis** developed by Lerner (Lerner, 1977; Lerner and Miller, 1978) there is a strong link between cause and effect (see Chapter 2) People have the feeling that they get what they deserve. In these circumstances a cynical view might be that people will be less likely to come to another's assistance. In rape cases it has sometimes been said of the victim, 'she had it coming to her'. Either she was out too late at night, or she was dressed provocatively. On the other hand, the Buddhist view would be to welcome the opportunity to help as a good deed which will eventually be to our benefit. In which direction we view the just-world hypothesis will depend on developmental influences, particularly in childhood. Also, others might argue that evidence of undeserved suffering gives the lie to the just-world hypothesis. Who can really argue that the class of infants in Dunblane, gunned down by a psychopath deserved what they got?

Social Norms of Behaviour

In childhood, **social norms of behaviour** are acquired through learning. These norms specify what behaviour is expected as normal and what is abnormal. They are the product of the culture in which we have grown up and they lay down what behaviour is expected within that culture. In almost every culture there is a norm which specifies that to be selfish is wrong; to be helpful is right. In most cultures it is prescribed that we do what we can to help other people.

Two social norms in particular have been cited as responsible for altruism:

1. The **principle of reciprocity**. This is the 'do as you would be done by' norm. Individuals have an obligation to reciprocate help which has been given them; the more so, if the help given is freely given and involves some sacrifice. The greater the sacrifice the greater the obligation it lays on us to reciprocate (Tesser *et al.*, 1968; Wilke and Lanzetta, 1970).

2. The **social responsibility norm**. People have a social obligation to afford help to those who need it. Membership of a community imposes upon individuals to help, without any expectation that this help will be reciprocated or rewarded. Such help is frequently given anonymously. Charity collectors call at your front door and if you do not give to them there are feelings of guilt. Of course, the just world hypothesis lays down that you give the most help to those whom you perceive as being in greatest need of help. You are more likely to contribute generously for poor children than to support a local football team. You are less obligated to help in the rehabilitation of drug addicts, perhaps, than in the support of disabled people. The former might be seen as having brought their misfortunes on themselves and so are less-deserving. The concept of the *deserving poor*, prevalent in Victorian times and re-emerging more recently, reflects this.

Culture and Altruism

It is evident that some cultures are far more prosocial than others. Child-rearing practices, religious training and education (in the broadest sense) may determine the extent to which people are motivated to help others. If people are led to believe that there is 'no such thing as society', but just individuals looking after their own interests, prosocial behaviour will not readily be fostered. Eisenberg and Mussen (1989) summarised cross-cultural research on children's prosocial tendencies and concluded that American children typically were less kind, considerate and cooperative than those reared in Mexican villages, Hopi Indian children reared on reservations, or Israeli children reared in Kibbutzim. There seem to be two separate kinds of cultures in this respect

- **Individualist** cultures, such as the USA, Canada, Australia and some European countries, where less emphasis is placed upon the responsibility each individual has for the welfare of others; more on the freedom individuals have to pursue their own goals.
- **Collectivist** cultures which include Japan and some other Asian countries, those from the former Communist block, many Latin American and native American cultures where the good of the group is held to be more important than individual wishes.

Empathy

Empathy, the vicarious experiencing of another's emotions, and its relationship with altruism, has been the basis for the **empathy–altruism hypothesis** developed by Batson and his colleagues (Batson, 1987, 1990; Batson and Oleson, 1991). Batson has suggested that empathy can produce genuinely altruistic motivation to help as distinct from egoistically-motivated helping. A person may be 'personally distressed' at seeing the suffering that someone else is experiencing, and their motivation for helping may be an egoistic one, to relieve their own distress. Alternatively, there may be genuine empathy, a sympathetic focus on the other person's suffering and a motivation to reduce it. Batson and his colleagues have demonstrated several times in experiments that participants who are genuinely aroused empathetically continued to help, when they could quite easily have relieved their own distress by escaping from the situation. The difficulty is to rule out other egoistically-based motives for helping (how you appear to other people, for example, or the good feelings which assisting someone in trouble may give you). Batson's later studies cast some doubt on whether apparently genuinely empathetic people might have such ulterior motives as these.

However, an alternative to the empathy–altruism hypothesis is Cialdini's **negative-state relief model** (Cialdini *et al.*, 1973, 1987). This model has suggested that people learn in childhood that it is gratifying to help, and that this gratification can help them to overcome sadness and guilt (that is, personal distress at the suffering of others and guilt that they are all right while someone else is suffering). These feelings of sadness are experienced also by those who empathise with the victim, but they help in order to reduce their own sadness rather than through an altruistic desire to relieve the victim's suffering. Cialdini's experiments were designed to test whether other means of lifting the negative feelings (sadness) – aroused by watching someone else suffer – might break the altruism–empathy link. He arranged for participants to receive – in one condition – an unexpected gift of money, or, in another, lavish praise. In yet another study participants were led to believe that their mood of sadness had been 'fixed' by a drug, so that even helping the victims would not relieve it. Schaller and Cialdini (1988) tried to relieve the 'sadness' using a comedy tape.

The results of these studies challenged the empathy–altruism hypothesis. While the surprise gift of money did not make any difference, the other attempts to relieve negative arousal states (lavish praise, belief that the feelings had been fixed, or a comedy tape) did lessen the motivation to help. Schroeder *et al.* (1988), however, found with highly empathetic individuals none of such mood-relieving strategies altered their motivation to help.

It has to be said that some of these studies are of somewhat doubtful ecological validity. Not only Cialdini's, but Batson's studies involved laboratory tests, where students (not, perhaps, a typical sample of the population at large) watched other students being given electric shocks (not something you see often everyday in real life). However, his research has led Batson to say that if research continues to suggest that empathetically aroused people often help for altruistic rather than egoistic reasons, present views about human nature and human capacity for caring need to be revised radically. That said, genuine concern for others is a 'fragile flower, easily crushed by egoistic concerns' (Batson *et al.*, 1983, p. 718). When highly empathetic people were asked to take a victim's place to receive painful shocks, but were perfectly free to leave if they wished to, 86 per cent opted to leave (Batson *et al.*, 1983).

Deciding Whether to Help

Two processes operate side by side to determine whether or not we give help when it appears to be needed:

1. *Cognitive processes*: this includes an evaluation and interpreting of the situation, weighing up the consequences of alternative courses of action.
2. *Emotional processes* which act as motivators to spur people on to action.

Piliavin's Bystander Calculus Model

Piliavin *et al.* (1981) have developed an **arousal/cost–reward model** (**also termed a bystander calculus model**) to explain what happens when decisions are taken as to whether to give assistance in emergencies. This consists of five distinct stages:

1. Becoming aware that someone needs help. This may be some-thing quite clear-cut such as screams, cries for help or smoke billowing out of an upstairs window in a house. But often the cues are ambiguous. It may be quite difficult to decide whether the noise heard from within a house represents an emergency situation.

2. Having become cognitively aware that there is an emergency and someone may need help there will a degree of emotional arousal. Physiologically, this will represent itself by a quickened pulse, butterflies in the stomach, and the other manifestations of strong emotion. (There is a full discussion of emotion in Malim *et al.*, 1992, *Perspectives in Psychology*, in this series: pp. 92–100.)

3. The bystander will need to interpret the physiological changes experienced, using cues from within the total environment. Piliavin stresses that arousal is a distressing thing which we are motivated to reduce. This is egoistic motivation rather than altruism. However, arousal might be due to empathy with the distress of the victim, which accords with Batson's empathy–altruism hypothesis. Arousal and our interpretation of it are important in determining whether or not we go to help. The more highly aroused we are the quicker we are to help, as evidenced by an a emergency staged by Gaertner and Dovidio (1977). Chairs appeared to have crashed down on a woman in the next room. Those bystanders who were most highly aroused (those who had the fastest heart rate and said that they felt most upset) were the quickest on the scene to help. But the arousal had to be labelled as a response to the 'emergency'. Gaertner and Dovidio tested this by giving one group of the bystanders a 'drug' (in fact a placebo), and telling them it would cause them to be aroused; while another group were told that the 'drug' they were given would not cause them to be aroused but might give them a dull headache. The former group attributed their arousal to the drug and were slower to help.

4. The next stage represents a cost–benefit analysis. What are the likely consequences of either helping or not helping? Costs might include some of the following:

- Effort and time expended;
- Loss of resources, including any benefits or rewards we might have to forego. (We might, for instance, have a train to catch.)
- Risks involved – of actual harm, of embarrassment, of social disapproval or emotional reaction to interacting with the victim.

On the other side of the balance sheet we weigh up the rewards:

- Monetary rewards for heroism.
- Increased self-esteem which comes from living up to the moral standards we have set ourself.
- Social approval.

And what about helping indirectly rather than directly (phoning the police or the fire service rather than going in ourselves)? or escaping from the scene? We weigh up the potential costs and benefits of these options as well *as we perceive them.*

The perceptions people make of the costs and benefits are individual ones, influenced perhaps by knowledge of their own abilities. There may also be some distortion, exaggerating the costs of helping or of not helping.

5. The decision stage: we decide whether or not to help.

Figure 4.9 shows a flow chart illustrating Piliavin's cost/arousal model.

A Commentary on Piliavin's Model

There is doubt whether people really do calculate in this detached way when there is an emergency. Latané and Darley (1970) have said that the very nature of most emergencies is that they are dangerous and unforeseen and consequently produce very high levels of arousal. Bystanders are less likely to take account of all the cues in the situation and then calmly weigh up costs and benefits

FIGURE 4.9
Piliavin's Cost/Arousal Model

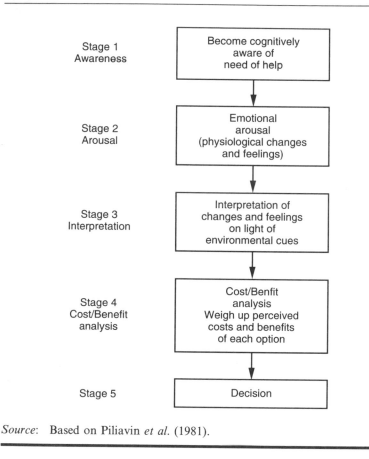

Stage 1 Awareness	Become cognitively aware of need of help
Stage 2 Arousal	Emotional arousal (physiological changes and feelings)
Stage 3 Interpretation	Interpretation of changes and feelings on light of environmental cues
Stage 4 Cost/Benefit analysis	Cost/Benfit analysis Weigh up perceived costs and benefits of each option
Stage 5	Decision

Source: Based on Piliavin *et al.* (1981).

than to act in an impulsive fashion, doing what to someone not directly involved might be seen as irrational. There is a distinction to be drawn between routine help and what happens in cases of emergency. There is not a great deal in common between, for instance, a routine commitment a person may have taken-on to get their elderly relative out of bed every morning, and reacting to smoke billowing from the windows of a house they happen to be passing.

Influences on Prosocial Behaviour

These include:

- Situational influences; what kind of a need is it?
- What is the relationship between the helper and the helped?
- What other people do.
- Personal influences (for instance, are men or women more helpful? do people receive more help in towns or in the country?).

Influences of the Situation

Latané and Darley conducted a series of experiments to determine what the situational factors might be which determine bystander intervention in emergencies. The stimulus to this research was the shocking affair of Kitty Genovese. In a respectable neighbourhood of New York city, Kitty Genovese was on her way home from work late at night. She was suddenly attacked by a man with a knife. At first her screams alarmed the man and he ran off. But when no one came to her aid, he returned, sexually assaulted her and stabbed her eight times. In the half hour during which the attack lasted, no one came to help her. After about half an hour an anonymous resident called the police but would not give his name, because 'he did not want to get involved'. The next day police interviewed neighbouring residents. No fewer than 38 people admitted hearing the screaming. The affair became a *cause célèbre*, exciting the attention, not only of the media but of social psychological researchers. Apathy, callousness, indifference and a loss of concern for others were cited (Latané and Darley, 1976).

Latané and Darley (1970) developed a cognitive model to determine whether or not bystanders decide to help in an emergency. This too had five stages:

1. *Noticing* the event and realising that help may be needed.
2. *Interpretation*: is the event a serious emergency? Are there cues which indicate distress, screaming, for example?
3. *Responsibility*: is it anything to do with me? Does the bystander accept responsibility? This may include factors such as other witnesses to the event, and also perception by the bystander of his or her competence to deal with the situation.

4. *Decision*: this might include direct intervention, indirect intervention (for example calling the police, perhaps) escape, or to do nothing.
5. *Action*: this will depend on the nature of the situation (emergency or not), knowledge of what to do, and the behaviour of other people.

Figure 4.10 represents a flow chart illustrating Latané and Darley's model

Latané and Darley's development of this model led to a series of experiments. In the first of these, participants (male students) were interviewed ostensibly about problems which they faced as students in a large university. They were given, to begin with, a questionnaire to complete and while they were doing this smoke began to pour from a vent in the wall. This continued for six minutes by which time

FIGURE 4.10
Latané and Darley's Cognitive Model of Bystander Intervention

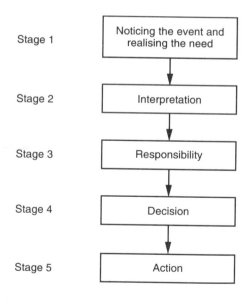

Source: Based on Latané and Darley (1970).

the room was full of smoke. In relation to the question of what influence other people have on decisions taken in such situations there were three conditions:

1. They were alone;
2. They were with two other participants whom they did not know;
3. They were with two confederates of the experimenter who ignored the smoke.

The hypothesis was that in such situations other people present exercise a crucial influence on decisions which are taken. Results supported this hypothesis. Of those who were alone, 75 per cent took positive action, reporting the matter. Of those in the company of two other strangers (condition 2) only 38 per cent took action. In the third condition, where there were two other people present who had had instructions to ignore the smoke, only 10 per cent took action.

Latané and Darley suggested that the presence of other people inhibits action; the more people the more inhibition. Where those who were present obviously ignored what was happening, the inhibition was greatest of all. There appear to be three issues which affect the decisions taken:

- **Diffusion of responsibility**: In a group, people will off-load their responsibility on to others (social loafing). In an emergency, the fact that there are others watching provides an ideal opportunity for **social loafing**. In fact they do not even have to be there watching or visible. The knowledge that others are around somewhere is enough.
- **Audience inhibition**. The presence of other people has another effect as well, to make people afraid of appearing foolish. They become self-conscious, and frightened that they are going to make a mistake.
- **Social influence**: People will look to others as models for what they should do; Chapter 6 will deal in greater detail with issues of social influence.

Latané and Darley (1976) set out in their most elaborate experiment to test each of these three issues. This became known as the 'three in one experiment' and is detailed in Box 4.6.

BOX 4.6
Latané and Darley's (1976) Three in One Experiment

Four conditions varied the communications between the participants and other bystanders:

1. Where they could see and be seen;
2. Where they could see but not be seen;
3. Where they could not see but be seen;
4. Where they could neither see nor be seen.

These conditions were achieved by means of television monitors and cameras. Participants were recruited to take part in a study of repression. The props used were a supposedly antique and unreliable shock generator. An emergency situation was created when the experimenter apparently received a violent shock from this generator, screamed, jumped into the air, threw himself against the wall and then fell to the floor out of camera range with his feet sticking up. Then he began to moan softly until help arrived or for about six minutes. The conditions used were as follows

- **Control or baseline condition**: no one is present with the participant. The video camera in the participant's room is pointed at the ceiling (the participant cannot be seen) and the monitor shows the ceiling of the second room (the participant cannot see).
- **Diffusion of responsibility**: the participant knows there is another person there but otherwise the same conditions apply (the camera points to the ceiling, the monitor shows only a ceiling).
- **Diffusion plus social influence**: the participant can see in the monitor another person working on a questionnaire. The camera still points to the ceiling. (the participant can see but not be seen).
- **Diffusion plus audience inhibition**: The camera points to the participant (he or she knows he/she can be seen), but the monitor just shows the next room's ceiling.
- **Diffusion plus social influence plus audience inhibition**: Each person is visible to the other via cameras and monitors.

Results

The results showed a cumulative effect. Where the participant was alone there was the greatest readiness to help. With just diffusion of responsibility there was slightly less readiness. With diffusion as well as inhibition (or influence) there was still less readiness. With diffusion as well as inhibition and influence there was least readiness of all.

The results supported Latané and Darley's suggestion that the factors of diffusion, influence and inhibition were additive.

Individual Differences in Helping Behaviour

Latané and Darley (1970) did not find any personality measure which accurately predicted whether someone would help. Attempts by other researchers (Bar-Tal, 1976; Schwartz, 1977) to single out Good Samaritans from the rest of the population have not been successful. There is some evidence, though, that there is a relationship between possession of specific skills and willingness to use them to help others (Midlarsky and Midlarsky, 1973; Schwartz and David, 1976). In a more general sense, the possession of emergency skills (first-aid training, for instance) makes it more likely that someone will intervene in an emergency.

Leadership and Followership

There is some evidence that some people are more likely to take the initiative in all kinds of action than others. There is clearly a skills component in this but, apart from this, Baumeister *et al.* (1988) have identified a more specific quality of leaders that they do not suffer to the same degree as do followers from diffusion of responsibility. But leadership and followership is the subject of Section 2 in Chapter 6.

Gender and Helping

Males are more likely to help females than vice versa. Cars are more likely to stop for a female than a male hitchhiker, or for a male and female pair (Pomazal and Clore, 1973). Those who are more physically attractive are likely to get more help. Przybyla (1985) manipulated the sexual arousal of participants by showing them sexually explicit videos. Seeing an erotic video made a male participant more likely to help a female in trouble, while when it was a male who was in trouble, participants were less likely to help and spent less time on it. Females, on the other hand, when aroused by an erotic video spent less time helping anyone, male or female.

The type of situation which presents itself makes a crucial difference. In dangerous emergencies men are more likely to intervene. It is conceived as part of the male role to act heroically in dangerous situations (Eagly and Crowley, 1986). Moreover, because men are in general stronger and more likely to have relevant skills, they perceive the costs of intervening as being lower than women do;

whereas women are more likely to provide help where emotional support is needed (Brody, 1990; Eagly and Crowley, 1986).

Town and Country

There seems to be something in the crowded noisy hectic environment of the big city which inhibits helping. Milgram (1970) proposed what he termed the **urban overload hypothesis** to explain why people in rural areas and in small towns are more helpful than those in big cities. In large cities, people had to be selective in the help they gave. The general levels of stimulation were so high that people had sometimes to ignore others in need and to be choosy about those they helped. Amato (1983) studied helping behaviour in different sizes of communities, and found that as the population of a community increased so helping decreased.

Mood and Helping

All kinds of things may put you into a 'good mood', being successful in something, having some good fortune, being happy, or even good weather. Isen (1987) manipulated the success factor and showed that it did indeed make participants more likely to help. George (1991) found that happy sales-people were more likely to go beyond the call of duty to be helpful. There is no doubt that the present trend towards more aggressive management and consequent unhappiness and insecurity do not make for helpful people. If we focus on our own good fortune we are more likely to be helpful, but if the focus rests on someone else's fortune then that makes you less helpful. Rosenhan *et al.* (1981) found that happiness at a good posting (to Hawaii) increased helpfulness; but the thought of a friend getting the posting actually decreased it.

Bad mood or ill-fortune do not seem to have the same effect. A feeling of guilt may stimulate helping behaviour (Carlson and Miller, 1987). As has been seen sadness can motivate people to help (Cialdini *et al.*, 1973). But if we are preoccupied with our own woes we will not be likely to help anyone else (Aderman and Berkowitz, 1983). What seems to matter is where the focus of attention is. If we focus on the misfortunes of others, we will be more likely to help; but if we focus on your own unhappiness, then we will not help others.

Some Conclusions

How can we have a more prosocial society? Maybe we need to start with how children are brought up. Young children are naturally egoistic but may become more prosocial as they grow up. They discover that adults approve of children who help others. Also, as they grow up they become more able to empathise with others, as their cognitive abilities improve. Piaget saw children becoming less egocentric as they grew older (see Birch, 1997, *Developmental Psychology*). Children can be encouraged to act more prosocially if they are reinforced for prosocial behaviour. But they need to develop intrinsic motives, and rewarding all good behaviour may inhibit this intrinsic motivation. Parents are the ideal models; where they practise what they preach and clearly set out the norms of behaviour which are expected they will encourage children to be prosocial (Eisenberg and Mussen, 1989). In the same way that violence on television may foster aggression, so television portrayals of people behaving prosocially may increase prosocial behaviour (Liebert and Sprafkin, 1988; Roberts and Maccoby, 1985). Children should have real opportunities to help, looking after younger brothers or sisters, helping with the cleaning and the washing-up and so on. We have already noted that individualist cultures foster less prosocial behaviour than do collectivist ones.

Adults, too, can be encouraged to be more prosocial. The ways in which charity fund-raisers increase the rewards of helping behaviour while minimising the costs could be studied. They give us little prizes and opportunities to win things. They make it easy. Just phone up with a credit card number. They put us in a good mood by putting on a show (Bob Geldof's 'Band Aid' was an example). Social approval can be mobilised. Jason *et al.* (1984) found that on a campus 31 per cent of students volunteered to give blood if they were directly approached by friends, while only 14 per cent volunteered when approached by people they did not know. When they do give blood, a good experience initially will encourage them to do it again until they become intrinsically and altruistically motivated.

Self-assessment Questions

1. Describe the sociobiological explanation of altruism. Do you find it convincing?

2. Outline and compare Batson's *empathy–altruism hypothesis* with Cialdini's *negative state relief model*. Which of these seems to be the best explanation of why people help others?
3. List the factors which Latané and Darley found inhibit bystanders from helping in emergencies. Does their complex 'three in one' experiment support the view that these factors are additive?
4. Is it possible to identify ways in which prosocial behaviour may be encouraged?

FURTHER READING

M. A. Hogg and G. M. Vaughan, *Social Psychology: An Introduction*, Chapter 13 (London: Prentice-Hall, 1995).

K. Deaux, F. C. Dane and L. S. Wrightsman, *Social Psychology in the 90s*, Chapter 11 (Pacific Grove, Cal.: Brooks Cole, 1993).

"SPEED, A QUICK START, COMFORTABLE SUSPENSION — EVERYTHING PROVES IT'S MUCH BETTER THAN THE ONE I *NEARLY* BOUGHT!"

Attitudes and Attitude Change 5

At the end of this chapter you should be able to:

1. Define what is meant by attitudes and identify the three components of an attitude.
2. Describe some theoretical models of attitudes including Pratkanis and Greenwald's socio-cognitive model, and Ajzen's theory of planned behaviour.
3. Identify some theories which relate to the formation of attitudes, including conditioning and cognitive theories.
4. Describe some theories relating to changing attitudes including balance and cognitive dissonance theories.
5. Describe and evaluate attempts which have been made to measure attitudes.
6. Identify some of the bases for prejudice and discrimination.
7. List some of the emphases which have been adopted in the study of prejudice.
8. List some of the ways in which prejudice and discrimination might be reduced.

SECTION I THE NATURE AND FUNCTION OF ATTITUDES

Since Allport (1935) referred to attitudes as the most indispensable concept in social psychology they have remained central. According to him an attitude is:

> a mental and neural state of readiness, organised through experience, exerting a directive and dynamic influence upon the individual's response to all objects and situations with which it is related. (Allport, 1935, p. 810)

McGuire (1989) has linked attitudes to a tripartite view of human experience which has ancient roots in philosophy:

> The trichotomy of human experience into thought feeling and action, although not logically compelling is so compelling in Indo-European thought (being found in Hellenic, Zoroastrian and Hindu philosophy) as to suggest that it corresponds to something basic in our way of conceptualisation, perhaps . . . reflecting three evolutionary layers of the brain, cerebral cortex, limbic sytem and old brain. (McGuire, 1989, p. 40)

Thus attitudes are widely held to have three components:

- **Cognitive** which includes perceptions of objects and events or reports or beliefs about them. For example, the belief that to live by a main road is likely to be noisy and dangerous.
- **Affective**, which includes feelings about, and emotional responses to, objects and events. For example, I may be continually worried and fearful about the effect that living on a main road is going to have on my family.
- **Behavioural** or **conative** components. This concerns intentions and predicts the way in which an individual may behave in relation to an object or event. For example, I am going to sell my house because I do not want to go on living on a main road.

This three-component model has had wide acceptance, but more recently doubt has been cast upon the behavioural component. It is hard to see how knowing someone's attitude towards something may realistically help us to predict his or her behaviour. Ajzen (1988) has suggested that people do not always behave in ways which are consistent with their attitudes. They may, for instance, be faced with conflicts between contradictory attitudes.

Functions of Attitudes

Attitudes function in much the same way as schemata or scripts. They represent packaged and memorised responses to people, events and situations, short cuts to the necessity of working out each time how we should respond. We no longer have to figure out from scratch how we should relate to objects, events and situations each time we come across them.

Fazio (1989) has suggested that one of the main functions of attitudes is to facilitate evaluation of objects. If I have a hostile attitude towards abortion, for example, it enables me to come to an instant appraisal of someone who is intending to undergo an abortion, without the necessity for a full appraisal of all the facts of the case.

A Socio-cognitive Model

Pratkanis and Greenwald (1989) have developed a **socio-cognitive model** of attitude structure. This might be described as a definition of attitude structure which draws upon ideas from social cognition. The reader will remember that social cognition centres around the storing in memory of social experiences which may be drawn upon at a later time to facilitate responses to particular situations (see Chapter 1). In Pratkanis and Greenwald's model the object, person or event towards which we have a particular attitude is represented in memory by three elements:

- A label for that object, person or event together with rules for applying that label.
- An evaluation or appraisal of the object, person or event.
- A knowledge-structure to support that appraisal, that is to say a cognitive basis for it.

The most important element in this is appraisal. It has to be borne in mind that there are two elements in evaluation. Breckler and Wiggins (1989a, b) have made some attempt to clarify the distinction between these two elements:

1. The emotional reaction to the object.
2. Thoughts, beliefs and judgements made about the object.

While the first of these two elements is clearly in the affective domain and relates to emotional responses, the second of the three components of attitudes mentioned above, the second is cognitive, relating to knowledge and thought. The behavioural component is not dealt with in their model, and this omission is discussed below. Figure 5.1 represents Pratkanis and Greenwald's model.

FIGURE 5.1
A Socio-cognitive Model of Attitudes

Elements in the representation
of attitudes   Function

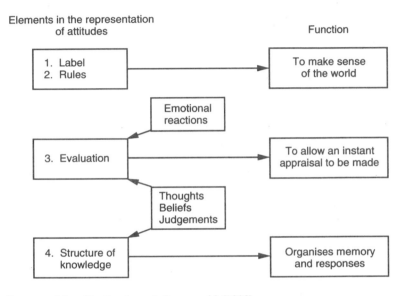

Source: After Pratkanis and Greenwald (1989).

An Information-processing Approach to Attitudes

Anderson (1971, 1980) stresses that we receive information about objects, people and events and as a result of that information attitudes are formed. The nature of the attitudes we form depends upon the way in which this information is received and combined. Some items of information will be received before others; some items will receive more emphasis than others. The importance that is attached to different pieces of information and the order in which they are received will materially effect the formation of attitudes. We evaluate all the information as it comes in, and then combine it with what is already stored. Anderson complicates this somewhat by the suggestion that individuals assemble a number of items of information, attach values to them and take the average of these values in order to form attitudes.

Attitudes and Behaviour

It is important to note that neither Pratkanis and Greenwald nor Anderson have dealt with the third component we mentioned, the behavioural element. The problem of trying to predict how people will behave by measuring attitudes in some way (measurement of attitudes will be dealt with in the next section) is full of pitfalls. La Piere (1934) conducted a classic study into the relationship between attitudes and behaviour. He was interested in attitudes towards the Chinese, and in particular towards two Chinese friends of his. Travelling right across America with his Chinese friends, they visited 66 hotels, autocamps and tourist homes as well as 184 restaurants and were only refused service once. Six months later he sent a questionnaire to all the places they had visited, asking 'Will you accept members of the Chinese race as guests in your establishment?' The replies he received indicated that 92 per cent would not accept Chinese customers.

This study has stimulated a huge amount of research into the relationship between attitudes and behaviour. In particular, Ajzen and Fishbein (1980) have argued that what La Piere and others were doing was to attempt to predict *specific* behaviour from *general* attitudes; that is general attitudes towards Chinese, and specific attitudes towards these two specific Chinese on these particular occasions. As a result they developed a **theory of reasoned action** (Fishbein and Ajzen, 1974; Ajzen and Fishbein, 1980).

Theory of reasoned Action

Ajzen and Fishbein's model contains the following components:

- *Subjective norm*: this is a guide to what is considered to be the 'proper thing to do'. It is arrived at by means of a perception of what 'significant others' believe.
- *Attitude*: for example, 'I do not like to serve Chinese people.'
- *Behavioural intention*: this amounts to a decision taken internally not to serve Chinese people.
- *Behaviour (in a specific case)*: what actually happened.

A specific action will be performed if:

1. The attitude is favourable.

2. The social norm is favourable; people who are important to us approve our action.
3. There is a high level of perceived behavioural control: that is, we perceive that there is a high degree of freedom to choose how to behave in a specific set of circumstances.

The third element in this model, conscious behavioural control, has assumed paramount importance in Ajzen's (1989) extension of it. This involves the extent to which it is easy or difficult to perform the action. Ajzen has referred to this extension as a **theory of planned behaviour**. An example might help to make this clearer. A student has a favourable attitude towards A-levels (i); the attitude which significant others (parents, teachers and peers) take towards A-levels is favourable (ii); perceived behavioural control (iii) is determined by his or her ability in relation to the task, how good the teaching and preparation for the exam, is and perhaps the content of the actual paper, things which the student perceives as being only partially within his or her control. Behaviour (passing the exam) and attitude are therefore only conditionally related. If the student gets in with a group of ne'er-do-wells (the social norm is not favourable), if it transpires that his or her ability does not match up to the task, or if the teaching is poor, then behavioural intention will not be closely linked to outcome. Figure 5.2 illustrates how these factors are related in this model.

Other Factors Linking Attitudes to Behaviour

Other factors which may influence the relationship between an attitude and a person's behaviour include accessibility (how easily an attitude is called to mind (Fazio, 1986)); strength of attitude (Fazio *et al.* (1986) claim that only a strong attitude may be automatically translated into action), personality and situational variables.

Attitude Formation

Means whereby individuals form attitudes include the following:

- Direct experience;
- Classical conditioning;
- Instrumental conditioning;

FIGURE 5.2
Theory of Planned Behaviour

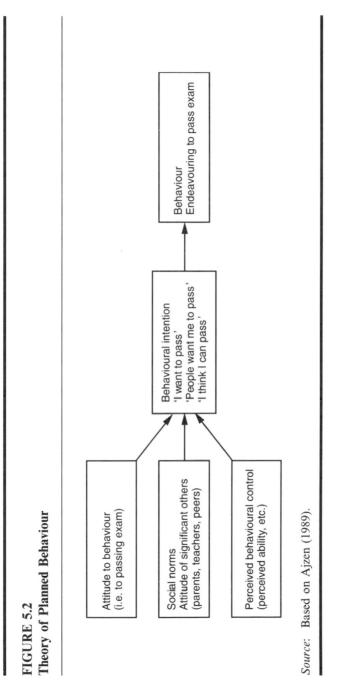

Source: Based on Ajzen (1989).

- Observational learning and modelling; and
- Cognitive development.

Direct Experience

In a great many instances the attitudes we hold are the result of direct experience of the object of the attitude. It might be the result of a traumatic event or of direct exposure. For instance, a holiday in Cyprus and trip into the mountains towards the 'green line' which separates the Turkish-occupied from the Greek part of the island caused this author to focus upon what the Turks had done when they invaded Cyprus in 1974 and radically changed attitudes towards them. Stroebe *et al.* (1988) focused upon changes in attitudes which resulted from student exchanges with foreign countries. Fishbein and Ajzen (1975) have suggested that these kinds of changes result from the information gained about the attitude object which leads to beliefs, and then influences the extent of our liking or disliking the object.

Zajonc (1968) has identified a **mere exposure effect**. The number of times we meet an attitude object will affect the evaluation we make of it. Repeated exposure strengthens the response we make to something or someone, whether that is a dish we have in a restaurant or an MP standing for election. This gives a sitting MP, a familiar dish or a place we know well from many visits to it, an advantage over the unfamiliar or the new. It may, of course, work in either direction. Familiarity or exposure may equally strengthen negative as well as positive attitudes. When Margaret Thatcher was Prime Minister, the level of exposure to her on the media was such that attitudes to her became polarised. The public either adored her or abhorred her.

Classical Conditioning

Under classical conditioning a repeated association between one stimulus and another may cause a previously neutral stimulus to elicit a reaction which was previously confined to another, non-neutral stimulus. For instance, we may form a romantic attachment with someone who is passionately fond of curries, to which we had been indifferent. Every occasion on which we go out with this person we go to a curry house. An association is formed between this individual and curry. Our liking for the individual is transferred to a liking for curry so that even when we are with someone else we will tend to choose curry. This might be said to be an extension of Zajonc's mere exposure effect, or perhaps an explanation of it. To take another example, a person grows up with great respect and fondness for his father who happens to be an ardent socialist. Long association may cause that person to have similar positive attitudes towards socialism as his father has. Figure 5.3 illustrates how this process might work.

Instrumental/Operant Conditioning

This is a second form of associative learning of attitudes. To put it at its simplest, responses which are reinforced (for example, followed by favourable outcomes) are strengthened, those that are not reinforced tend to die away. Parents use this form of conditioning to form the attitudes of their children. They try to ensure that acceptable behaviour, children's cooperation with their siblings for instance, wins praise; conflict and fighting with them does not. Hence a negative attitude is formed towards fighting, and a positive attitude towards peaceful cooperation.

Observational Learning or Modelling

The work of Bandura (1973) has already been discussed in other contexts. Suppose that we had a very happy childhood with our mother staying at home full-time to devote her time to the family. We have modelled our positive attitude to mothers staying at home on the successful outcome we experienced.

Cognitive Development

Cognitive approaches to formation and changing of attitudes give less weight to the external outcomes or reinforcements associated with a particular attitude, and more with what is going on internally in the mind. Heider's **balance theory** or Festinger's concept of **cognitive dissonance** are instances.

Balance Theory

Balance theory stems from Heider (1946). It is concerned with the balance between three elements which form a triad:

FIGURE 5.3
Classical Conditioning of Attitudes

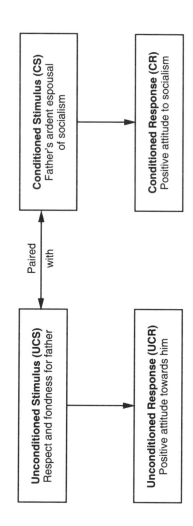

1. A person (P);
2. Another person (X);
3. An attitude object (O).

These triads may be either 'balanced' or 'unbalanced'. The relationships between the elements may be positive ($+$) or negative ($-$). A 'balanced' state exists when there are either three positive relationships, or when there are two negatives and a positive as in Figure 5.4.

Other combinations are unbalanced as shown in Figure 5.5. Heider suggested that where unbalanced states occur there is tension. Wherever there is an odd number of negative relationships there is an unbalanced relationship. Forces are likely to build up to restore balance. For instance, Charles might try to overcome his dislike of riding in 1. Angela may come to like Charles in 2. Charles may profess to disliking riding in 3.

Heider's balance theory has been used to explain the way in which people vote in elections. People try to achieve a balance between:

1. Their attitude towards an issue;
2. Their attitude towards a candidate; and
3. The candidate's attitude towards an issue.

If there is a balanced relationship they might be more likely to vote for the candidate. For instance, if an individual felt that Mr Ashdown held a positive attitude towards European integration and he or she liked Mr Ashdown, that individual would be likely to vote for him if he or she also had a positive attitude towards European integration.

Cognitive Dissonance Theory

A second theory relating to consistency in attitudes is **cognitive dissonance theory**. This was proposed by Festinger in 1957. Cognitive dissonance exists when there is a conflict between two related cognitions (thoughts, beliefs or attitudes). This might also include behaviour. For example, if an individual was a member of a church which was strongly committed to Sunday observance and was personally committed to Sunday observance, there might be dissonance if circumstances (the arrival of an unexpected guest, for example) made it necessary for him or her to purchase provisions at

the supermarket on Sunday morning. Attitudes to Sunday observance are at odds with behaviour and this is uncomfortable.
Festinger talks about cognitive elements which may be:

1. consonant,
2. dissonant, or
3. irrelevant.

Figure 5.6 illustrates the concept. The size of the conflict (and
therefore of the tension it produces) is related to:

- The importance to the person of the elements.
- The ratio of consonant to dissonant elements. The greater the
  number of dissonant elements the greater the dissonance.
- The amount of cognitive overlap. The less two events have in
  common, the greater the potential dissonance. For example, a
  choice between going to the theatre and going fishing would
  create greater dissonance than one between the theatre and the
  cinema.

The importance of this theory is that dissonance is uncomfortable,
so that there is motivation to alter one or more of the elements in
order restore consonance between the elements. An extension of the
basic idea is the notion of **forced compliance**. The suggestion is that
pressure of some kind to adopt a public attitude which is at odds
with another thought, belief or behaviour will reduce the amount of
the dissonance and so of the discomfort that results. Box 5.1 (on
p. 164) shows details of a classic experiment by Festinger and
Carlsmith (1959) which aimed to test this notion.

This evident exception to what has become a very basic rule of
learning, that the stronger the reinforcement the greater the change
in behaviour will be, has been challenged by Bem (1967, 1972).
Bem's self-perception theory, described in Chapter 2, proposed that
attitudes are determined from behaviour. We are aware of what we
are doing and so get to 'know our own attitudes, emotions and other
internal states . . . partially by inferring them from observations. of
overt behaviour.' Bem described Festinger and Carlsmith's study to
participants in a study of his and asked them to predict the results.
Their predictions were not unlike the results of the original experiment. $1 was not enough money to persuade someone to lie, so that
participants had looked back at the experiment and decided that
they had enjoyed it. After all they had *said* they had enjoyed it!

FIGURE 5.6
Examples of Cognitive Dissonance

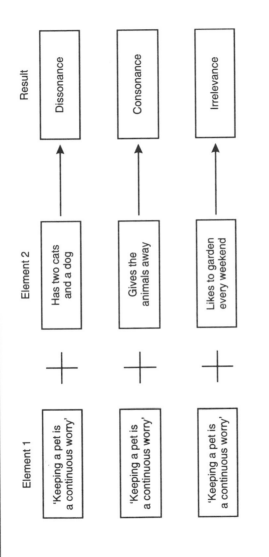

Element 1		Element 2		Result
'Keeping a pet is a continuous worry'	+	Has two cats and a dog	→	Dissonance
'Keeping a pet is a continuous worry'	+	Gives the animals away	→	Consonance
'Keeping a pet is a continuous worry'	+	Likes to garden every weekend	→	Irrelevance

Source: Based on Festinger (1957).

BOX 5.1
Festinger and Carlsmith's Experiment on Forced Compliance

Festinger and Carlsmith (1959) paid participants either a small amount of money ($1) or a larger amount ($20) to promote publicly a position which they did not hold privately. After being asked to spend a long period on a very boring and meaningless task they were paid to represent it to other potential participants as interesting and very worthwhile. Those who were paid the larger sum altered their *private* opinion of the task much less than did the group who had only received $1. Presumably, the larger sum of money was sufficient to justify their behaviour, lying to the other participants; those who were only offered a trifling sum had to find some other justification and this was that they really did find the boring task interesting and worthwhile. It was clear that there might be circumstances where a smaller reward produced a larger attitude change. This runs quite counter to the accepted laws of reinforcement that a greater reward will produce a greater change in behaviour.

The controversy between Festinger on the one side and Bem on the other raged for some considerable time, with each side mustering empirical support. Finally, the debate ended with a review of the research by Fazio *et al.* (1977) which concluded that there was right on both sides! It all depended how great the discrepancy was between attitudes and behaviour. In most ordinary situations where the discrepancy was fairly small, Bem's self-perception theory was right, but where the discrepancy was very large Festinger's dissonance theory provided the better explanation.

A further review of the research on dissonance by Cooper and Fazio (1984) led them to state that dissonance arousal depends upon two criteria:

1. The consequences of the behaviour must be aversive. That is to say, it has to result in an event that runs counter to self-interest. As Cooper and Fazio say, 'an event that one would rather not have occur'. For example, in the instance mentioned above, we are on our way to the supermarket on Sunday morning, already uncomfortable because we are doing something which is contrary to our beliefs and we meet the pastor of the church.
2. There has also to be an assumption of personal responsibility. A person has to attribute the event to some personal internal factor. We feel personally responsible for not having made

adequate provision for the possibility of someone coming to lunch. This is most likely to occur when the individual has some choice in the matter and can foresee the consequences.

When these two criteria are met, dissonance may be aroused provided that the behaviour involved is not inconsistent with an individual's self-concept (Scher and Cooper, 1989). In very nearly every case where attitude change has resulted from dissonance reduction, Steele (1988) argues that behaviour is involved which is inconsistent with a person's self concept. When there is a threat to our self-concept from behaviour we perceive ourselves to be engaged in – for example lying to someone else, acting in a foolish way or arguing against our own self-interest, there are really only two alternatives:

1. To change our self-concept, which is not likely to happen, or
2. To change our attitudes to make them more consistent to the behaviour we are engaged in.

Thus, we have seen members of government who see themselves as honourable men, and who certainly would not conceive themselves to be liars, justifying telling less than the truth – what has been termed 'being economical with the truth' – before the House of Commons. They have not altered their concept of themselves as honourable men who would not lie, but they have altered their attitude to truth. This attitude change occurs as a result of **self-affirmation**. They have responded to a threat to their self-esteem by enhancing some other aspect of the self-concept, perhaps a concern for security. It has to be borne in mind that the conclusions Steele has come to were arrived at in a laboratory setting. This might not be the same as would happen 'in real life'. He provided alternative means for self-affirmation where participants found themselves engaged in activities inconsistent with their attitudes by, for instance, completing questionnaires about values. Figure 5.7 provides as an algorithm, an updated version of cognitive dissonance theory, incorporating the modifications of Cooper and Fazio and of Steele.

Post-decisional Dissonance

When we make a decision – perhaps an agonising one between alternatives of nearly equal attractiveness – dissonance is likely to

166

FIGURE 5.7
Cognitive Dissonance Updated

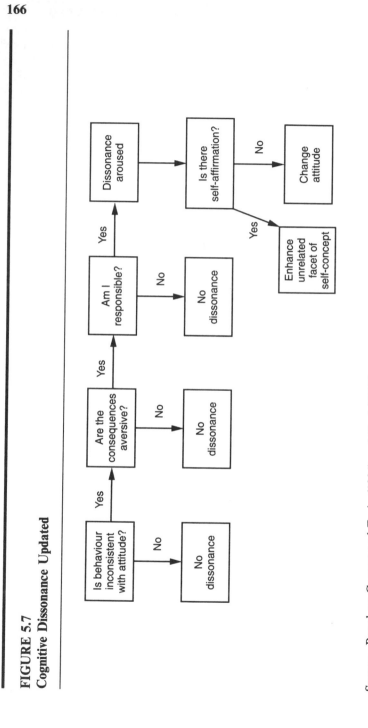

Source: Based on Cooper and Fazio (1984) and Steel (1988).

arise between our attitude to the non-chosen alternative and our behaviour in choosing the other one.

Box 5.2 shows details of an experiment by Knox and Inkster (1968) into post-decisional dissonance.

BOX 5.2
Post-decisional Dissonance. An Experiment by Knox and Inkster

Knox and Inkster (1968) went to a racecourse in Vancouver to interview those waiting to place their bets. Most admitted not being very confident that the horse they had chosen would win. However, interviewed again after they had placed their bets they were much more certain that their choice was the right one. The suggestion was that the act of deciding upon one horse rather than another created dissonance which motivated people to alter their attitudes, not only to the chosen horse but also to the non-chosen one. By boosting the merits of the chosen option, dissonance is reduced and reduced still more by downgrading the other choice.

We go into a car showroom in a state of ambivalence about the merits of two models of car. Finally, we make up our mind to select one of them which stirs up dissonance. This is uncomfortable so that attempts are made to reduce it. Emphasis is placed on the good points of the one chosen, while highlighting the disadvantages of the other. This process will even go so far as **selective exposure**. We seek out information which supports our choice and avoid information which does the opposite.

Self-assessment Questions

1. Identify the components of an attitude. Why is it true to say that the link between attitude and behaviour is a fragile one?
2. List some of the ways in which attitudes are formed. Which of these seems to you to be the most convincing?
3. Describe what is meant by balance in relationship to attitudes. How does imbalance generate attitude change?
4. Cognitive dissonance theory has been influential in explaining some of the ways in which attitudes change. What are the important elements of dissonance theory? Identify some of the practical implications.

process, but a study by Hovland and Sherif (1952) did not support this. They found a definite bias in the way in which black judges, or those who were sympathetic to black people, sorted statements as compared to those who were unsympathetic to black people.

• Finally, Thurstone assumed that the data obtained from this procedure were interval scale data (the assumption was made that a score of 6, for instance, was twice as favourable as a score of 3). In fact, because the judges are not totally objective we only have an ordinal scale of measurement, that is, putting participants into a rank order.

Osgood's Semantic Differential

The **semantic differential** (Osgood, Suci and Tannenbaum, 1957) focuses upon the effective component of attitudes, the emotion or feeling attached to a word or concept. The concept is rated on a seven-point bipolar scale. Pairs of adjectives are produced such as:

FIGURE 5.8
Osgood's Semantic Differential

	1	2	3	4	5	6	7	
Fair	_	_	_	X	_	_	_	Unfair
Large	_	X	_	_	_	_	_	Small
Bad	_	_	_	_	_	X	_	Good
Clean	_	X	_	_	_	_	_	Dirty
Valuable	_	_	_	_	_	X	_	Worthless
Weak	X	_	_	_	_	_	_	Strong
Active	_	_	_	_	_	_	X	Passive
Cold	_	_	_	_	X	_	_	Hot
Fast	_	_	_	X	_	_	_	Slow

The respondent places an X at a point on the seven-point scale. Three dimensions are represented by the pairs of adjectives chosen, evaluation (good, clean) potency (strong), and activity (active, fast). This approach does have the advantage that the researcher does not have to make up a series of statements, but can use a fairly standard set of adjectives. It yields a great deal of information and is generally reliable, but does demand careful analysis.

Bogardus Social Distance Scale

Bogardus' scale (1925) was an early attempt to measure attitudes from behaviour. It is based upon the degree of intimacy with which respondents feel comfortable in contacts with other racial or social groups. Questions such as:

● I would accept these people to close kinship through marriage;
● I would accept these people as visitors only to my country;
● I would exclude these people from my country.

are taken as indications of attitude to members of other races or social groups, and are assigned numerical values to provide an attitude measure. This technique is obviously quite limited in application, though Triandris (1971) has used it to measure attitudes to religion and race.

Unobtrusive Measures of Attitudes

Webb *et al.* (1969) suggested that attitudes might be inferred from watching what people do, from archival records and from physical traces. For instance, it might be possible to count the number of noseprints on a museum display case to determine the attitude of the visitors to that particular display, and measure the height of the noseprints to give some indication of the ages of the interested visitors. By examining the changes in roles played by male and female characters in children's books, changes in sex-role attitudes might be inferred. The kinds of books people borrow from libraries are another source of information about people's attitudes. After the introduction of TV, more non-fiction books were borrowed but fewer fiction, indicating a change in people's attitudes to books. A successful television version of a book, *Middlemarch* for instance, or *Pride and Prejudice* might increase the popularity of the book from which the adaptation came, as evidenced from demands to borrow from the library. The ways in which people seat themselves in a room can also be an index of attitudes. When there is good feeling between people they will tend to sit closer together.

Bogus Pipeline Technique

There have been attempts to get over the reluctance of people to reveal their true feelings which has made it hard to measure attitudes. Jones and Sigall (1971) introduced what has become known as a **bogus pipeline technique** to overcome this problem. Participants in their studies were connected to a machine resembling a lie-detector and were told that the machine could measure the strength and direction of their true attitudes so that there was no point in lying. Cialdini *et al.* (1981) successfully used the technique in investigating cognitive dissonance. They were attempting to ascertain whether the attitudes they reported were genuine or whether they reflected **impression management**, that is to say attempts to appear to others to be consistent.

Expectancy-value Technique

It was noted earlier that Fishbein and Ajzen had debated the relationship between attitudes and behaviour and had arrived at what they termed a theory of planned behaviour. They suggested that attitudes and behaviour might be linked more closely if there was an evaluative as well as a belief component. Fishbein developed a technique for measuring attitudes which incorporated this. He combined a rating scale with a scale of evaluation. For instance, in investigating attitudes towards the use of nuclear energy for power generation he might ask participants to rate nuclear power stations with the instruction: 'Rate the degree to which you believe the following statements to be true or untrue (0 = not true at all, 10 = absolutely true),

nuclear power stations are

safe,
economical,
sustainable,
environmentally unfriendly.

Now rate the value you place upon each of the attributes ($-10 =$ extremely undesirable, $0 =$ neutral, $+10 =$ extremely desirable),

  safe,
  expensive,
  sustainable,
  environmentally unfriendly'.

The strength of the belief can then be combined with the value attached to provide a numerical value for the attitude strength.

Conclusions

The measurement of attitudes is difficult. The approaches used have been linked to the components of attitudes and this is part of the problem. It is hard to separate cognitive from effective components or either of these from the behavioural aspect. There is little certainty that holding a particular attitude is inevitably linked to a particular sort of behaviour. In addition, there is a problem of interpretation. The assumption is frequently made that everyone will interpret the question in the same way. This is not always the case. Nevertheless, it remains a worthwhile enterprise to make the attempt, because so many of the choices we make in everyday life are linked to the attitudes we adopt.

Self-assessment Questions

1. Describe the measurement of attitudes by means of a Likert Scale. Which component of attitudes does this measure?
2. What measures have been adopted to attempt to measure the behavioural component of attitudes? What are the limitations of these attempts?
3. Do you feel that the Fishbein's expectancy-value scale solves the problem of the fairly tenuous link between behaviour and attitude?

SECTION III   PREJUDICE AND DISCRIMINATION

Introduction

Prejudice refers to the making of assumptions about people's characteristics (usually to their detriment) on the basis of the identification of a salient characteristic and behaving in accordance with these assumptions. For instance, a Bosnian Serb might identify someone as being a Muslim and immediately characterise that individual as being associated with a supposed Islamic threat to take over their country. **Discrimination** follows from this and implies that simply on the basis of an identification made, an individual is treated differently from the way in which someone not so identified might be treated. Behaviour such as that known as ethnic cleansing might well follow. An employer might, for instance, have a prejudiced view of the abilities and commitment of members of ethnic minorities. In evaluating the abilities and experience of applicants for a job, it may be assumed that members of an ethnic group would not be suitable so that once identified they are ruled out of contention.

While most people would consider prejudiced behaviour and discrimination unacceptable behaviour – indeed, it is used as a term of abuse to call someone bigoted – nevertheless prejudice is extremely pervasive. It is a part of the social cognition structure of each individual that experience and learning has built up in us and which allows us to take short cuts in our judgements about people and things.

It is usual to consider prejudice to be an **attitude** towards a particular set of people, objects or events. Allport (1954) has said that attitudes have three component parts:

- **Cognitive**: This amounts to a set of beliefs about the object of prejudice.
- **Affective**: Feelings or emotions related to the person or object in question.
- **Conative**: Intentions to behave in a particular way towards the person or object.

In more general terms, prejudice refers to *negative* emotional responses to particular people and the consequent intolerant, unfair and unfavourable attitudes towards them. We have already considered stereotyping (Chapter 2) which consists of assigning a range of characteristics (usually negative) to a group as a whole. Once an individual has been identified as belonging to that group, it is assumed that he or she possesses those characteristics.

Devine (1989) has shown that the primary difference between prejudiced and unprejudiced people may rest in the way in which unprejudiced people are able to inhibit or to disregard negative stereotypical beliefs. Where a stereotypical belief exists, it will be spontaneously triggered upon identification of a member of the group which is the subject of the stereotypical belief. Elimination of stereotypical beliefs is likely to be a difficult and protracted process, but conscious control may allow people to inhibit or disregard negative beliefs, so that prejudiced behaviour does not occur (see Figure 5.9).

Note that in this model there are two stages:

1. The unconscious stage where identification triggers the existing stereotype.
2. The consciously controlled stage where a non-prejudiced person may inhibit prejudiced beliefs to prevent a prejudiced response,

---

FIGURE 5.9
Devine's Model of Prejudice

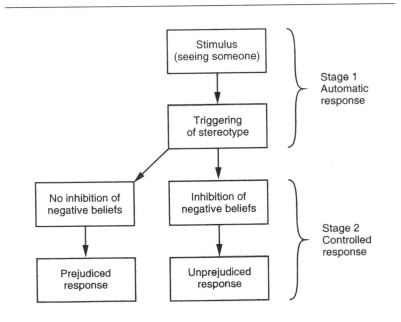

Source: Based on Devine (1989).

prejudiced thought. This again is social cognition. Life experience has established patterns of thinking about people which can be hard to change.

The way in which success or failure is differentially attributed to men and to women is another manifestation of the way in which people have been programmed to think. Deaux and Emswiller (1974) found that in tasks which traditionally might be regarded as 'male', success was attributed overwhelmingly to ability or to effort in the case of a man; to luck or to the fact that it was an easy task in the case of a woman. On traditionally female tasks this difference in attribution did not occur.

There is evidence, however, that efforts to reduce sex stereotyping and sex discrimination have had some effect. In the 1960s, for instance, Goldberg found that identical pieces of work were differently evaluated when attributed to a man as compared to a woman (Goldberg, 1968). A replication of this study done by Swim *et al.* (1989) found that this differential evaluation was no longer evident.

Racism

In Germany in Hitler's time, Jews were subjected to gross prejudice and discrimination culminating in the Holocaust. More recently in Rwanda, prejudice and discrimination by one tribal group towards another resulted in mass genocide. Similarly, in Bosnia there has been genocide by Serbs against Muslims and Croats, and violence by all three groups. Whereas in places such these, racism has resulted in many deaths and vast numbers of people being displaced from their homes, elsewhere in Western countries laws enacted against discrimination have done something to reduce the more blatant forms of racism. However, it is still widespread in a less blatant or more covert way. Pettigrew (1987) has examined the very pervasive way in which racism persists even among those who have made conscious efforts to resist it. The automatic stereotypical reactions which Devine reported (1989) are hard to eradicate:

> Many Southerners have confessed to me . . . that even though in their minds they no longer feel prejudice towards Blacks, they still feel squeamish when they shake hands with a Black. These feelings are left over from what they learned in their families as children.
> (Pettigrew, 1987, p. 20)

This has been termed **symbolic racism** (Kinder and Sears, 1981) or **modern racism**. Individuals who hold deep-seated attitudes based upon racial fears and upon stereotypes learned very early in life to express these attitudes in more socially acceptable ways. For instance, schemes established to give preference in awarding public contracts to firms run by and employing black workers are opposed on the grounds that they interfere with the free operation of the marketplace. Symbolic racial attitudes have been harder to measure than blatant racism. One technique used involved some of the methods of cognitive psychology. Gaertner and McClaughlin (1983) paired positive and negative descriptive adjectives with racial labels (for example black or white) and asked participants to say whether they fitted together. They predicted that where the pairing represents an existing attitude, participants would respond more quickly than where the trait is not associated with an existing racial group. There was a tendency for positive adjectives paired with 'white' to be responded to more rapidly than negative adjectives. Similarly, when 'black' was paired with negative adjectives there was also a more speedy response.

Ageism

In countries such as the UK, Canada, the USA and some European countries such as the Netherlands, the extended family has to a large extent been replaced by nuclear families. Instead of there being uncles and aunts and grandparents living close at hand and supplementing the support given to children by their parents, families in these countries typically tend to be nuclear; that is mother, father and children only. Youth tends in these societies to be very highly valued; old age is much less highly valued. Increasingly unfavourable stereotypes are being attached to older people. Indeed **ageism**, as this prejudice against older people may be termed, starts earlier and earlier. In competition for some jobs, to be over 40 is now considered to be too old! Brewer *et al.* (1981) have shown that older people are treated as relatively worthless and powerless members of the community.

Other Forms of Prejudice

Other focuses of prejudice include homosexuals and people with various kinds of disability. The prejudice which exists against homosexuals can be seen in the refusal by senior officers in the armed services to allow those who have been discovered to be homosexual to continue serving. In the USA, President Clinton faced great opposition to his proposal that there should be no bar to homosexuals serving in the US armed forces. The HIV epidemic and AIDS have focused attention upon homosexuals and there has been some increase in prejudice against them, though in most communities they are not considered deviant and immoral in the way they once were. Oscar Wilde would not have been thrown into Reading gaol had he lived 100 years later. However, a survey done in the United States in 1974 by Levitt and Klassen did show that a majority of people thought that homosexuals were 'sick'.

Similarly, there has been a marked change in the level of prejudice against disabled people of all kinds. Once they were regarded as freaks and kept out of sight as a family secret. Hitler's Final Solution' embraced not only Jews but mentally-ill people as well. Mentally handicapped children in Romania were found after the fall of the Ceaucescu regime to be living like animals in a bleak castle. Szasz (1967) in his book *The Myth of Mental Illness* argues that labels are important. If a person is labelled as 'mad', prejudice and discrimination follows. It is not until mental illness is treated in exactly the same way as any other illness that this will be diminished. Where there is a physical cause, then it is just an illness. Where there is not it is just 'a problem of living'.

How do Prejudice and Discrimination Manifest Themselves?

As we have seen, blatant prejudice and discrimination against individuals and groups is not common and often illegal. What is much more common is **subtle discrimination**. For example, a landlord may turn away a potential tenant on discovering that he or she is black on the pretext that the flat has already been let. It is, in effect, discrimination against either women or single parenthood where single mothers cannot find work where the flexible working hours are available which would allow them to take a job.

Sometimes a trivial movement is made towards helping members of a group which is being discriminated against in order that more meaningful help can be written off as unnecessary. Rosenfield *et al.* (1982) had participants in their study do a small favour for a black stranger. Subsequently, when asked to participate in more demanding forms of helping they were more reluctant to do so than other people who had not already 'helped'. This is **tokenism**.

Positive (or reverse) discrimination is where a positive step is taken to reverse what are seen to be results of prejudice. The Labour Party has taken the step of insisting on all-women short-lists for some of its most winnable seats in parliament. This step was taken because there was felt to be discrimination against women trying to enter parliament. It may well have a positive effect in getting more women elected. But Fajardo (1985) has demonstrated that this kind of reverse discrimination can have negative effects as well, particularly on the self-esteem of the individuals on the receiving end. In this study, identical essays attributed to black students were marked more leniently than when they were attributed to white students. Self-esteem was damaged when reality impinged on them. In the same way, women elected to parliament from all-women shortlists might feel that they somehow got elected too easily, with consequent loss of self-esteem.

Causes of Prejudice

Allport (1954) in his book *The Nature of Prejudice* (Chapter 13) identifies six emphases or approaches to causal theories of prejudice, and these are displayed graphically in Figure 5.10 and listed as follows:

1. The historical or economic emphasis;
2. The socio-cultural emphasis;
3. The situational emphasis;
4. The approach via personality dynamics and structure, the psychodynamic emphasis;
5. The phenomenological emphasis; a holistic approach via stimulus object.

The Historical/Economic Emphasis

Historians have suggested that we cannot properly understand the causes of prejudice without examining the history which surrounds any particular conflict. For example, prejudice against black people in the United States has its roots in slavery. Slave owners in the south of the USA treated their slaves like chattels. The prejudice of

FIGURE 5.10
Emphases in Causal Theories of Prejudice

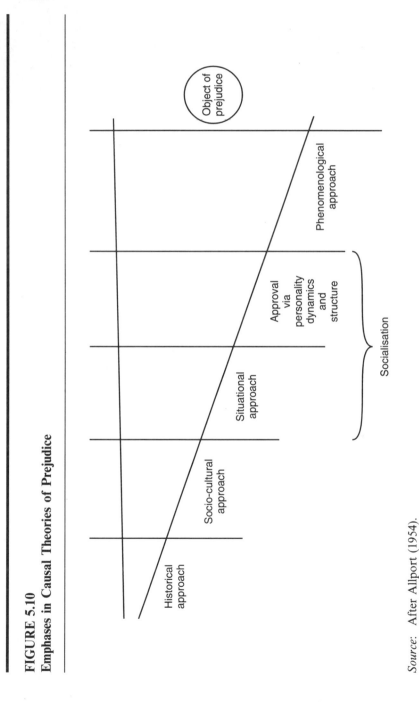

Source: After Allport (1954).

Protestants in Northern Ireland towards Catholics stems from what happened when William III overcame James at the Battle of the Boyne in 1688. They then became 'top dogs' and identified closely with the Protestant regime in England. These are just two examples but it might be argued that virtually all cases of prejudice have an historical root.

In many instances the economic circumstances are determinants of the roots of prejudice. Cox (1948) has summarised the **exploitation theory** of prejudice in these terms:

> Race prejudice is a social attitude propagated among the public by an exploiting class for the purpose of stigmatizing some group as inferior, so that the exploitation of either the group itself or its resources may be justified. (Cox, 1948, p. 393)

Prejudice against native populations rose to a peak during the period of European colonial expansion in the nineteenth century, Cox has claimed, because there was need for justification of the way in which indigenous populations were treated. People in colonial territories were variously described as 'inferior', 'requiring protection', belonging to a 'lower form of evolution' or being 'a burden' which the colonialists had to bear altruistically. Sexual and social taboos (for example 'clubs' for colonialists which native people were not allowed to enter except in the capacity of servants; or a complete ban on intimate relationships) reinforced the inequality. It allowed colonialists to rationalise exploitation – 'Orientals only need a handful of rice a day'. 'Some of "these people" are so primitive they would not know how to use money if they had it! They would only use it for drink.'

There are flaws in this argument, though. There are many examples of prejudice which do not fit this exploitation theory:

- Jews cannot really be said to be victims of economic exploitation. The cause there seems to be jealousy; they were altogether too successful in prospering when others had economic difficulties (for example in Germany in the 1930s).
- Quakers and Mormons were at various times victims of prejudice without being exploited. It was their difference which made them victims.
- Immigrant groups such as the Irish in the USA suffered exploitation but did not suffer the same prejudice as did the

Jews and the black population of America. White tenant farmers suffered exploitation as 'sharecroppers'.

Community Pattern Theory

A network of historic hostilities exists in Europe where cities and lands have changed hands. For example the hostility of Lithuanians, Latvians and Estonians towards the Russians who came to live among them when the USSR included the Baltic States. The native Baltic people see them as intruders. There is hostility among Poles in Silesia towards the Germans, and among Germans in what was once East Prussia towards the Poles and the Russians. Closer to home, some of the animosity between the two communities in Northern Ireland stems from the fact of settlers from Scotland being brought in and given privileged status over the indigenous population.

The Socio-cultural Emphasis

This is the causal explanation favoured by sociologists and anthropologists. Factors which are cited include:

- *Urbanisation, mechanisation and the increasing complexity of life* Ill-educated people flocked to the cities when times were hard on the land, for example during the depression years in the United States or at the time of the potato famine in Ireland. There they were only capable of doing menial work. At the same time advertising encouraged a desire for more goods and more luxury. The poor were not able to reach the standard of material possessions which was considered the norm. They were therefore treated with contempt.
- *Materialism in the city* We hate the city and its materialist values. These are personified in dislike of those who have done well; those who may be dishonest, sneaky, too clever by half, vulgar and noisy. Jews have received opprobrium as the symbol of all that is hated in the city; hence anti-Semitism.
- *Upward mobility of certain groups* There are feelings of condescension towards those who have not 'made the grade'.
- *Increases in population coupled with limitations on housing and available usable land* It was the clamour for 'Lebensraum' which led to Hitler's rise.

- *Inability among many people to develop their own standards internally* They relied upon others for leadership and conformed to the behaviour of those others (for example in Nazi Germany).
- *The role and function of the family changed and also the standard of morality altered* There is prejudice in some British cities against immigrants from Asia or the Caribbean because their family values and patterns of living are not the same as those of the original population; Asian girls coming to school wearing shalwars under their skirts, or being sent back to India, Pakistan or Bangladesh for an arranged marriage; West Indian families holding noisy parties late at night, many individuals crowded into one dwelling.

The Situational Emphasis

This is the individual level of explanation which tends to be favoured by psychologists as opposed to sociological or historical explanations. It focuses upon conformity with others as being a strong influence on the growth of prejudice. Stereotypes of national or of racial groups tend to change according to situational changes. For instance, stereotypes of Russians during the period of the 'cold war' tended to see them as hostile and prepared to go to almost any lengths to inflict damage on the Western powers. Since the overthrow of the communist regime in Russia they have been seen as muddled, confused and in need of help. The situational emphasis is what is left after we have removed the historical element from the socio-cultural perspective. Allport (1954) highlights the importance of *atmosphere*. He recounts an incident which illustrates the impact of atmosphere upon attitudes:

An inspector of education in a British African colony wondered why so little progress was made in learning English in a certain native school. Visiting the classroom he asked the native teacher to put on a demonstration of his method of teaching English. The teacher complied, first making the following preface to the lesson in the vernacular which he did not know the inspector understood: 'Come now, children, put away your things, and let us wrestle for an hour with the enemy's language.

(Allport, 1954, p. 208)

Other situational theories may place emphasis on such things as:

- The *employment situation*. It is necessary, it might be argued, to discriminate against those over 50 because they are no longer as quick on the uptake as they were, and would not allow the firm to compete in the current economic situation. Ageism is therefore justified as situationally necessary.
- *Upward or downward social mobility*. Those on the way up separate themselves from those they have left, no longer frequenting the same venues and so becoming prejudiced against those who do. 'spending an evening at "Bingo" is not something that people like us do!' Bingo is therefore characterised as mind-blowingly dull and those who go to Bingo as stupid.
- *The types of contact between groups*. Those who like to spend their time going to concerts or to the theatre and who meet their friends there, look down on those who frequent football matches or spend evenings in pubs. There is, they claim, a lack of intellectual stimulus from the people they meet there.
- *The density of groups*. We might hear it said, 'I cannot see how they stand the crush of shopping in the superstore on a Saturday.' Those who prefer to shop at more select High Street shops show prejudice against the crowds shopping at Tesco's.

Figure 5.11 illustrates this situational emphasis.

The Psychodynamic Approach

This is to do with conflict. Again, it is essentially a psychological emphasis and concentrates on such things as stress. Within this area is the **frustration** theory of prejudice. Allport quotes from Bettelheim and Janowitz (1950) to illustrate the violent prejudice of a World War II veteran:

> When asked about possible employment and a future depression he replied: 'We'd better not have it. Chicago 'll blow wide open. On South Park the niggers are gettin' so smart. We'll have a race riot that'll make Detroit like a Sunday school picnic. So many are bitter about the part the Negro played in the war. They got all the soft jobs – the quartermasters, engineers. They're no good for anything else. The white got his ass shot off. They're pretty bitter.

FIGURE 5.11
Situational Emphasis on Causes of Prejudice

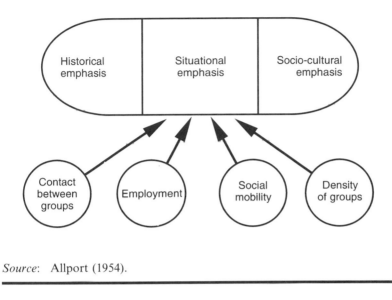

Source: Allport (1954).

If both whites and niggers get laid off, that'll be bad. I'm gonna eat. I know how to use a gun.

(Bettelheim and Janowitz, 1950, p. 82)

Deprivation or the frustration of not being able to get work is causing or intensifying prejudice. Hostility boils up and if it is not controlled will burst out against ethnic minorities. These minorities become demons against whom feelings of anger are directed. The frustration of not being able to get a job has caused and intensified prejudice.

This frustration theory has sometimes been termed **a scapegoat theory.** The anger which has been engendered as a result of the frustration or deprivation suffered is displaced upon a logically irrelevant victim. Two problems with this 'scapegoat' theory are:

1. It does not explain why the pent-up hostility is vented upon a particular victim.

Rosenfield (1978) found that racial attitudes among children were determined more by how much contact they had with members of other races than by the way in which they were brought up by their parents. We could therefore reduce prejudiced behaviour in Northern Ireland more by ensuring that children were educated together in mixed Protestant/Catholic schools than by any attempt to change children's upbringing in their home surroundings.

2. *The permanence of the authoritarian personality*. A further problem is the notion that, once engendered in childhood, authoritarianism remained a permanent personality style. All the evidence is that there can be sudden and dramatic changes in people's attitudes in the light of events. In Germany, extreme anti-Semitism arose during about 12 years (the period of Nazi dominance from 1932 to 1945). This is far too short a period for parents to adopt new child-rearing styles which might form the basis for authoritarian personality. Other examples include attitudes towards the Japanese after the bombing of Pearl Harbour in 1941; attitudes towards the Argentinians after the invasion of the Falkland Islands in 1982; and attitudes towards the French as a result of the resumption of nuclear testing on Muroroa atoll in 1995. As situations change, so prejudices alter.

Within the same psychodynamic field and closely allied to the authoritarian personality is Rokeach's (1948, 1960) theory of **dogmatism**. Rokeach focused upon cognitive style. The characteristics of the dogmatic personality include:

1. Isolation of contradictory belief systems from one another.
2. Reluctance to change beliefs in the light of new information.
3. Appeals to authority to justify the correctness of existing beliefs.

The scales which Rokeach used to measure dogmatism are reliable and correlate highly with measures of authoriarianism, but the same problems remain. It overlooks the socio-cultural and situational influences. What is essentially a group phenomenon is reduced to individual personality predispositions.

Belief Congruence Theory

At the same time as his dogmatism theory, Rokeach produced, separately, a belief congruence theory of prejudice. Individuals use their belief systems as anchoring points; when others agree with your beliefs it confirms and validates them. This congruence of beliefs is therefore reinforcing. We tend to be attracted to, and to have positive empathy with, people who share our beliefs. The converse also applies; we have negative feelings towards those whose beliefs are not congruent with ours. As far as Rokeach was concerned, prejudiced behaviour and social discrimination is more likely to be caused by incongruity in beliefs than ethnic or racial differences.

However there are problems with this:

1. Rokeach excludes circumstances where prejudice is institutionalised or where the prejudice has received social sanction. In those cases it is a matter of group membership. This excludes many of the most obvious manifestations of prejudice.
2. The research on which Rokeach's theory has been based is quite seriously flawed. Participants in his study had to rate their attitude towards a number of individuals in a repeated measures design. Some of these individuals were of the same race, some of a different race. All had different beliefs. There was therefore no homogeneity of belief within the racial groups, and no separation of belief between groups. The focus was therefore on individual differences, with participants responding not as members of a racial group but as individuals. The research design had therefore written out in advance racial or ethnic group membership as an explanation, which leaves only the belief variable.

The Phenomenological Emphasis

This is the holistic emphasis. The overall impression created by the stimulus object or person is what matters. We may label a person or a group of persons as 'dirty' or 'stupid' and that is a defining label. Clearly the historical and cultural background from which perceptions originate contributes to the perception. A couple of examples might make this clearer:

1. We might come from a background where cleanliness is a paramount virtue. To use Kelly's term (1955) it is a personal construct which helps us to make sense of the world. When we meet someone or a group of people, perhaps a group of 'travellers', they are identified as 'dirty' and that is the overriding

and defining perception. Negative feelings towards that person or that group arise from that source; we feel hostility and are prejudiced against them.

2. The context from which we perceive the world is that of passive and compliant women and more aggressive and assertive men. If we meet a woman whose behaviour is more assertive than most, even though it is less assertive than that of most men, we are more hostile to her than we would be towards a man behaving in exactly the same way. We are prejudiced and discriminate against her.

Emphasis on Earned Reputation

The focus here is on the minority groups who are the object of prejudice and discriminatory behaviour. It suggests that the characteristics of such groups may have provoked that hostility. Both Triandis and Vassiliou (1967) and Brigham (1971) have come to the conclusion that there is a 'kernel of truth' in stereotypes. The traits which identify a particular group tend to be commonly agreed upon by different respondents. That is not to say that stereotypes are *justified* even though they may be relatively accurate. Asians tend to display emotions facially less than do Europeans; hence they tend to be stereotyped as impassive and unemotional (Ekman *et al.*, 1987). La France and Mayo (1976) found that black people make less eye contact with others than white people; hence there exists a stereotype of shiftiness. This may help in understanding the origins of prejudice and discrimination.

The Reduction of Prejudice and Discrimination

In the discussion of prejudice a wide variety of emphases have been brought in and strategies to reduce prejudice relate to these. It is evident that prejudice is extremely complex so that attempts to combat it must be multi-faceted, but we shall not attempt to disentangle the facets. Education must inevitably play a great part. Formal education in schools can only have a marginal impact if the children are subjected to bigotry at home. It helps to reinforce prejudice if the historical victories of one group are celebrated and remembered. This is what happens with such events as the Apprentice Boys parade in Londonderry in Northern Ireland. Men adorned in orange sashes march through the city to commemorate events which took place in 1688 when apprentice boys closed the gates of the city against Catholic King James.

Box 5.5 (on the following page) details some other experiments on prejudice. 'In the light of earlier comments upon the ethical status of experiments such as those of Milgram and Zimbardo which have been described (pp. 263–8) you might like to consider whether these experiments by Elliot (reported by Zimbardo), by Weiner and Wright and Clore were justified from an ethical standpoint. Perhaps it is worthwhile to re-read the section on ethics in Chapter 1 Section III, and consider to what extent they were within the ethical guide-lines set out in this section. The extent to which the understandings which result from these studies justify any 'abuses' of ethical principles is a matter of debate and does need careful evaluation.'

Superordinate Goals

Sherif's summer camp studies, which have been fully discussed earlier in Chapter 4, showed that by imposing superordinate goals on groups which had become hostile to one another, inter-group tension might be reduced. The problems with the water supply at the camp were not solvable by either of the groups on their own, but by cooperating they were able to overcome the problem. Cooperation in turn reduced prejudiced and discriminatory behaviour. But superordinate goals have to be achieved. Worchel *et al.* (1977) artificially created cooperative, competitive relationships between two groups and then imposed superordinate goals which were either achieved or not. Relations between the group improved except where there had been competition and the superordinate goal was not achieved. In this case relations actually got worse. Where the failure to achieve the goals can be attributed to the other group, rightly or wrongly, then inter-group relations worsen. If there are external reasons for the failure then inter-group relations may improve. Hogg and Vaughan (1995) have suggested that this might have been the case in Argentina in 1982 at the time of the Falklands war. The junta controlling Argentina was suffering factional conflict and the invasion of the Falklands was introduced as a superordinate goal. Its failure could be blamed on the junta and so the factional conflict worsened and the junta fell. It could be argued that there was a similar situation on this side of the Atlantic. Margaret Thatcher was faced with divisions in her party, some members of which felt strongly that her 'experiment' had failed and were ready

BOX 5.5
Experiments on Prejudice

1. One way in which children may be helped to feel what it is like to be a victim was demonstrated in an experiment conducted by Jane Elliot, a teacher with a third grade class in Iowa, and reported by **Zimbardo (1979).** She announced to the class that it was a well-known fact that blue-eyed children were brighter and generally superior to those with brown eyes. The brown-eyed children were told that they were inferior and had to look up to and respect the blue-eyed ones. They were forced to sit at the back of the class, use paper cups instead of drinking from the drinking fountain, to stand at the end of the line, and wear special collars to enable the blue-eyed ones to identify them immediately, even from behind. Blue-eyed children were accorded special privileges, such as second helpings at lunch and extra time at break. After the first hour the effects began to show up. The school work of the brown-eyed ones deteriorated; they became angry and depressed and began to describe themselves as stupid. To quote Zimbardo 'What had been marvellously cooperative, thoughtful children became nasty, vicious discriminating third graders' (Zimbardo, 1979 p. 638).

   The next day Elliot informed the children that she had made a mistake. It was really the brown-eyed children who were brighter and blue-eyed children were inferior. Almost at once there was a switch in attitude and behaviour. Brown-eyed children's work began to get better and the blue-eyed children began to lose their self-confidence.

2. A second experiment was reported by **Weiner and Wright (1973)** which closely follows Elliot's experiment. White children in a third-grade class were assigned randomly to be either green or orange people. They wore orange or green armbands to distinguish them. To begin with, the orange people were regarded as superior. They were told that they were brighter and cleaner than the greens. The greens were regarded as inferior and denied privileges. The second day the situation was reversed. The group which was discriminated against lost self-confidence, felt inferior and did poorly in their schoolwork. Then at a later date the children who had been through the experiment were asked if they would like to go on a picnic with black children from a nearby school. 96 per cent agreed as compared with only 62 per cent of a control group who had not been through the orange/green experiment. These experiments mirror the experiences of black people, especially in the southern states of the USA, who had historically first been slaves and then had been regarded as inferior.

   Equal status contact can help. When people are made aware that members of minority groups share their goals, ambitions and feelings prejudice may be reduced. There needs to be personal contact between groups on an equal footing (Cook and Pelfrey, 1985).

3. Clore (1976) set up a unique summer camp for children. It was administered by one white and one black male, and one white and one black female. Blacks were equally divided in power, privileges and duties. Instead of always seeing blacks in a servile or subordinate role (which of course harks back to the historical fact of slavery), there was contact between the races on an equal basis. Tests showed that children attending the camp had significantly more positive attitudes towards opposite race children after attending the camp than they did before.

to depose her. The Falklands expedition served as a superordinate goal, which because it succeeded, improved inter-group relations within the Conservative party dramatically.

Contact

Taking the situational emphasis, prejudiced or discriminatory behaviour which results from high unemployment (ageism for instance, or discrimination against ethnic minorities) might be changed by altering the situation; by creating more jobs, for instance, where unemployment is high. Increased contact between groups is important in this context. Groups may be separated by a wide range of differences – educational, cultural, occupational and material. The suggestion is made that greater intergroup contact would reduce prejudice and conflict. Stephan and Stephan (1984) have claimed that ignorance is a factor. Allport (1954) proposed the **contact hypothesis**. However, he has stressed that the *nature* of the contact is important, and discussed six different kinds of contact:

1. *Casual contact* Where an individual lives in a place where members of a minority group also live, for example in Bradford where there is a high concentration of people of Asian origin, people may say that they know Asian people because they meet so many of them; but it is a superficial contact. Alternatively, where there is segregation it may be frozen into relationships between subordinates and those in positions of authority. The evidence is that such contacts do more to increase prejudice than to dispel it. The reasoning behind this is as follows. Perceiving a

member of an out-group casually triggers rumour, hearsay, tradition and stereotypes linked to that out-group. The greater the frequency of the casual contact, the more the adverse mental associations are strengthened and we are sensitised to perceive signs that confirm the stereotype. If a dozen Asians are behaving impeccably in a Bradford street, and one is not, we will select the one who is misbehaving to confirm our preconceptions. Allport quotes an imaginary instance to illustrate this process:

> An Irishman and a Jew encounter each other in casual contact . . . Neither, in fact has any initial animosity towards the other. But the Irishman thinks, 'Ah, a Jew; perhaps he'll skin me, I'll be careful'. The Jew thinks, 'Probably a Mick; they hate the Jews; he'd like to insult me.' With such an inauspicious start, both men are likely to be evasive, distrustful and cool. The casual contact has left things worse than before.
>
> (Allport, 1954, p. 252)

2. *Acquaintance*   True acquaintance lessens prejudice. Gray and Thompson (1953) found that there was a uniform tendency by people to rate higher on an acceptability scale (the Bogardus Social Distance Scale, see Chapter 4) those groups in which they had five or more acquaintances. A way, therefore, of reducing prejudice is to increase knowledge through closer acquaintance. There are various ways of doing this:

- *Academic teaching in schools* – anthropological facts can be taught as well as reasons why different customs have developed in other ethnic groups.
- *Social travel* – this is aimed at giving students direct experience with other groups. Smith (1943) has evaluated an experiment in social travel where 46 graduate students travelled to Harlem for a week-end, were entertained in black people's homes there and met prominent black doctors, editors, writers, artists and social-workers. Twenty-three students were unable to travel and so acted as a control. Attitudes towards blacks were measured both before and after the week-end. Even after a year had elapsed only 8 out of the 46 failed to show more favourable attitudes towards black people. This was not the case with the control group. It is worth noting that all the black people in this study were of high status (at least as high as the visitors' status).

- *Intercultural education* – which may involve role play. A white adult with anti-black attitudes might be asked to play the role of a black musician trying to get a room in a hotel and being refused by the receptionist, when it is known to both that rooms are free.

3. *Residential contact* The question here is whether integrated housing serves to increase or to lessen prejudice as compared to segregated housing. As has been seen in Northern Ireland, segregation in housing means segregation in schooling, shopping, medical facilities and churches. Friendships across group residential boundaries become very hard to form.

  A minority group becomes much more visible if it is segregated. Black people represent a mere 10 per cent of the metropolitan population of New York. If they were randomly distributed they would not seem significant, yet concentrated in Harlem they are seen as a dangerously expanding threat.

  It is at the boundaries of segregated areas that tension is likely to occur particularly if there is pressure from within the segregated area from an expanding population. Integrated housing removes barriers to effective communication. Once these barrriers are removed fallacious stereotypes are reduced and realism replaces fear and autistic hostility.

4. *Occupational contact* Black people tend to be near the bottom of the occupational ladder, and this may have its roots in the historical fact of slavery. With menial jobs come poor pay and low status. Similarly, women have historically been seen to have their place at home rather than at work. When they enter the job market it is frequently in jobs with low pay and low status. Occupational contacts with members of out-groups who are of equal status are important for the reduction of prejudice. Equal Opportunities legislation can help, but there is also a task of persuasion to be done. Those who have authority should lead by example. Haas and Fleming (1946) have suggested:

> The smart personnel man will always start his non-discrimination program with the appointment of a Negro in his own department or on the top management level.

Members of minorities which have been victims of prejudice have contact on an equal basis once they have been appointed to posts in the higher echelons of employment, and this will help to break down prejudice.

5. *Pursuit of common objectives*   Occupational contacts of this kind are fine, but suffer from an inherent limitation. Contact, even if it is on the basis of equal status may remain dissociated from prejudiced behaviour at a more generalised level unless it leads people to do things together. A multi-ethnic team has a common goal and the ethnic composition becomes irrelevant. Common participation and common interests are more important than mere equal status contact.

6. *Goodwill contacts*   Goodwill contact with minority groups is likely to achieve very little unless there are concretely defined objectives. DuBois (1950) was establishing a neighbourhood festival and invited members of ethnic minorities, Armenians, Mexicans, Jews and so on, to recollect what each used to do in autumn festivals in their childhoods. Universal values common to all ethnic groups were in this way brought out and grounds for acquaintance established. An agenda for the improvement of community relationships was evolved which might be strengthened by cooperative endeavour.

So far as the psychodynamic emphasis is concerned some of the frustrations which lie at the root of scapegoat theory can be alleviated. Poverty, poor housing and lack of employment opportunities are capable of remedy. The authoritarian personality seems to be the result of particularly harsh child-rearing practices and so may be reduced, in time, with patient education. Indeed there is evidence that child-rearing has become more liberal, so that perhaps it is reasonable to expect that authoritarian and dogmatic personality structures will become less common.

Self-assessment Questions

1. List the various emphases which have been employed in attempts to explain prejudice and discrimination. Can it realistically be said that the emphasis used depends upon the discipline of the observer; psychologists favouring psychodynamic explanations, historians and sociologists favouring historical/economic or sociocultural explanations, and so on?

2. Describe the authoritarian personality. Is it realistic to explain prejudice in terms of a natural disposition to be prejudiced? Where do the flaws lie in this explanation?
3. Allport has put forward a contact theory for prejudice reduction. Specify which kinds of contact between groups are likely to be most helpful in reducing prejudice.
4. Superordinate goals have been suggested as a way of reducing prejudice and hostility. Explain how such goals may be used in a practical way to reduce conflict.

FURTHER READING

G. W. Allport, *The Nature of Prejudice* (New York: Doubleday Anchor, 1958).

K. Deaux, F. C. Dane and L. S. Wrightsman, *Social Psychology in the 90s*, 6th edn, Chapter 7 (Pacific Grove, Cal.: Brooks Cole, 1993).

"BEFORE YOU EXERCISE YOUR LEGITIMATE POWER TO USE COERCIVE POWER, SIR, I HAPPEN TO HAVE THIS INFORMATIONAL POWER . . . "

Social influence 6

At the end of this chapter you should be able to:

1. Distinguish between conformity and compliance.
2. Describe some of the research on conformity to social norms by Asch and others.
3. Identify what is meant by foot-in-the-door, door-in-the-face, that's-not-all and low-ball techniques.
4. Describe and comment upon Milgram's experiments on obedience, particularly in respect of the ethics involved.
5. Indicate the relative importance of situation and personality in the emergence of leadership.
6. Describe Fiedler's contingency model of leadership.
7. Describe the effects on decision-making of different communication structures within an organisation.
8. Identify what are meant by deindividuation and dehumanisation in relation to crowds of people.

SECTION I CONFORMITY AND COMPLIANCE

The distinction made here between these two terms, which have frequently been used interchangeably, is this: while conformity relates to responses to indirect pressure, compliance relates to how we respond to direct requests. Conformity would be involved in dressing appropriately for whatever situation we may find ourselves in, *because of the pressure exerted on us by others to do so*. We appear at a wedding in our best dress, because to appear in jeans and trainers would be frowned upon. However, if the invitation stipulated formal morning dress we would comply with that request.

Conformity

When an individual is part of a group, the individual is influenced by that group in relation to the way in which he or she responds to stimuli. The earliest studies of conformity include the work of Sherif (1936). He studied the responses of individuals in groups of various sizes and also when alone to what is known as the autokinetic effect. We are in a darkened room and there is a stationary pin point of light at the far side of it. Looking at the light we see that the light appears to move. Our eyes have no other reference point. Sherif believed that where there is ambiguity, **social norms** tend to emerge to reduce the uncertainty. Participants in Sherif's study made a large number of judgements about how far the point of light had moved. Over a number of trials a frame of reference or a range of variation emerged within which the estimates were made; each individual working alone developed a different frame of reference so that they gradually, over the course of, say, 100 trials, narrowed the range of their estimates of how far the light had moved. However, when participants were together in a group calling out their estimates, other participants' estimates began to be used as a frame of reference so that eventually they were giving virtually identical estimates. Their individual estimates had converged on a group norm. This group influence was powerful enough to remain with the individuals when they later made estimates on their own. It had become internalised.

Later, Asch (1951) argued that it was the uncertainty and ambiguity which made people conform to a norm. If the stimulus had been entirely unambiguous, judgements made would be entirely individual and not influenced at all by other people. To test this, he set up what has become a classic experiment. Male students were recruited for what they thought was a visual discrimination task. Seated round a table in groups of between seven and nine they were presented with a card on which were three comparison lines (as in Figure 6.1), A, B and C. A standard line was shown to them and they took turns to call out which of the comparison lines was the same length as the standard. In reality, all but one of the 'students' were confederates of Asch's, primed to give wrong answers on 12 of the trials, in six cases picking a line that was too short and in six one that was too long. In each of the 18 trials the real naive student answered second to last. To control for ambiguity, there was also a condition where participants made their judgements privately with no group influence. There were less than 1 per cent errors in this condition.

FIGURE 6.1
Materials Used in Asch's 1956 Study

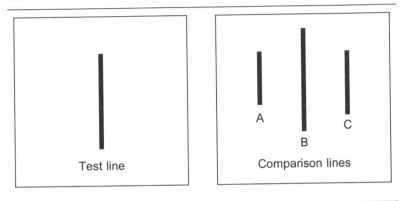

Test line   Comparison lines

Results

The results were not as Asch had predicted. While there were 25 per cent of participants who relied on their own judgement throughout and were not influenced by others at all, 50 per cent conformed to the judgement of the erroneous majority on six or more trials out of the 12 where there had been manipulation by confederates. Five per cent conformed on all 12 trials. The average conformity rate was 33 per cent.

When they were debriefed, participants gave various reasons for conforming to the erroneous majority. Initially they experienced uncertainty and self-doubt. They had, after all, a disagreement on what was a straightforward perceptual judgement. Then there was fear of social disapproval, anxiety and loneliness. Some really thought that they had perceived the lines in a different way from the others, that the group was right and their eyesight must in some way be defective. Others simply went along with the majority so as not to 'rock the boat'. There were even some who maintained that they actually saw the lines as the majority said they did.

Why Do People Conform?

Deutsch and Gerard (1955) suggested that there were two different kinds of influence which persuaded participants to conform:

- **Informational influence** The other people in the group provide a source of information in a case of ambiguity and uncertainty – such as in the Sherif studies.
- **Normative influence** Where there was little ambiguity, as in Asch's experiments, group norms and a strong social pressure not to be deviant, not to be the odd one out, persuaded people to conform. Deutsch and Gerard replicated the Asch studies and found that when participants were explicitly identified as group members, normative influence ensured that 'conformity' was greater.

More recently Abrams and Hogg (1990b) have proposed another influence which may operate to underpin both the above influences, **self categorisation**. As soon as we know a little about someone we meet we tend to place him or her in a category or categories. It may be 'male' or 'female', 'young' or 'old', 'well educated' or 'ill-educated' or we may perhaps put a class label on them. Abrams and Hogg suggest that the same processes operate as far as we ourselves are concerned. Membership of a group is very important to us, and what we do has to be consistent with membership of the group. Even something as transitory as being on a panel helping with an experiment confers membership of a group. We identify with the group in order to maintain our self-concept – and membership of the group is included as part of that – we need to conform.

This self-categorisation theory provides us with an explanation of why some people remain independent and why some people are anti-conformists, trying desperately hard not to be like everyone else. It may be part of someone's self-concept that he or she is not like everyone else, either fiercely independent, not taking any account of what others do, or fiercely different, taking account of others' behaviour but deliberately not conforming to it. Abrams and Hogg used a situation similar to that used by Sherif. There were six participants in a darkened room, three of whom were confederates of the experimenters. Using Sherif's procedures (q.v.) they consistently estimated the movement of the point of light as 5 cm greater than the rest of the group, thus creating the impression that there were two sub-groups. They then set up a competitive task, pitting the three confederates against the other three participants, so that *explicit* groups were set up. In this situation, the discrepancy between the estimates (of light movement) was significantly greater than in the non-explicit group originally set up.

Thus self-categorisation operates to strengthen both informational and normative conformity as well as anti-conformity and independence (as Deutsch and Gerard found).

Factors which influence the degree of conformity include:

Group Size

As the size of a group increases so does its influence. The larger the group, the greater the number of reasons they are able to provide for conforming. Also, as Insko *et al.* (1985) have found, the chances become greater that there will be someone in the group with sufficient power to exert pressure to comply; but the group must be seen as acting as individuals.

Group Decision

Wilder (1977) showed that the more closely (in an Asch-type situation) the 'confederates' are seen as cohering, the less the conformity is likely to be by a single individual who does not see himself or herself as belonging to that cohesive group. Conformity is greater when there are, for instance, four individuals making erroneous judgements, apparently independently of one another, than when they are seen as a single group. In that case the pressure to conform is little more than it would be with a single individual making erroneous judgements. But, notwithstanding that, when the individual sees himself or herself as *belonging*, the pressure is greater.

Unanimity

Where there is not unanimity among those making erroneous judgements, but rather a clear majority and minority view, then conformity becomes much less. The minority itself becomes a source of influence. This happens in the case of jury deliberations when a unanimous verdict has to be arrived at. A single individual who cannot make up his or her mind has pressure exerted on him or her from either side, those who would vote for conviction as well as those who favour acquittal. But the pressure will be greater from those who are in the majority. As more of the jury decides to convict, the pressure on the one undecided juror to convict increases as Campbell *et al.* (1986) showed.

Individual Difference in Conformity

Crutchfield (1955) replicated Asch's research but with significant modifications. Participants in his study were military men attending a three-day assessment programme. They did not confront one another, however, but were in individual cubicles in which were electrical panels. They responded to questions projected on the wall using these panels and received feedback on other participant's responses via the panels, which were in fact connected not to the other participants' panels but to the experimenter's. The apparent order in which the responses appeared (from the display of lights) to be made could be varied by the experimenter as well as the proportions of agreement or disagreement. The questions were wider, involving amongst other things attitudinal statements such as 'I believe we are made better by the trials and hardships of life' or 'Free speech is a privilege rather than a right; it is permissible to suspend free speech when a society feels threatened'; as well perceptual questions like those of Asch.

The results were similar to Asch's. In addition Crutchfield found that conformers and non-conformers showed different personality characteristics, in that non-conformers were higher than conformers in the following traits:

Intellectual effectiveness
Ego strength
Leadership ability
Maturity in social relationships
Efficiency
Ability to express themselves
Naturalness
Lack of pretension
Self-reliance

Conformers were found to be:

Submissive
Narrow
Inhibited
Lacking in insight.

He also found that females are more conforming and also more conservative than men. However, later research, such as that of

Zimbardo and Leippe (1991) and Cacioppo and Petty (1980) have found that much of this difference is due to the particular research setting, where men had an informational advantage. Where women know less about the subject they conform more, but men also conform more than women when they know less about the subject. Eagly and Carli (1981) found that in face-to-face interaction, women conform more than men. This they suggested is because women are socialised to a greater extent to regard harmony as important, so that they are likely to go along with the group and yield to pressure rather than risk disharmony.

In general, the consensus seems to be that situational rather than individual factors are of greatest importance.

Compliance

As has been mentioned, conformity refers to indirect pressure, compliance to responses to direct requests. Suppose we have been invited to a wedding. There is pressure to conform to particular standards of appearance. Men are likely to wear suits, probably with a carnation in their buttonholes; women will wear smart dresses or suits and probably a hat. However, the invitation might specify 'formal dress' which is a direct request for men to wear morning suits and top hat. To go along with such a direct request is compliance. This happens all the time. We are buying a house: the solicitor calls and asks us to come to his office to sign some papers; we do so. Our friend asks us to buy something for him (her) while we are in town; we buy it.

Foot-in-the-Door Effect

Much of the research into compliance relates to salesmanship. The **foot-in-the-door** effect relates to the notion that once we have been induced to comply with a small request, we will be more likely to comply later with a larger demand. Freedman and Fraser (1966) sent undergraduate experimenters to present women in their homes with a small request, to sign a petition about road safety or to place a small notice in their window. Then two weeks later different experimenters approached the same women with a more substantial request, to put a large billboard on their front lawn to promote road safety. Others approached a control group (who had not had the first request) with the same request. Those who had had the 'foot in the door' were much more likely to comply.

De Jong (1979) suggested that the reasons behind this effect relate to **self-perception**. Complying with the first request leads the individual to see himself or herself as basically a 'helpful person'. Then at the second request he or she is reluctant to lose this image of helpfulness which is seen as a positive one even if complying with the request is irksome. It is suggested that there are two necessary conditions to produce this effect:

1. The first request has to be sufficiently large that the individual thinks about it before complying. What are the implications of complying?
2. There has to be free choice. If there were any external pressure applied to comply there is no longer any reason why the individual should attribute compliance to being helpful (that is, the self-perception of a positive disposition). If women were offered money to grant the first request, Zuckerman *et al.* (1979) found that to be sufficient justification in itself and the effect was lost.

Door-in-the-Face Effect

This is in effect the obverse of the foot-in-the-door effect. Cialdini *et al.* (1975) suggested that there were occasions when refusal of an initial request actually made it *more* likely that a second request would be acceded to. In their study, college students were approached with a very demanding request – to serve as voluntary counsellors in a juvenile detention centre for two years. In nearly every case this initial request was refused. However, when the same people were approached a second time with a much less onerous request – to chaperon juveniles on a trip to the zoo – there was much greater compliance, 50 per cent complied compared to 17 per cent where there had been no larger first request. De Jong's self-perception explanation would suggest that there should be less compliance on the second request. The persons approached have already refused one request and so have begun to see themselves as unhelpful. This should, in theory, have coloured their response to the second request and they should have been less likely to accede to it. Again, it has been suggested that there are two conditions which have to be met for the door-in-the-face effect to operate:

1. The initial request has to be sufficiently onerous for them not to think badly of themselves if they refuse it.
2. The second request has to be made by the same person who made the first one. According to Cialdini and his colleagues, the second request is then seen as a concession and complying with it is seen as a reciprocal gesture.

If we put our hand into icy water and then into lukewarm water, the water feels hot: this contrast effect, it is suggested, lies behind the door-in-the-face phenomenon. We might go into a car show-room to buy a used car. The salesman asks us how much we want to spend. We say, perhaps, £2000. We are shown a few very well used and high-mileage vehicles for around that price before being shown a much better-looking car for £3000. It appears a so much better bargain that we cannot pass it by. This is the door-in-the-face technique in action.

That's-Not-All Effect

Allied to the door-in-the-face is the **that's-not-all** technique. In this technique we go into the showroom and are shown a car at around our price and before we have the chance to say 'yes' or 'no' the salesperson says we can have it for £500 less than the advertised price, and we will get free insurance as well. According to Burger (1986), the difference between this and the door-in-the-face technique is that the consumer does not have the chance to refuse an offer before a more favourable one is made. Burger's comparison of the two techniques showed 'that's not all' to be the more effective. In both techniques a concession is made.

Low-Ball Technique

Cialdini *et al.* (1978) investigated a technique prevalent among dealers in new cars. This **low-ball technique** consists of offering a much better deal than any of the competitors, a discount on the list price or a very high trade-in price for our old car. We agree to the deal and all the papers are prepared when the sales person goes to check with the boss. Then he or she comes back and apologises that the boss will not agree to the deal. We can have the car for the list price. In many cases such as this, the customer will still go ahead with the deal because they are committed and reluctant to back out.

Cialdini demonstrated the low-ball technique by getting students to agree to take part in an experiment and only then telling them that they had to be there by 7 a.m. Others, told initially of the early start, were much less likely to agree to take part. Cialdini (1985) suggested reasons for the effectiveness of low-ball techniques. When people receive the initial offer or request and make a commitment, they develop justifications for that commitment. When one of the justifications (the low price, for example) is removed the remaining justifications still remain.

A variation on the low-ball technique is the **lure**. We go to buy a pair of shoes and see just what we want on the shelf for a very attractive price. We tell the salesperson we would like this pair but in a different size and colour. The salesperson goes out to the back to look for a pair the right size and returns to apologise that the size (or colour) which we want is not available, but we can have another similar pair in the right size and colour but it is not 'in the sale'. Because we have made a commitment and justified that commitment to ourself we go ahead with the purchase. Joule *et al.* (1989) set out to test this. Students were asked to volunteer for a boring hour-long study which involved memorising numbers. No payment was mentioned. Only 15 per cent agreed. A second group were asked to volunteer to take part in an interesting half-hour study which involved watching a film. They would be paid 30 francs (about £4); 47 per cent agreed. When they arrived to take part they were told that the study which they had agreed to take part in had been completed the day before. They could take part in the boring memory study, though, but unfortunately they could not be paid for it. They all accepted. They had made a commitment to take part in an experiment and stood by that commitment.

Theory of Politeness

Brown and Levinson (1987) developed what they termed a **theory of politeness** to explain why people comply. It relates to impression management. What matters is to give the best impression to people we meet. Goffman (1967) referred to face-saving in this context. When we ask someone to do something for us, we are asking to be allowed to impose our will on the other person. He or she may lose 'face' if he/she complies. Similarly, when we ask someone to do something for us and he/she refuses, that may involve loss of face on our part. Polite requests involve less face-threatening than more peremptory demands and so are more likely to be complied with. Brown and Levinson developed a hierarchy of strategies to obtain compliance. Those which might involve loss of face (force, threats, bribery, deception) are likely to be less successful than those which do not (such as polite requests, invoking personal reasons or expertise or bargaining for a favour).

Power Bases

Whether we are able to induce someone to comply with a request may depend upon the power which we can exercise. French and Raven (1959) identified five types of power:

1. *Coercive power.* This amounts to the ability to administer punishment of some kind. A teacher, for example, or a parent has sanction which can be applied to ensure compliance.
2. *Reward power.* The ability to reward someone for compliance. A parent may reward a child for doing what he or she is asked, for example.
3. *Expert power.* This stems from superior knowledge, ability or expertise.
4. *Referent power.* Power may be exercised because we look up to, identify with, or wish to emulate someone.
5. *Legitimate power.* If we are elected or appointed to an official position we may exercise power by virtue of that. A headteacher exercises power over pupils and staff because of his or her appointment to that position.

Raven (1965) added an additional source of power, *informational power*. If we know that our boss has been claiming expenses to which he or she was not entitled, for example, and he or she knows that we know, this can be very influential in gaining compliance to requests. It is very hard sometimes to separate sources of power. In fact several sources may be exercised at the same time. A teacher may have legitimate power because he or she is a teacher; expert power because he or she has knowledge; referent power if a pupil identifies with him or her; and reward or coercive power because the ability to administer rewards or punishment rests with him or her. The circumstances will often determine the likelihood of compliance. When a parent or a teacher is there, coercive power may be more effective than when they are not. Legitimate power is vested in

present wore white lab coats. Milgram ran one experiment in a run-down inner-city office block. Obedience dropped in these surroundings to 48 per cent. Bushman (1984, 1988) tested the effect of the legitimacy of authority and so the possibility that participants might be able to abdicate responsibility for what they do. The scenario was someone fumbling for change by a parking meter. Bushman had confederates, variously dressed, in uniform, in a neat suit or in shabby clothes stop passers by and order them to give the person change for the meter. 70 per cent obeyed the uniformed confederate compared with 50 per cent of those who were not in uniform and even fewer of those who were shabbily dressed. When questioned as to why they had obeyed, those who obeyed the uniformed confederate said they did so 'because they were told to', while the reason given for obeying the non-uniformed confederates was more frequently that they wanted to be helpful.

Replications of Milgram's work carried out elsewhere produced similar results. Mantell (1971) in Germany found an even higher rate of obedience. Shanab and Kahya (1977) in Jordan found 80 per cent obedience in children. High levels of obedience were also found in Australia by Kilham and Mann (1974).

A Question of Ethics

Much of the debate which centred around Milgram's research into obedience has been concerned with the ethics of what he did. While participants in his studies did not *actually* inflict pain or suffering on the supposed 'victims', they thought they were doing so and this caused stress. On the other hand, there is no evidence that any of them suffered psychological harm, and in fact at a later date (Milgram, 1992) 83.7 per cent of them indicated that they were glad they had taken part. Only 1.3 per cent had any misgivings.

The ethical questions in this research centre upon three issues:

- Can the amount of stress to which the participants were subjected be justified in terms of the importance of the research itself and its outcomes?
- Were the participants free to withdraw at any time? While they were free in the sense that no one tied them down, it was never made explicit to them that they could withdraw, and withdrawal was a large part of what was being measured. The fact that they

were paid also places a certain obligation upon them not to back out.

- The third issue is about whether they gave 'informed consent' to what they were about to be asked to do As part of the design of the experiment the participants had to be naïve about it true purpose. They could not therefore give *informed* consent.

Some further points have been made in Chapter 1 in the context of a discussion of ethics in a more general sense. Milgram's defence to charges of ethical misconduct centre around precautions taken beforehand to ensure that none of the participants was in any way unstable, and around the care taken in debriefing them afterwards. Nevertheless, Bettelheim, quoted in Miller (1986) was moved to say:

> These experiment are so vile, the intention with which they were engaged is so vile, that nothing in these experiments has any value. (Miller, 1986, p. 124)

One of the results of this debate is a set of guidelines for psychological research which makes it unlikely that the exact procedures of Milgram's research could now be replicated. The code of practice includes three key points:

1. That there must be informed consent.
2. That participants must be explicitly told that they are free to withdraw at any time, without any repercussions.
3. There must full and honest debriefing at the end.

Generalisability

It was also suggested by Baumrind (1964), among others, that it was not possible to generalise these findings into 'real life'. There was the prestigious nature of the institution to be taken into account as well the fact that the participants were paid volunteers. It is known that volunteers do not constitute a typical sample.

Other Studies Involving Obedience

Other studies into obedience include the work of Hofling *et al.* (1966). The researchers looked at nurse/doctor relationships in a hospital setting. Nurses were instructed by telephone to give 20 mg of the drug 'Astrofen' to a patient, Mr Jones. The doctor would come to see the patient in 10 minutes and would sign for the drug then; 21 out of 22 nurses complied in spite of the fact that three rules were broken:

1. The maximum dose for this drug was 10 mg.
2. Written authority was required for its administration.
3. Nurses were required to check the genuineness of a doctor.

Zimbardo *et al.* (1973) conducted an experiment into social power in a more general sense. Details of their experiment are shown in Box 6.2.

BOX 6.2
Zimbardo's Prison Experiment

Twenty-five volunteer participants were selected after extensive psychological tests to take part in an experiment for a generous fee. The context was a simulated prison and the participants were to role play being either prisoners or guards. The toss of a coin determined which role each person would play. To start with, the 'prisoners' were arrested, charged with felony and underwent all the procedures associated with this. They were de-loused, strip-searched, given a prison uniform with a number front and back and a manacle on one ankle. The 'guards' on the other hand were given military style uniforms reflective sunglasses to prevent eye contact, clubs, whistles, handcuffs and keys. They were encouraged to shout orders and push the 'prisoners' around. Anything was allowed short of physical violence. While the 'prisoners' were locked up for 24 hours a day, the 'guards' worked eight hour shifts. In quite a short time a perverted relationship began to develop between 'prisoners' and 'guards'. The 'guards' became more aggressive; 'prisoners' became more passive. Within 36 hours one 'prisoner' had developed symptoms of depression and had to be released. Soon, others also showed symptoms of stress and the whole experiment had to be called off after six days, though it had been scheduled to last a fortnight.

Zimbardo was subjected to similar criticisms as to the ethics of his experiment as Milgram had been. It remains unclear whether the dubious ethics of the programme were justified by the uncovering of normal human beings' propensities to behave in an evil manner.

Self-assessment Questions

1. Describe Asch's experiments on conformity. Do you think they reflect at all what happens in real life?
2. List some of the techniques used to ensure compliance. How effective are they?
3. Were the samples in Milgram's experiments representative? If not, why not?
4. What were the factors which caused participants in Milgram's experiments to obey, even when they were apparently inflicting pain on others?
5. List some of the criticisms made of these experiments. Do you think they were justified?
6. Make some comparison of Milgram's work with either that of Hofling or of Zimbardo. Can you draw any conclusions about human nature from these experiments?

SECTION II   LEADERSHIP AND FOLLOWERSHIP

In this section we shall be considering why it is that some individuals become leaders in whatever they become involved with, while others are content to follow the lead of others. This division between leaders and followers seems to subsist as much in teams, committees, gangs and so on, as in the larger context of countries, political parties and councils. It seems at least possible that there are factors which can be isolated which provide a clue as to why this should be the case. These factors include:

- *Personality*   Can it be said that those who persistently emerge as leaders in whatever field possess certain personality traits which mark them out so that it can be predicted who will lead?
- *Situation*   Is it the situation in which individuals find themselves and the requirements of those situations which allow certain individuals to emerge as leaders, while others are content to be led?
- *Behaviour or style*   Do leaders behave consistently in ways which might be termed *leaderlike* while others adopt the behaviour of followers?

Personality Correlates of Leadership

The question here is whether there is such a thing as a **'great person'** personality and if so, is it a trait or traits which are inherited? Stogdill (1974) and others have reviewed attempts to link the personality traits of leaders to their effectiveness, and identified a number of personality characteristics which correlated with leadership, albeit weakly. Leaders tend to be above average in size, health, physical attractiveness, intelligence, self-confidence, talkativeness and the need for dominance. Mann (1959) found intelligence to be a reliable factor. Mullen *et al.* (1989) isolated talkativeness. Intelligence would seem to be needed because leaders have to be able to think and respond quickly and develop the ability to gain access to information quickly and accurately. Being talkative makes a person the centre of attention so that everyone looks to that person for a response to the situation. However, the search for the personality of the great leader has not been successful. Correlations among traits, and between traits and effective leadership have been low. Great events in history, however, have by popular consent been associated with 'great' individuals. We talk about the 'Thatcher years' when referring to the changes which took place in Britain in the 1980s. Churchill is identified with standing alone against the world in 1940; Hitler is identified with the phenomenon of Nazism in Germany in the 1930s. Similarly, great trends in thought and in science are associated with particular individuals. Plato, Socrates, Freud and Isaac Newton spring to mind. It makes easier sense for people to interpret complex events and ideas in a straightforward way, and what could be more straightforward than to lay them at the door of particular individuals.

Situational Factors

If it is not easy to predict who will assume leadership from personality traits, then perhaps there are features in situations which will allow us to predict who will emerge as leader. Different situations call for different qualities of leadership. Bales (1950) identified, as part of his analysis of interactions among people in groups, two distinct functions of leaders within groups, task-oriented leadership and socio-emotional leadership. In the former, the task of a leader is primarily to ensure that the job in hand gets done and that the objectives are reached; in the latter, that relations between the individuals in the group remain buoyant and happy. In some cases the leader will perform both of these functions, not only ensuring that the job gets done but also that the members of the group get on well with each other while doing it. In other cases there may be one person providing task leadership and another socio-emotional leadership. Their functions may be complementary. In Sherif's studies of boys' summer camps, described in Chapter 4 (Sherif, 1961, 1966) it was found that when the situation changed from one of establishing group cohesion (stage 2) to one of inter-group conflict, leadership changed and a person more capable of leading the group in these circumstances emerged. On a national scale, when a war situation arose in 1939–40, the individual who had led failed in attempts to maintain the peace, Neville Chamberlain, was replaced by Winston Churchill. During the previous decade Churchill had been relegated to a backwater of politics and then emerged as the right leader in the right place at the right time. After the war was over, in 1945, the situation changed to one which demanded different qualities and Churchill was rejected in his turn.

Behavioural Factors

If it is possible to separate one's personality from one's behaviour, then perhaps leadership is related to the ways in which individual people behave towards one another. Lippitt and White (1943) studied leadership in the context of after-school activities in clubs for boys. The parameters of effectiveness studied were morale, task achievement and group atmosphere. Box 6.3 details the experiment carried out by Lippitt and White.

While this was a valuable addition to what was known about leadership, it was limited in that it was concerned only with juveniles and only boys at that. Studies done at Ohio State University focused upon the distinction between task-oriented and socio-emotional aspects of leadership. Distinctions were found as a result of questionnaires completed by military and industrial participants between the **initiating** structure of leadership and **consideration**. This roughly corresponds to the distinction Bales (1950) drew in his Interaction Process Analysis (IPA) between Task Area interactions and Socio-emotional interactions. There seemed to be two distinct types of leader, a task-oriented and a socio-emotional type of leader. In the Ohio study the distinction was as follows:

BOX 6.3
An Experiment in Leadership Style

The leaders of the clubs were confederates of the experimenters who
had been trained to exercise three distinct leadership styles:

1. *Autocratic leadership:* the prime focus was on achievement. The
   leader issued orders, praised or censured boys without giving
   reasons, discouraged communication between the boys and behaved in an aloof an impersonal way towards them.
2. *Democratic leadership:* the leader helped the boys plan their
   projects by means of discussion, allowed them to choose their
   own workmates and communicate freely with each other. When
   comments were made they were fully explained and the leader
   joined in group activities.
3. *Laissez-faire leadership:* the boys were left very much to themselves.
   Advice and help were only given when the leader was directly asked
   for it and no praise, blame or other comment was offered at all.

Each group was assigned a particular leadership style. One confederate
was the leader for seven weeks, and then the confederates changed
round. It was important that each group was exposed to only one
leadership style, though to three leaders. In this way Lippitt and White
were able to separate leadership style from a specific leader who was
behaving that way. They were thus able to rule out personality
explanations of differences in leadership outcomes
The democratic style of leadership led to the boys liking their
leaders more than in either of the two other styles. The atmosphere
engendered was friendly. Productivity was relatively high and the boys
got on with their tasks whether the leader was there or not. In the case
of the autocratic leadership style the atmosphere engendered was quite
different. It was aggressive but dependent and self-oriented. Productivity was high but only while the leader was there. The *laissez-faire*
style of leadership created a friendly but play-oriented atmosphere.
Productivity was low and increased only when the leader was not there

- *Initiating structure* relates to the leader's behaviour in defining
  the relationship between himself or herself and the members of
  the group, establishing patterns of organisation, channels of
  communication and methods of procedure (Halpin 1966). The
  leader has the task of motivating the group towards its defined
  goal. This may also involve identifying and agreeing on the goal.
- *Consideration*: Halpin sees consideration as behaviour indicative
  of friendship, mutual trust, respect and warmth in relation to
  other group members.

The flaw in this approach is that it concentrates solely on the behaviour of the leader. Deaux *et al.* (1993) have suggested that these researchers had fallen prey to fundamental attribution bias (see Chapter 2), in that they overemphasised the importance of the dispositional characteristics of leaders as opposed to situational factors.

Recognition of this failing and the need for an interactionist approach has led to the development of what have been called **contingency models** of leadership. These were developed by Fiedler (1964, 1967) and have received considerable empirical support from, for example, Chemers (1983, 1987).

Fiedler's Contingency Model of Leadership

There are four components of the model, the first related to disposition, the other three to situation.

1. *The personality of the leader:* Fiedler devised an instrument called the **least preferred co-worker (LPC) scale**. Participants using the scale are asked to think of all the people with whom they have ever worked, and identify the one person they found most difficult to work with. Eighteen bipolar scales are used for this (for example pleasant/unpleasant, boring/interesting, friendly/unfriendly and so on). High LPC scores indicate that the leader has a favourable attitude towards the least preferred co-worker; low LPC scores indicate an unfavourable attitude. In more explicit terms, a low LPC score indicates a task-oriented leadership style; a high LPC score a relationship-oriented one.
2. *Relations between the leader and the members of the working group*: these can range from very good to very poor. The leader may be liked and respected, or disliked, distrusted and rejected.
3. *Task structure*: there are three elements here:

   (a) *Task definition:* some tasks are very clearly defined in terms of goals, while others are much less clearly structured. The tasks before workers on an assembly line in a factory are likely to be much more clearly delineated than, for example, those before members of a committee working out policy for the factory.
   (b) *Solution specificity:* this relates to whether there is more than one solution to the problem, or more than one way of completing the task.

(c) *Verifiability:* how easy it is to determine whether the decisions taken are the right ones.

4. *What power and authority are vested in the leader?* Can he or she hire and fire? Has the leader the authority to raise the pay and status of an individual worker? What backing does the leader get for decisions made? To take examples: a person is responsible for a group of canvassers in an election campaign, they are volunteers and the leader would ordinarily be able to exercise very little positional authority over them; whereas the commanding officer of a military unit would have extremely high positional authority.

There are thus eight situational variables, as illustrated in Figure 6.2. In Category I, the situational control is at its highest; in Category VIII at its lowest.

A low LPC results in the most effective leadership where situational control is either very high or very low: at intermediate levels of situational control a high LPC score produces maximum effectiveness.

This model goes some way towards explaining why it has proved difficult empirically to show that particular personality characteristics or particular behavioural patterns explain effective leadership. It seems clear that effective leadership is the result of fairly complex interactions between personality, behaviour and situational factors.

Self-assessment Questions

1. What personality traits have been found to be associated with effective leadership?
2. What differences did Lippitt and White find in the effectiveness of different styles of leadership in the context of boys' clubs?
3. Do you feel that Fiedler's *contingency model* of leadership adequately solves the problem of whether effective leadership is associated with the personality, the behaviour of leaders, or the situation in which leadership is needed? Explain your answer.

SECTION III GROUP DECISION-MAKING

Following on from the previous section on leadership, this section aims to examine the influence of group membership on the beha-

FIGURE 6.2
Fiedler's Eight Situational Control Categories

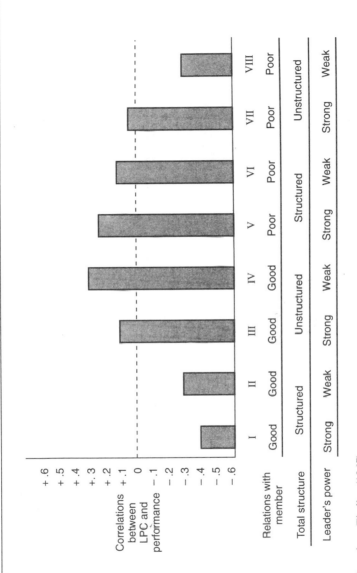

Source: Based on Fiedler (1967).

viour of members of the group, with particular reference to the way in which decisions are taken.

Characteristics of Groups

First, it is necessary to be clear what a group is. Perhaps, Bales' (1950) proposal is relevant so far as size is concerned:

> Provided that each member receives some impression or perception of each other member, distinct enough . . . that he can give some reaction to each of the others as an individual person then a collection of people can be termed a small group. (p. 33)

Johnson and Johnson (1987) have identified seven features of a group:

1. *Interaction:* a group is a collection of individuals who are interacting with one another.
2. *Perception of belonging:* a group consists of two or more persons who perceive themselves to belong to a group.
3. *Interdependence*: group members are interdependent.
4. *Common goals:* a group is a collection of individuals who join together to achieve a goal.
5. *Need satisfaction:* individuals who belong to a group are trying to satisfy some need through membership of it.
6. *Roles and norms:* members of a group structure their interactions by means of roles and norms. Roles consist of sets of obligations and expectations. The role of 'student', for example, embodies obligations to attend class, listen to the teacher and attempt to do what is asked of him or her; it also embodies expectations that the teacher will provide the means to achieve the goals set. Norms imply established ways of behaving; that is, uniformities among people in the ways they behave.
7. *Influence:* a group is a collection of individuals who influence each other.

Group Size

For our purposes, a group, therefore, is not just a collection of people waiting for a bus; most of the features listed above would not apply. There is certainly a limitation in size; a single person cannot interact with each of the members of a group of 200 people. Most experimental research has concentrated on groups of between three and ten people.

Group Cohesivenesss

Group cohesiveness relates to the way in which members of a group hang together; how tightly or how loosely knit it is; what degree of mutual support or uniformity of behaviour there is. Where there is very low cohesiveness, a collection of individuals almost ceases to be a group. Festinger *et al.* (1950) defines cohesiveness in terms of the attractiveness of the group to its members, and the attractiveness of members of the group to each other, and the degree to which the group satisfies the goals of individual members and acts on those members.

Communication Networks

Most of the features of a group mentioned above presuppose communication between its members. The relationships between members of a group depend upon the channels of communication which exist between them. The pattern of these channels may in turn be determined by a number of factors, for example:

- *Location*: the physical relationship of one group member to another (they may be in different buildings most of the time, for example) may have an effect on ease of communication.
- *Formal rules or chains of command:* in military units, individuals may not communicate directly with, for example, the commanding officer, but need to go through a chain of command – platoon commander, company commander and so on.
- *Personal factors*: these may include personal liking or dislike. Two members of a group may not be on speaking terms and communication between them may be solely through intermediaries

Leavitt (1951), Shaw (1964, 1978) and Steiner (1972, 1976) are among those who have studied communication networks. Leavitt used some of the networks shown in Figure 6.3 to investigate the relative efficiency of five-person groups with different structures in solving simple identification problems.

FIGURE 6.3
Communication Networks

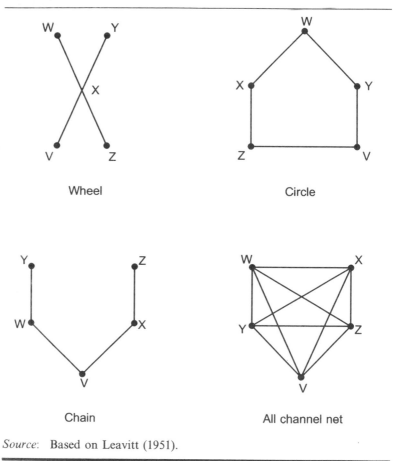

Wheel

Circle

Chain

All channel net

Source: Based on Leavitt (1951).

The form of communication links is important in that it determines the way in which the group functions. Wheel, Y and chain
networks tend to lead to a centralised organisation because the
person at the centre of the wheel, the intersection of the Y, or the
middle of the chain is pivotal. The central person is likely to emerge
as leader. By contrast, in less-centralised communication patterns
such as the circle or all channel net, where everyone can commu-

nicate with everyone else, the structure of communication does not influence who emerges as leader, and individuals' personalities and skills become more important. These latter also take full advantage of the contributions which each member of a team may make. Where a particular individual or individuals are absent, the negative impact of this is less because channels of communication are less likely to be interrupted. Romzek and Dubnick (1987) have reported that a factor which led to the loss of the *Challenger* space shuttle was that concerns about the performance of a key component, the O-ring seals, was not channelled to the appropriate individuals because two key members of the communication network had left.

Roles in Groups

Within a group, the roles to be occupied by individuals emerge and develop. This includes the leadership role which has been explored in the previous section. This process of **role differentiation** has been explored by Forsyth (1983). Where there is a new group one individual may assume the task-leadership role (keeping the group working towards a goal) and another may assume the morale-leadership role, corresponding to the *initiating structure* and *consideration* elements mentioned earlier. Where the group has been in existence for some time and a member of the group leaves, a newcomer may be specifically assigned to take over the role – whatever it might have been – of the leaver. The new person will probably modify the role in the course of time. But to begin with the role is associated with the position to be filled rather than with the individuals who fill them (Katz and Kahn, 1976; McGrath, 1984).

Norm Formation

As the group develops, so also do the expectations members have about what rules and procedures might be appropriate to develop. This is the process of the establishment of **group norms**. For example, during Sherif's studies of conformity in relation to the autokinetic effect (described in Section I of this chapter), where judgements were made by members of a group they were much less variable than those made by individuals and this 'group norm', once established, persisted even when those who had established the norm left the group to be replaced by others. Among the norms which develop in this way are **status characteristics**. These involve rules or expectations concerning the characteristics of individuals who will be accorded the highest status and authority within the group. For example, experience might be conceived of as the most important characteristic of group membership, so that individuals with the most experience are accorded the highest status within the group. Berger *et al.* (1980) have developed a model called **status characteristics theory** to explain how these principles emerge.

Within this model, status characteristics may be **specific** or they may be **diffuse**. In the former case, the characteristics of an individual which cause him or her to be given the accorded status and authority within the group may be closely linked to the task in hand. Suppose a group has been convened to plan for the establishment of a new laboratory for a school. Within the group are individuals with specific knowledge and experience of laboratory work in a school context, perhaps the head of the science department, alongside members of the governing body and perhaps the head teacher. This individual is likely to have high status *within* the group, though maybe not outside it, in recognition of his or her expertise (his or her *specific* status characteristics).

At another level there will be individuals who have *diffuse* status characteristics. These are less closely linked to the task in hand, but who nevertheless throw up expectations about performance. The head teacher, in the group mentioned above, might be a case in point. Within this category of status characteristics can be included considerations of gender, perhaps, or race. Suppose the group mentioned above is planning for an engineering laboratory, the female members of the group might be accorded lower status than the male ones because of the assumption, perhaps totally erroneous, that women have less skill in domains that include mechanical and mathematical abilities. On the other hand, were the group planning a nursery rather than an engineering laboratory, the female members of the group might have higher status on the unwritten, and perhaps unwarranted, assumption that small children are women's domain.

Decision-making in Groups

Given that one of the most important functions which groups perform is that of decision-making, it is worthwhile to spend a little time on the processes by which decisions are reached within groups. Davis (1973) in a model called **social decisions schemes** has related the strictness of the rules adopted in discussions leading to the forming of decisions, to the concentration of power. Where there is maximum strictness (as, for example, in cases where a unanimous decision is to be reached; in a jury situation for example) there is least concentration of power. Egalitarian rules such as unanimity tend to spread power among all the members; authoritarian rules concentrate it on one or on a few members. Majority decision-making rules concentrate power more. Where the final decision is left to the chair there is maximum power concentration.

Generating Ideas

The ability of a group to generate ideas is important to decision-making. Osborn (1957) popularised the technique of **brainstorming** to achieve this end. Members of a group are encouraged to put forward as many ideas as they can irrespective of quality, and to build upon others' ideas where they can. However, there is no evidence that brainstorming is effective in producing more novel ideas than the individual members of the group might produce on their own. Paulus *et al.* (1993) have suggested three reasons for this:

1. Individuals tend to censor their ideas because they are concerned to make a good impression. Productivity is therefore reduced. This has been termed **evaluation apprehension.**
2. Individuals have a tendency to leave it to others. It has been suggested that the larger the group, the greater the amount of **social loafing**, as it has been called.
3. The difficulty of having to deal with the ideas produced by others at the same time as generating your own has been termed **production blocking**.

Group Memory

As a result of experiments carried out, Clark and Stephenson (1989) have concluded that groups recall more material than individuals, and more than the individual in the group with the best memory. There do seem to be qualifications about this, however. Where the material to be memorised is simple and artificial, group superiority in memory is greater than for complex and realistic tasks.

A quite different and separate aspect of the advantages of groups over individuals in terms of memory lies in Wegner's ideas about

transactive memory (Wegner, 1986: Wegner *et al*. 1991). Individuals within a group can share a memory load so that each individual is responsible for memory of part of what is needed to be recalled. When a group is formed individual members are assigned, on the basis of stereotypes, domains of information related to their social categorisation. One member, for example, categorised as a technical expert might remember technical details; while another might recall organisational facts, the programme of events for instance. Areas of expertise may be assigned explicitly or implicity.

Groupthink

In most cases groups come together in order to work out the best solution to the problems that confront them. It may be that they are *ad hoc* groups set up as 'working parties' to deal with specific problems, or they are committees set up to run an organisation, the academic board of a college, for example, or the board of directors of a firm. Groups may differ in the degree of their cohesiveness. Cartwright (1968) has described 'cohesivness' as the total of all the forces attracting members to a group. When all or nearly all the members of the group are strongly attracted to it, the group is highly cohesive; less-cohesive groups may be those with a number of members who are *ex officio* or who feel that their interests ought to be represented. Janis (1982) defined **groupthink** as 'a mode of thinking that people engage in when they are deeply involved in a cohesive in-group when members' striving for unanimity overrides their motivation to realistically appraise alternative courses of action.' Five antecedent conditions of groupthink have been described by Janis and Mann (1977), and more recently McCauley (1989) has added a sixth. These are:

1. *High cohesiveness.*
2. *Uncertainty of approval.* This refers to the extent to which a group member feels able to count on the acceptance of his or her ideas by other members of the group.
3. *Insulation.* This relates to the extent to which the group is cut off from outside influence. A board of directors, for example, insulates itself from the judgement of qualified outsiders because they are not members of the board. McCauley relates this insulation to two events which happened during the time

President Kennedy was in power, the abortive invasion of Cuba which became known as the Bay of Pigs episode, and the Cuban Missile Crisis when Soviet missiles were discovered to have been based in Cuba, targeted on American cities. In the former, decisions were taken by a cohesive group around the President himself with disastrous consequences. American forces were forced into a humiliating retreat. In the latter Kennedy encouraged debate, appointed a 'devil's advocate' and brought outsiders with differing opinions into his discussions on the crisis. The US was able to face down the threat and the crisis was averted.

4. *Lack of methodical procedures for search and appraisal.*
5. *Highly directive leadership.*
6. *High levels of stress and low levels of hope of finding a better solution than the one advocated by the leader or by other influential persons.*

The above antecedent conditions lead to symptoms of groupthink becoming apparent. These include:

- Mind guards. The conscious protecting of the group from information which might shatter its complacency and lay it open to doubt
- The illusion of invulnerability.
- Collective rationalisation.
- Belief in the inherent morality of the group.
- Unfavourable stereotyping of out-groups.
- Pressure applied directly on dissenters.
- Self-censorship.
- The illusion of unanimity.

The closed-mindedness described above is destructive of efficient decision-making. Alternative policies are not adequately explored, objectives are not fully surveyed, the risks inherent in the chosen policy are not fully examined, information is only partial, and the processing of it is biased and contingency plans are not worked out. Most of us can identify cases where groupthink has resulted in poor decisions being taken, sometimes with disastrous consequences. However, Hogg (1992) and Turner *et al.* (1992) have suggested that groupthink has not been fully explained. For one thing, group cohesiveness has not been defined precisely enough. It could amount to a group consisting of close friends with strong emotional and friendship ties to each other. It could merely imply that members of the group get on reasonably well together. It has also been suggested that groupthink is not a discrete phenomenon at all but merely a specific case of 'risky-shift'. This is explained below.

Risky Shift Phenomenon

Contrary to what appears to be common sense, the outcome of group discussions appears to be more extreme than the sum of the views of the members would lead you to suppose. There is a **group polarisation** which takes place during discussion. Stoner (1961) found in some very important research that group decisions were riskier than ones taken by individuals on their own. For example, a committee looking into the spending of a large sum of money on a new laboratory is likely to be less cautious than a single executive might have been, making the same decision. This finding became known as the **risky shift** phenomenon. This term is, however, something of a misnomer. Research over the years between Stoner's original research and the present has suggested that the shift resulting from group discussion was not necessarily in the direction of greater risk, but in the direction of the initial opinions of the group. This might well be towards a more conservative line. Kaplan (1987) has explained this phenomenon in terms of two types of influence:

1. *Normative influence*   Within a group, individuals have a chance to assess the opinions of others. Pressures to conform encourage them to move towards a position of perceived agreement. This may be for one of two reasons:

   (a) Desire for a favourable evaluation by group members;
   (b) A concern for self-presentation.

   A bandwagon effect may also be evident whose influence depends on the extent to which individual members see themselves as 'belonging' to the group.
2. *Informational influence*   Learning results from exposure to the group discussion itself. Members are persuaded to change their opinions by the arguments advanced by other members of the group.

Both of these influences may operate on a group at any given time. Where the emphasis is upon getting the job done and on right answers to problems, informational influences are stronger. Where the emphasis is upon the group rather than the task and where there is no one right answer but solutions depend upon judgement, then normative influences come to the fore. Unanimous decisions (such as jury decisions, for example) are the result of both normative and informational influences. (Kaplan and Miller, 1987). Members need to convince others holding different opinions to change them, and this involves informational influence. At the same time the unanimity rule means that there is emphasis on group harmony and this brings normative influence into play.

Self-assessment Questions

1. Describe two types of communication network within groups. What effect is each of these likely to have on the influence exerted by particular members?
2. What is *transactive memory?* How may this operate to make groups more effective than individuals?
3. Describe the phenomenon of the *risky shift?* Is this really a proper description of it and why does it occur?

SECTION IV   THE INFLUENCE OF THE CROWD

Le Bon (1908) observed events during a period of great social turmoil in France, read accounts of crowd behaviour in the French Revolution of 1948 and in the Paris Commune in 1871, and claimed that 'the crowd is always intellectually inferior to the isolated individual . . . mob man is fickle credulous and intolerant, showing the violence and ferocity of primitive beings'.

This primitive behaviour was attributed to three things:

- *Anonymity*: individuals cannot be easily identified in a crowd.
- *Contagion*: ideas and emotions spread rapidly and unpredictably.
- *Suggestibility*: the savagery which is just below the surface is released by suggestion.

Freud (1921) saw the crowd as unlocking the unconscious mind. The socialisation process has submerged the *id* as the *ego* and the *superego* develop. The leader in a crowd acts as a hypnotist, replacing the *superego*. In Freud's terms the *id* represents a person's basic animal impulses, the *ego* the modification of these impulses as a result of the impact of those around us, and the *superego* is the internalised sense we develop of right and wrong. The primitive impulses of the *id* come under the leader's control because each of us has the instinct to regress to the 'primal horde'. McDougall (1920) believed strongly in the instinctive motives within human beings. Fear and anger are the strongest and most widely shared of these instincts. Where these strong primitive instincts are brought to the surface there is wide consensus so that they spread and strengthen in the crowd as each individual provides stimulus to the others. The effect is, as Le Bon has suggested, a lowered sense of responsibility and anonymity.

Deindividuation

Festinger *et al.* (1952) was the first person to use the term **deindividuation** for the loss of personal responsibility and the anonymity which comes upon people in a crowd situation. In a series of experiments by Festinger himself, and by Zimbardo (1970), participants were deindividuated by being made to wear uniform laboratory coats, or in Zimbardo's case cloaks and hoods reminiscent of the Klu-Klux-Klan, or dressed as prison guards in a simulated prison (for a full account of this experiment see Section I of this chapter). In each study, participants were found to be ready to behave in ways which were quite foreign to their normal behaviour, making negative comments about their parents in Festinger's study, or behaving quite brutally to 'prisoners' in Zimbardo's study.

Diener (1976) had children engage in 'trick or treat' activities wearing costumes which concealed their identities. Children were invited into homes in Seattle where they were asked to take just one piece of 'candy' from a plate. Some of them were asked their names and so were individuated to an extent; others were not. As many as 80 per cent of the deindividuated children took more than one piece of candy as opposed to 8 per cent of the individuated ones. It is questionable whether this was an ethical experiment in terms of what was discussed in Chapter 1, Section II.

Self-awareness

People are normally aware of themselves as individuals and as a consequence monitor their own behaviour. When a person is deindividuated this **self-awareness** is reduced and the monitoring process no longer operates to ensure that restraints on behaviour are in place. He or she is no longer concerned about what others may think. In many instances this loss of restraint leads to aggression and anti-social behaviour, though this is not inevitable. It might equally manifest itself in the kind of euphoria that was evident in the rally held in Sheffield by the Labour party before the 1992 general election. Those present, while not aggressive, behaved in an unrestrainedly euphoric manner. Other researchers including Carver and Scheier (1981) have distinguished public and private deindividuation. It is only when we become less attentive to how we want others to evaluate us, and do not care any longer what others think, that behaviour begins to be released from the social norms which restrain it and may become anti-social.

Emergent Norm Theory

Turner's (1974) explanation takes a somewhat different approach. A crowd of people probably have no common prior association with each other and have come together just on this one occasion for a particular purpose. For example, the crowds which rioted in protest at the imposition of a flat rate of 'poll tax' in the late 1980s, which paid no regard to individuals' means or ability to pay, brought together very diverse people with little in common and therefore few pre-existent common norms of behaviour. There was nothing to tell them how to behave and in such cases norms of behaviour begin to emerge which are peculiar to that particular crowd. Attention is drawn to individuals who stand out from the crowd and to their behaviour, and they begin to supply the norms of behaviour. There is pressure on the previously inactive majority in the crowd to conform to these emergent norms.

There are some difficulties with this theory, though:

• Diener (1980) claims that the emergence of norms implies self-awareness. People do not need to comply with norms unless they feel that they are identifiable. Mann *et al.* (1982) conducted an experiment which supported this view. Participants were found to be more aggressive when anonymous, irrespective of what norms had been established, but when the norm established was an aggressive one, this aggression increased.

• Reicher (1982, 1987) rightly stated that crowds do not usually come together except with a specific purpose (to get rid of the poll tax, for example), and this purpose implies shared norms. We do not usually find a crowd coming together for no purpose at all. Any purpose, whether it be supporting a football team or demonstrating against a perceived injustice, in itself establishes norms.

Social Identity Theory

As often as not, crowd behaviour involves confrontation, one group against another. Striking miners against the police, for example in the Miners' Strike in the early 1980s; or supporters of one football team confronting those of another. Reicher (1982, 1984) relates social identity theory to crowd behaviour. This has been discussed earlier (p. 125) in a different context. So far from losing their identity, members of the crowd replace their idiosyncratic personal identities with a social identity as a crowd member (or perhaps, more correctly, a faction member within the crowd). They categorise themselves as, for example, supporters of the England Football Team and identify others as 'the enemy', supporters of Italy, for example. Group membership produces group norms of conduct, very often mediated by leaders or prominent individuals. The police in a strike confrontation may behave in one way governed by their norms of conduct; strikers in another governed by their norms. Reicher has used the theory to explain what happened in the riots in St Paul's in Bristol in the early 1980s. The following points emerged:

1. The rioters were selective in their attack; police, the bank and entrepreneurial merchants who were seen as representing the power or the state.
2. The crowd did not stray from the boundaries of St Paul's.
3. A strong sense of social identity was engendered as members of the St Paul's community.

The riot was a protest against the government by a community which felt itself to be deprived. There was very high unemployment in St Paul's even in a time of national high unemployment.

Football Crowds

Marsh *et al.* (1978) conducted an ethogenic study of football crowds. They observed social behaviour and analysed the accounts which football fans gave of what was going on. The conclusions which they arrived at suggested that violence when it occurs does not come from a deindividuated mob. There is a great deal of ritualised aggression but little actual damage. While fans might talk about the opposition getting their 'heads bashed in', actual aggression was limited to chasing the opposing fans back to the railway station, being careful not to catch them up. It was the chase and the ritualised aggression which was important. This has its parallels in the animal world where defence of territory may result in ritualised aggression which stops short of actual injury, which would be counterproductive. Actual conflict involves the risk of injury or even death to either party. A severely injured animal is likely to be unable to pass on its genes. Marsh suggested in the context of football crowds that outbreaks of uncontrolled violence are more likely to occur when the ritual is upset by the interference of outside authority. Excessive control removes the known pattern of ritualised behaviour and replaces it with a much less well-controlled violence. The 'hooligans 'of the football terraces are in fact part of a well defined and structured social pattern.

Social Disorder

Most political demonstrations are peaceful affairs which pass off without injury or violence. However, there are occasionally violent altercations. The St Paul's riot in Bristol has already been mentioned as well as the poll tax riots. A specific event, such as the raid by the police on the Black and White Café in St Paul's provided a flashpoint from which more generalised violence erupted. But to say that such flashpoints *caused* the violence is too simplistic Waddington *et al.* (1987) have proposed a model which might be used to analyse different kinds of social disorder. In their model there are six levels of analysis:

1. *Structural* Wider issues of social structure need to be considered. For instance in the St Paul's area there was very high unemployment among the black people, which led to frustration and alienation.

2. *Political or ideological* A particular sector of society might feel aggrieved about a piece of legislation which has imposed social controls on them to unacceptable levels. The recent Police and Criminal Justice Act has provided this focus of discontent for 'travelling' groups.

3. *Cultural* Social representations (see Chapter 4) are ways in which we see the world and include such things as beliefs about rights. A different cultural group within a society may have different social representations of the elements of a problem. The police, for example, in St Paul's see the world quite differently from young unemployed black people: the problem will be defined quite differently. As far as the police were concerned it was about drugs; so far as the community of St Paul's were concerned it was an invasion of territory.

4. *Contextual* This includes the particular time when the incident occurs and the sequence of events which have led up to this particular incident.

5. *Spatial* This includes the physical setting in which the confrontation has occurred, the lay-out of open spaces and buildings, and the symbolic significance any of these may have for the participants. The Black and White Café, for example, represents a focus for the black community in the St Paul's area and so has importance as a centre of the community's 'territory'. In the eyes of the police, on the other hand, the café was a centre for drug-dealing.

6. *Interactional* This concerns the nature of the interactions which took place between the people involved. It might be argued that the police overstepped the established norms of behaviour in dealing with a particular community. Was a 'raid' on the Black and White Café an appropriate way of responding to a suggestion of drug-dealing? The arrest or the rough treatment of a prominent member of the community, a local politician or a trades union official, might be seen as 'out of order'. Waddington *et al.* stressed that interpersonal style could be as important as the political context.

Waddington *et al.* conducted an analysis of two public rallies which took place during the miners' strike in 1984, of which one was disorderly and involved violence between the police and demonstrators. The second, in a similar context, was peaceful. Researchers used participant observation, both while the events were taking place and in the run up to them. They used the model above and concluded that at the structural, ideological and cultural levels, there was no difference between the two events. The differences were at the situational, contextual and interactional levels. The second, peaceful, event was carefully planned with consultation with the local police. The setting was carefully organised so as to channel the crowd's responses into peaceful activity with entertainments laid on. To control the movements of the crowd without recourse to police intervention barriers were erected beforehand. The control of the crowd was undertaken by the organisers themselves, the police carefully avoiding any confrontation.

As a result of this, work Waddington's team concluded that crowd violence was not unpredictable. Action can be taken at any or all of the above levels to ensure that it does not occur. On a practical level, Waddington outlined five steps which can be taken to ensure peaceful crowd control:

1. *Self policing* Confrontation is more likely to be avoided if the control of the crowd is left in the hands of the organisers of the rally.
2. *Liaison* There should be close cooperation and liaison between the organisers and the police, both before and during the event.
3. *Minimum force* A policy should be adopted of the police using minimum force. For them to be deployed in riot gear presupposes that they expect trouble.
4. *Training in interpersonal skills* Those involved in managing and controlling crowds should have had appropriate training.
5. *Accountability* Police and enforcement agencies should be seen as wholly accountable for their actions. The use of overalls which deliberately conceal the numbers of individual officers to give them anonymity is not acceptable.

Self-assessment Questions

1. Describe what is meant by deindividuation. What are its causes and results?
2. What is meant by emergent norm theory? How far is it reasonable to say that a group of people is without common norms of behaviour at any time?

3. Can it reasonably be said that crowd violence is an unpredictable thing which cannot be prevented? What steps does the evidence suggest may be taken to avoid it occurring?

FURTHER READING

K. Deaux, F. C. Dane and L. S. Wrightsman, *Social Psychology in the 90s*, (6th ed) (Pacific Grove, Cal.: Brooks-Cole, 1993).

N. Hayes, *Foundations of Psychology* (London: Routledge, 1994).

M. A. Hogg and G. M. Vaughan, *Social Psychology: an Introduction* (London: Prentice-Hall, Harvester Wheatsheaf, 1994).

Bibliography

Abdalla, I. A. (1991) 'Social support and gender responses to job stress in Arab culture', *Journal of Social Behaviour and Personality*, 6 (7), 273–88.

Abelson, R. P. (1981) 'Psychological status of the script concept', *American Psychologist*, 836, 715–29.

Abrams, D. and Hogg, M. (1990a) *Social Identity Theory: Constructive and Critical Advances* (London: Harvester Wheatsheaf).

Abrams, D. and Hogg, M. (1990b) 'Social identification, self-categorisation and social influence', *European Review of Social Psychology*, 1, 195–228.

Adams, J. (1965) 'Inequity in social exchange', in L. Berkowitz (ed.), *Advances in Experimental Social Psychology*, Vol. 2 (New York: Academic Press).

Aderman, D. and Berkowitz, L. (1983) 'Self-concern and the unwillingness to be helpful', *Social Psychology Quarterly*, 46, 293–301.

Adorno, T. W., Frenkel-Brunsik, E., Levinson, D. J. and Sanford, R. M. (1950) *The Authoritarian Personality* (New York: Harper).

Ainsworth, M. D. S. and Bell, S. M. (1969) 'Some contemporary patterns in mother infant interactions in the feeding situation', in A. Ambrose (ed.), *Stimulation in Early Infancy* (London: Academic Press).

Ainsworth, M. D. S., Blehar, M. C., Waters, E. and Wall, S. (1978) *Patterns of Attachment: A Psychological Study of the Strange Situation*, Hillsdale, NJ: Erlbaum.

Ajzen, I. (1988) *Attitudes, Personality and Behaviour* (Milton Keynes: Open University Press).

Ajzen, I. (1989) 'Attitude structure and behaviour', in A. R. Pratkanis, S. J. Breckler and A. G. Greenwald (eds), *Attitude Structure and Function* (Hillsdale, NJ: Erlbaum).

Ajzen, I. and Fishbein, M. (1980) *Understanding Attitudes and Predicting Social Behaviour* (Englewood Cliffs, NJ: Prentice-Hall).

Allport, G. (1935) 'Attitudes', in C. M. Murchison (ed.), *Handbook of Social Psychology* (Worcester, Ma: Clark University Press).

Allport, G. W. (1954) *The Nature of Prejudice* (Reading, Ma: Addison-Wesley).

Altman, I. and Chemers, M. (1980) *Culture and Environment* (Monterey, Ca: Brooks/Cole).

Amato, P. R. (1983) 'Helping behaviour in urban and rural environments: field studies based on taxonomic organisation of helping episodes', *Journal of Personality and Social Psychology*, 45, 571–86.

Anderson, C. A. (1989) 'Temperature and aggression: Ubiquitous effects of heat on occurrence of human violence', *Psychological Bulletin*, 106, 74–96.

Anderson, C. A. and Sechler, E. S. (1986) 'Effects of explanation and counter-explanation on the development and use of social theories', *Journal of Personality and Social Psychology*, 50, 24–34.

241

Anderson, C A. and Anderson, D.C. (1984) 'Ambient temperature and violent crime: Tests of linear and curvilinear hypotheses', *Journal of Personality and Social Psychology*, 46, 91–7.

Anderson, N. H. (1971) 'Integration theory and attitude change', *Psychological Review*, 78, 171–206.

Anderson, N. H. (1980) 'Integration theory applied to cognitive responses and attitudes', in R. E. Petty, T. M. Ostrom and T. C. Brock (eds), *Cognitive Responses in Persuasion* (New York: Erlbaum).

Andreeva, G. (1984) 'Cognitive processes in developing groups', in L. H. Strickland (ed.), *Directions in Soviet Social Psychology* (New York: Springer-Verlag).

Archer, D., Iritani, B., Kimes, B. B. and Barrios, M. (1983) 'Face-ism: five studies of sex differences in facial prominence', *Journal of Personality and Social Psychology*, 45, 725–35.

Argyle, M. and Henderson, M. (1985) 'The rules of friendship', *Journal of Social and Personal Relationships*, 1, 211–37.

Asch, S. E. (1951) 'Effects of group pressure upon the modification and distortion of judgements', in H. Guetzkon (ed.) *Groups Leaderships and Men* (Pittsburgh, Pa: Carnegie Press).

Association for Teaching Psychology (1992) *Ethics in Psychological Research: Guidelines for Students at Pre-Degree Levels* (Leicester: Association for Teaching Psychology).

Averill, J. R. and Boothroyd, P. (1977) 'On falling in love in conformance with the romantic ideal', *Motivation and Emotion*, 1, 235–47.

Azrin, N. H., Hutchinson, R. R. and Hake, D. F. (1966) 'Attack, avoidance and escape reactions to aversive shock', *Journal of Experimental Analysis Of Behaviour*, 9, 191–204.

Bachy, V. (1976) 'Danish permissiveness revisited', *Journal of Communication*, 26, 40–5.

Bales, R. F. (1950) *Interaction Process Analysis: A Method for the Study of Small Groups* (Cambridge Ma: Addison-Wesley).

Bandura A. (1977) *Social Learning Theory* (Englewood Cliffs: Prentice-Hall).

Bandura, A. (1973) *Aggression: A Social Learning Analysis* (Englewood Cliffs NJ: Prentice-Hall).

Bar-Tal, D. (1976) *Prosocial Behaviour: Theory and Research* (Washington, DC: Hemisphere Press).

Baron, R. A. (1971) 'Reducing the influence of an aggression model: The restraining effects of discrepant modelling cues, *Journal of Personality and Social Psychology*, 20, 240–45.

Baron, R. A. (1974) 'Aggression as a function of a victim's pain cues, the level of prior arousal and exposure to an aggressive model', *Journal of Personality and Social Psychology*, 99, 117–24.

Baron, R. A. (1977) *Human Aggression* (New York: Plenum).

Baron, R. A. (1989) 'Personality and organisational conflict: The Type A behaviour problem and self-monitoring', *Organisational Behaviour and Human Decision Processes*, 44, 281–97.

Baron, R. A. and Ball, R. L. (1974) 'The aggression-inhibiting influence of non-hostile humour', *Journal of Experimental Social Psychology*, 10, 23–33.

Baron, R. A. and Ransberger, Y. M. (1978) 'Ambient temperature and the occurrence of collective violence: The "long hot summer" revisited', *Journal of Personality and Social Psychology*, 36, 351–60.

Batson, C. D. (1987) 'Prosocial motivation: Is it ever truly altruistic? *Advances in Experimental Social Psychology*, 20, 65–122.

Batson, C. D. (1990) 'How social an animal? The human capacity for caring', *American Psychologist*, 45, 36–46.

Batson, C. D. and Oleson, K. C. (1991) 'Current status of the empathy–altruism hypthesis', *Review of Personality and Social Psychology*, 45, 706–18.

Batson, C. D., O'Quin, K., Fultz, J., Vanderplas, M. and Isen, A. M. (1983) 'Influence of self-reported distress and empathy on egoistic versus altruistic motivation to help', *Journal of Personality and Social Psychology*, 45, 706–18.

Baumeister, R. F., Chesner, S. P., Senders, P. S. and Tice, D. M. (1988) 'Who's in charge here? Group leaders do lend help in emergencies', *Personality and Social Psychology Bulletin*, 14, 17–22.

Baumrind, D. (1964) 'Some thoughts on the ethics of research: after reading Milgram's study of obedience', *American Psychologist*, 19, 421–3.

Bem, D. J. (1967) 'Self-perception: An alternative interpretation of cognitive dissonance', *Psychological Review*, 74, 183–200.

Bem, D. J. (1972) 'Self-perception theory', in L. Berkowittz (ed.), *Advances in Experimental Social Psychology*, Vol. 6 (New York: Academic Press).

Berger, J. Rosenholz, S. J. and Zelditch, M. Jr (1980) 'Status organizing process', *Annual Review of Sociology,* 6, 479–508.

Berkowitz, L. (1962) *Aggression: A Social Psychological Analysis* (New York: McGraw-Hill).

Berkowitz, L. (1965) 'Some aspects of observed aggression', *Journal of Personality and Social Psychology*, 2, 359–369.

Berkowitz, L. (1972) 'Frustrations, comparisons, and other sources of emotion arousal as contributors to social unrest', *Journal of Social Issues*, 28, 77–91.

Berkowitz, L. (1983a) 'Aversively stimulated aggression', *American Psychologist*, 38, 1135–44.

Berkowitz, L. (1983b) 'Experience of anger as a parallel process in the display of impulsive "angry" aggression', in R. G. Geen and E. Donnerstein (eds), *Aggression: Theoretical and Empirical Reviews* (New York: Academic Press).

Berkowitz, L. (1989) 'Frustration–aggression hypothesis: Examination and reformulation', *Psychological Bulletin*, 106, 59–73.

Berkowitz L. and Alioto, J. T. (1973) 'The meaning of an observed event as a determinant of its aggressive consequences', *Journal of Personality and Social Psychology*, 28, 206–17.

Berry, D. S. (1990) 'The perceiver as naive scientist or the scientist as naive perceiver? An ecological view of social knowledge acquisition', *Contemporary Social Psychology*, 14, 145–53.

Berscheid, E. (1985) 'Interpersonal attraction', in G. Lindzey and E. Aronson (eds), *Handbook of Social Psychology*, 3rd edn, vol. 2 (New York: Random House).

Berscheid, E. and Walster, E. (1978) *Interpersonal Attraction*, 2nd edn (Reading, Ma: Addison-Wesley).

Bettelheim, B. and Janowitz, M. (1950) *Dynamics of Prejudice: A Psychological and Sociological Study of Veterans* (New York: Harper).

Bharati, A. (1985) 'The self in Hindu thought and action', in A. J. Marsella, G. Devos and F. L. K. Hsu (eds), *Culture and Self: Asian and Western Perspectives* (London: Tavistock Publications).

Birch, A. and Hayward, S. (1994) *Individual Differences* (Basingstoke: Macmillan).

Birch, A. (in preparation) *Child Development: From Infancy to Old Age* (2nd ed.) (Basingstoke: Macmillan).

Blais, M. R., Sabourin, S., Boucher, C. and Vallerand, R. J. (1990) 'Toward a motivational model of couple happiness', *Journal of Personality and Social Psychology*, 59, 1021–31.

Blake, R. R. and Mouton, J. S. (1961) 'Reactions to intergroup competition under win/lose conditions', *Management Science*, 7, 420–35.

Bogardus, E. S. (1925) 'Measuring social distance', *Journal of Applied Sociology*, 9, 299–308.

Borden, R. J. (1975) 'Witnessed aggression: Influence of an observer's sex and values on aggressive responding', *Journal of Personality and Social Psychology*, 31, 567–73.

Bowlby, J. (1969) *Attachment and Loss: Vol. 1. Attachment* (New York: Basic Books).

Bowlby, J. (1973) *Attachment and Love: Vol. 2. Separation: Anxiety and Anger* (New York: Basic Books).

Bowlby, J. (1980) *Attachment and Loss: Vol. 3. Loss* (New York: Basic Books).

Breckler, S. J. and Wiggins, E. C. (1989a) 'On defining attitude and attitude theory: once more with feeling', in A. R. Pratkanis, S. J. Breckler and A. G. Greenwald (eds), *Attitude Structure and Function* (Hillsdale, NJ: Erlbaum).

Breckler, S. J. and Wiggins, E. C. (1989b) 'Affect versus evaluation in the structure of attitudes', *Journal of Experimental Social Psychology*, 25, 253–71.

Breckler, S. J. Pratkanis, A. R. and McCann, C. D. (1991) 'The representation of self in multi-dimensional cognitive space', *British Journal of Social Psychology*, 30, 97–112.

Brehm, J. W. (1992) *A Theory of Psychological Reactance* (New York: Academic Press).

Brehm, S. S. (1988) 'Passionate love', in R. J. Sternberg and M. L. Barnes (eds), *The Psychology of Love* (New Haven, Ct: Yale University Press).

Brewer, M. B. (1988) 'A dual process model of impression formation', in T. K. Srull and R. S. Wyer (eds), *Advances in Social Cognition: A Dual Process Model of Impression Formation*, Vol. 1 (Hillsdale, NJ: Erlbaum).

Brewer, M. B. and Kramer, R. M. (1985) 'The psychology of intergroup attitudes and behaviour', *Annual Review of Psychology*, 36, 219–43.

Brewer, M. B. and Kramer, R. M. (1986) 'Choice behaviour in social dilemmas: The effects of social identity, group size and decision framing', *Journal of Personality and Social Psychology*, 50, 543–9.

Brewer, M. B., Dull, V. and Lui, L. (1981) 'Perceptions of the elderly: Stereotypes as prototypes, *Journal of Personality and Social Psychology*, 41, 656–70.

Brewer, M. B. and Schneider, S. (1990) 'Social identity and social dilemmas: A double edged sword', in D. Abrams and Hogg, M. (eds), *Social Identity Theory: Constructive and Critical Advances* (London: Harvester Wheatsheaf).

Brigham, J. C. (1971) 'Ethnic stereotypes', *Psychological Bulletin*, 76, 15–38.

British Psychological Society (1991) *Code of Conduct, Ethical Principles and Guidelines* (Leicester: British Psychological Society).

Brody, E. M. (1990) *Women in the Middle: Their Parent Care Years* (New York: Springer).

Broverman, I. K., Vogel, S. R., Broverman, D. M., Clarkson F. E. and Rosencrantz, P. S. (1972) 'Sex-role stereotypes: a current appraisal', *Journal of Social Issues*, 28, 59–78.

Brown, G. W. and Harris, T. (1978) *Social Analysis of Depression* (London: Tavistock).

Brown, P. and Elliot, R. (1965) 'Control of aggression in a nursery school class', *Journal of Experimental Child Psychology*, 2, 103–7.

Brown, P. and Levinson, S. (1987) *Politeness: Some Universals in Language Use* (Cambridge: Cambridge University Press).

Brown, R. (1965) *Social Psychology* (New York: Free Press).

Bryan, J. H. and Test, M. A. (1967) 'Models and helping: Naturalistic studies in aiding behaviour', *Journal of Personality and Social Psychology*, 6, 400–7.

Burger, J. M. (1986) 'Increasing compliance by improving the deal: The "that's-not-all" technique', *Journal of Personality and Social Psychology*, 51, 277–83.

Bushman, B. J. (1984) 'Perceived symbols of authority and their influence on compliance', *Journal of Applied Social Psychology*, 14, 501–8.

Bushman, B. J. (1988) 'The effects of apparel on compliance: A field experiment with a female authority figure', *Personality and Social Psychology Bulletin*, 14, 559–67.

Bushman, B. J. and Geen, R. G. (1990) 'Role of cognitive emotional mediators and individual differences in the effects of media violence', *Journal of Personality and Social Psychology*, 58, 156–63.

Buss, A. H. (1961) *The Psychology of Aggression* (New York: Wiley).

Buss, A. H. (1967) 'Instrumentality of aggression, feedback and frustration as determinants of physical aggression', *Journal of Personality and Social Psychology*, 3, 153–62.

Buss, A. H. (1971) 'Aggression pays', in J. L. Singer (ed.), *The Control of Aggression and Violence* (New York: Academic Press).

Buss, D. M. (1984) 'Toward a psychology of the person-environment (PE) correlation: The role of spouse selection', *Journal of Personality and Social Psychology*, 47, 361–77.

Buss, D. M. and Barnes, M. (1986) 'Preferences in human mate selection', *Journal of Personality and Social Psychology*, 50, 559–70.

Byrne, D. (1971) *The Attraction Paradigm* (New York: Academic Press).

Byrne, D. and Clore, G. L. (1970) 'A reinforcement model of evaluative responses', *Personality: An International Journal*, 1, 103–28.

Byrne, D. Clore, G. L. and Smeaton, G. (1986) 'The attraction hypothesis: do similar attitudes affect anything? *Journal of Personality and Social Psychology*, 51, 1167–70.

Cacioppo, J. T. and Petty, R. E (1980) 'Sex differences in influencability: toward specifying the underlying process', *Personality and Social Psychology Bulletin*, 6, 651–6.

Campbell, D. T. Tesser, A. and Fairey, P. J. (1986) 'Conformity and attention to the stimulus: Some temporal and contextual dynamics', *Journal of Personality and Social Psychology*, 51, 315–24.

Carlson, M. and Miller, N. (1987) 'Explanation of the relation between negative mood and helping', *Psychological Bulletin*, 102, 91–108.

Cartwright, D. (1968) 'The nature of group cohesiveness', in D. Cartwright and A. Zander (eds), *Group Dynamics: Research and Theory*, 3rd edn (London: Tavistock).

Carver, C. S. and Glass, D. C. (1978) 'Coronary-prone behaviour pattern and interpersonal aggression', *Journal of Personality and Social Psychology*, 36, 361–6.

Carver, C. S. and Scheier, M. F. (1981) *Attention and Self-Regulation: A Control Theory Approach to Human Behaviour* (New York: Springer-Verlag).

Cash, T. F., Kehr, J. A., Polyson, J. and Freeman, V. (1977) 'Role of physical attractiveness in peer attribution of psychological disturbance', *Journal of Consulting and Clinical Psychology*, 45, 987–93.

Chaplin W. F., John O. P. and Goldberg L. R. (1988) ' Conceptions of states and traits: dimensional attributes with ideals as prototypes', *Journal of Personality and Social Psychology*, 54, 541–57.

Chemers, M. M. (1983) 'Leadership theory and research: a systems/process integration', in P. B. Paulus (ed.), *Basic Group Processes* (New York: Springer-Verlag).

Chemers, M. M. (1987) 'Leadership processes: Intrapersonal, interpersonal and societal influences', *Review of Personality and Social Psychology*, 8, 252–77.

Cialdini, R. B. (1985) *Influence: Science and Practice* (Glenview, Ill: Scott Foresman).

Cialdini, R. B., Baumann, D. J. and Kenrick, D. T. (1981) 'Insights from sadness: A three step model of the development of altruism as hedonism', *Developmental Review*, 1, 207–23.

Cialdini, R. B., Cacioppo, J. T., Basset, R. and Miller, J. A. (1978) 'Low-ball procedure for producing compliance: Commitment then cost', *Journal of Personality and Social Psychology*, 36, 463–76.

Cialdini, R. B., Darby, B. L. and Vincent, J. E. (1973) 'Transgression and altruism: A case for hedonism', *Journal of Experimental Social Psychology*, 9, 502–16.

Cialdini, R. B., Schaller, M., Houlihan, D., Arps, K., Fultz, J. and Beaman, A. L. (1987) 'Empathy based helping: Is it selflessly or selfishly motivated?', *Journal of Personality and Social Psychology*, 52, 749–58.

Cialdini, R. B., Vincent, J. E., Lewis, S. K., Catalan, J., Wheeler, D. and Darby, B. L. (1975) 'A reciprocal concessions procedure for inducing compliance: Door-in-the-face technique', *Journal of Personality and Social Psychology*, 21, 206–15.

Clark, M. S. (1984) 'Record keeping in two types of relationship', *Journal of Personality and Social Psychology*, 51, 333–8.

Clark, M. S. and Mills, J. (1979) 'Interpersonal attraction in exchange and communal relationships', *Journal of Personality and Social Psychology*, 37, 12–24.

Clark, N. K. and Stephenson, G. M. (1989) 'Group remembering', in P. B. Paulus (ed.), *Psychology of Group Influence*, 2nd edn (Hillsdale, NJ: Erlbaum).

Clore, G. L. (1976) 'Interpersonal attraction: An overview', in J. W. Thibaut, J. T. Spence and R. C. Carson (eds), *Contemporary Topics in Social Psychology* (Morristown, NJ: General Learning Press).

Clore, G. L. and Byrne, D. (1974) 'A reinforcement–affect model of attraction', in T. L. Huston (ed.), *Foundations of Interpersonal Attraction* (New York: Academic Press).

Clore, G. L. and Kerber, K. W. (1978) 'Toward an affective theory of attraction and trait attribution', unpublished manuscript (University of Illinois, Champaign).

Coates, B., Pusser, H. E. and Goodman, I. (1976) 'The influence of *Sesame Street* and *Mister Roger's Neighbourhood* on children's prosocial behaviour in preschool', *Child Development*, 47, 138–44.

Cohen, C. (1987) 'Nuclear language', *Bulletin of the Atomic Scientist*, June, 17–24.

Coke, J. S., Batson, C. D. and McDavis, K. (1978) 'Empathic mediation of helping: A two-stage model', *Journal of Personality and Social Psychology*, 36, 752–66.

Condry, J. (1977) 'Enemies of exploration: Self-initiated versus other-initiated learning', *Journal of Personality and Social Psychology*, 35, 459–77.

Cook, S. W. and Pelfrey, M. (1985) 'Reactions to being helped in cooperating interracial groups: A context effect', *Journal of Personality and Social Psychology*, 49, 1231–45.

Cooley, C. H. (1902) *Human Nature and the Social Order* (New York: Scribners).

Cooper, H. M. (1979) 'Statistically combining independent studies: A meta-analysis of sex differences in conformity research', *Journal of Personality and Social Psychology*, 37, 131–46.

Cooper, H. M. (1990) 'Meta-analysis and integrative research review', *Review of Personality and Social Psychology*, 11, 142–63.

Cooper, J. and Fazio, R. H. (1984) 'A new look at dissonance theory', in L. Berkowitz (ed.), *Advances in Experimental Social Psychology*, Vol. 17 (New York Academic Press).

Coopersmith, S. (1968) 'Studies in self-esteem', *Scientific American*, 218, 96–106.

Cox, O. C. (1948) *Caste, Class and Race* (New York: Doubleday).

Crocker, J., Fiske, S. T. and Taylor, S. E. (1984) 'Schematic bases of belief change', in J. R. Eiser (ed.), *Attitudinal Judgement* (New York: Springer-Verlag).

Crook, J. H. (1973) 'The nature and function of territorial aggression', in M. F. A. Montagu (ed.), *Man and Aggression*, 2nd edn (New York: Oxford University Press).

Crutchfield, R. S. (1955) 'Conformity and character', *American Psychologist*, 10, 191–8.

Cunningham, M. R. (1981) 'Sociobiology as a supplementary paradigm for social psychological research', *Review of Personality and Social Psychology*, 2, 69–106.

Cunningham, M. R. (1986) 'Measuring the physical in physical attraction: Quasi-experiments on the sociobiology of female beauty', *Journal of Personality and Social Psychology*, 50, 925–35.

Cutrona, C. E. (1988) 'Behavioural manifestations of social support: A microanalytic investigation', *Journal of Personality and Social Psychology*, 51, 201–8.

Dane, F. C. and Harshaw, R. (1991) 'Similarity-attraction versus dissimilarity-repulsion: The establishment wins again', Paper presented at the South Eastern Psychological Association, New Orleans, March 1991.

Davies, J. C. (1969) 'The J-curve of rising and declining satisfaction as a cause of some great revolutions and a contained rebellion', in H. D. Graham and T. R. Gurr (eds), *The History of Violence in America: Historical and Comparative Perspectives* (New York: Praeger).

Davis, J. H. (1973) 'Group decision and social interaction: A theory of social decision schemes', *Psychological Review*, 80, 97–125.

De Jong W. (1979) 'An examination of self-perception and the foot-in-the-door effect', *Journal of Personality and Social Psychology*, 37, 2221–39.

Deaux, K. (1985) 'Sex and gender', *Annual Review of Psychology*, 36, 49–81.

Deaux, K. and Emswiller, T. (1974). 'Explanations of successful performance on sex-linked tasks: What is skill for the male is luck for the female', *Journal of Personality and Social Psychology*, 29, 80–5.

Deaux, K. and Lewis, L. (1983) 'Components of gender stereotypes', *Psychological Documents* 13, 25 (Ms. no. 2583).

Deaux, K., Dane, F. C. and Wrightson L. S. (1993) *Social Psychology in the 90s* (Belmont, California: Brookes/Cole).

Deci, E. L. and Ryan, R. M. (1985) *Intrinsic Motivation and Self-determination in Human Behaviour* (New York: Plenum).

Dembroski, T. M. and MacDougall, J. M. (1978) 'Stress effects and affliation preferences among subjects among subjects possessing the Type A coronary-prone behaviour pattern', *Journal of Personality and Social Psychology*, 36, 23–33.

Derlega, V. J., Lewis, R. J., Harrison, S., Winstead, B. A. and Costanza, R. (1989) 'Gender differences in the initiation and attribution of tactile intimacy', *Journal of Non-Verbal Behaviour*, 13, 83–96.

Deutsch, M. (1958) 'Trust and suspicion', *Journal of Conflict Resolution*, 2, 265–79.

Deutsch, M. (1975) 'Equity, equality and need: What determines which value will be used as a basis of distributive justice?', *Journal of Social Issues*, 31, 137–49.

Deutsch, M. and Gerard, H. B. (1955) 'A study of normative and informational social influences upon individual judgement', *Journal of Abnormal and Social Psychology*, 51, 629–36.

Devine, P. G. (1989) 'Stereotypes and prejudice: Their automatic and controlled components', *Journal of Personality and Social Psychology*, 56, 5–18.

Devos, G. (1985) 'Dimensions of the self in Japanese culture', in A. J. Marsella *et al.* (eds), *Culture and Self: Asian and Western Perspectives* (London: Tavistock Publications).

Diab, L. N. (1970) 'A study of intragroup and intergroup relations among experimentally produced small groups', *Genetic Psychology Monographs*, 82, 49–82.

Diener, E. (1976) 'Effects of prior destructive behaviour, anonymity, and group presence on deindividuation and aggression', *Journal of Personality and Social Psychology*, 33, 497-507.

Diener, E. (1980) 'Deindividuation: The absence of self-awareness and self-regulation in group members', in P. B. Paulus (ed.), *Psychology of Group Influence* (Hillsdale, NJ: Erlbaum).

Dion, K. L., Berscheid, E. and Walster, E. (1972) 'What is beautiful is good', *Journal of Personality and Social Psychology*, 24, 285–90.

Dipboye, R. L., Arvey, R. D. and Terpstra, D. E. (1977) 'Sex and physical attractiveness of raters and applicants as determinants of resumé evaluations', *Journal of Applied Psychology*, 61, 288–94.

Dittes, J. E. (159) 'Attractiveness of group as function of self-esteem and acceptance by group', *Journal of Abnormal and Social Psychology*, 89, 77–82.

Dittes, J. E. and Kelley, H. H. (1956) 'Affects of different conditions of acceptance upon conformity to group norms', *Journal of Abnormal and Social Psychology*, 53, 100–7.

Dodge, K. A. and Crick, N. R. (1990) 'Social information processing bases of aggressive behaviour in children', *Personality and Social Psychology Bulletin*, 16, 8–22.

Dollard, J., Doob, L. W., Miller, N. E., Mowrer O. H. and Sears, R. R. *Frustration and Aggression* (New Haven, Ct: Yale University Press).

Donnerstein, E. (1982) 'Erotica and human aggression', in R. G. Geen and F. Donnerstein (eds), *Aggression: Theoretical and Empirical Reviews* (New York: Academic Press).

Donnerstein, E., Donnerstein, M. and Evans, R. (1975) 'Erotic stimuli and aggression: Facilitation or inhibition, *Journal of Personality and Social Psychology*, 34, 237–44.

Donnerstein, M. and Wilson, D. W. (1976) 'The effects of noise and perceived control upon ongoing and subsequent aggressive behaviour', *Journal of Personality and Social Psychology* 34, 774–81.

Doob, A. N. and Gross, A. E. (1968) 'Status of frustrator as an inhibitor of horn honking responses', *Journal of Social Psychology*, 76, 213–8.

Dreiser, T. (1929) *A Gallery of Women* (New York: Boni & Liveright).

DuBois, R. D. (1950) *Neighbours in Action* (New York: Harper).

Duck, S. (1988) *Relating to Others* (Milton Keynes: Open University Press).

Duck, S. (1992) *Human Relationships*, 2nd edn (London: Sage).

Durkin, K. (1995) *Developmental Social Psychology from Infancy to Old Age* (Cambridge, Ma: Blackwell).

Eagly, A. H. and Caili, L. L. (1981) 'Sex of researchers and sex-typed communications as determinants of influenceability: A mega-analysis of social influence studies', *Psychological Bulletin*, 90, 1–20.

Eagly, A. H. and Crowley, M. (1986) 'Gender and helping behaviour: A meta-analytic review of the social psychological literature', *Psycholgical Bulletin*, 100, 283–308.

Eagly, A. H. and Steffen, V. J. (1986) 'Gender and aggressive behaviour: A meta-analytic review of the social psychological literature', *Psychological Bulletin*, 100, 309–30.

Eagly, A. H. and Wood, W. (1991) 'Explaining sex differences in social behaviour: A meta-analytic perspective', *Personality and Social Psychology Bulletin*, 17, 306–15.

Eisenberg, N. and Mussen, P. H. (1989) *The Roots of Prosocial Behaviour in Children* (New York: Cambridge University Press).

Ekman, P., Friesen, W. V., O'Sullivan, M., Chan, A., Diacoyanni-Tarlatzis, I., Heider, K., Krause, R., Lecompte W. A., Pitcairn, T., Riccibitti, P. E., Scherer, K., Tomita, M. and Tzvaras, A. (1987) 'Universals and cultural differences in the judgements of facial expressions of emotion', *Journal of Personality and Social Psychology*, 53, 712–17.

Epstein, L. C. and Lasagna, L. (1969) 'Obtaining informed consent', *Archives of Internal Medicine*, 123, 682–8.

Eron, L. D. (1980) 'Prescription for the reduction of aggression', *American Psychologist* 35, 244–52. Bushman, B. J. and Geen, R. G. (1990) 'Role of cognitive – emotional mediators and individual differences in the effects of media violence', *Journal of Personality and Social Psychology*, 58, 156–63.

Eron, L. D. (1982) 'Parent-child interaction, television violence and aggression of children', *American Psychologist*, 37 197–211.

Fajardo, D. M. (1985) 'Author race, essay quality and reverse discrimination', *Journal of Applied Social Psychology*, 15, 255–68.

Farr, R. M. and Moscovici, S. (eds) (1984) *Social Representations* (Cambridge: Cambridge University Press).

Fazio, R. H. (1986) 'How do attitudes guide behaviour?', in R. M. Sorrentino and E. T. Higgins (eds), *Handbook of Motivation and Cognition* (New York: Guilford Press).

Fazio, R. H. (1989) 'On the power and functionality of attitudes: The role of attitude accessibility', in A. R. Pratkanis, S. J. Breckler and A. G. Greenwald (eds), *Attitude Structure and Function* (Hillsdale, NJ: Erlbaum.

Fazio, R. H., Sanbonmatsu, D. M., Powell, M. C. and Kardes, F. R. (1986) 'On the automatic activation of attitudes', *Journal of Personality and Social Psychology*, 50, 229–38.

Fazio, R. H., Zanna, M. P. and Cooper, J. (1977) 'Dissonance and self perception: An integrative view of each theory's proper domain of application', *Journal of Experimental Social Psychology*, 13, 464–79.

Feshbach, S., Stiles, W. B. and Bitter, E. (1967) 'The reinforcing effect of witnessing aggression', *Journal of Experimental Research in Personality*, 2, 133–9.

Festinger L., Pepitone, A. and Newcombe, T. (1952) 'Some consequences of deindividuation in a group', *Journal of Abnormal and Social Psychology*, 47, 382–9.

Festinger, L. (1950) 'Informal social communication', *Psychological Review*, 57, 271–8.

Festinger, L. (1957) *A Theory of Cognitive Dissonance* (Stanford, Ca: Stanford University Press).

Festinger, L. and Carlsmith, J. M. (1959) 'Cognitive consequences of forced compliance', *Journal of Abnormal and Social Psychology*, 58, 203–10.

Fiedler, F. E. (1964) 'A contingency model of leadership effectiveness', in L. Berkowitz (ed.), *Advances in Experimental Social Psychology* (New York: Academic Press).

Fiedler, F. E. (1967) *A Theory of Leadership Effectiveness* (New York: McGraw-Hill).

Fischer, C. S. (1963) 'Sharing in pre-school children as a function of the amount and type of reinforcement', *Genetic Psychology Monographs*, 68, 215–45.

Fishbein, M. and Ajzen, I. (1974) 'Attitudes towards objects as predictors of single and multiple behaviour criteria', *Psychological Review*, 81, 59–74.

Fishbein, M. and Ajzen, I. (1975) *Belief Attitude, Intention and Behaviour: An Introduction to Theory and Research* (Reading, Ma: Addison-Wesley).

Fisher, R. J. (1990) *The Social Psychology of Intergroup and International Conflict Resolution* (New York: Springer-Verlag).

Fiske, S. T. and Taylor, S. E. (1984) *Social Cognition* (Reading, Ma: Addison-Wesley).

Forsyth, D. R. (1983) *An Introduction to Group Dynamics* (Pacific Grove, Ca: Brooks-Cole).

Fowler, C. A., Wolford, G., Slade, R. and Tissinary, L. (1981) 'Lexical access without awareness', *Journal of Experimental Psychology: General*, 13, 281–90.

Freedman, J. L. and Fraser, S. C. (1966) 'Compliance without pressure: The foot-in-the-door technique', *Journal of Personality and Social Psychology*, 4, 195–202.

French, J. R. P. Jr and Raven, B. H. (1959) 'The bases of social power', in D. Cartwright (ed.), *Studies in Social Power* (Ann Arbor, Michigan: University of Michigan Press).

Freud, S. (1921) 'Group psychology and the analysis of the ego', in J. Strachey (ed.), *Standard Edition of the Complete Psychological Works*, Vol. 18 (London: Hogarth Press).

Freud, S. (1938) *The Basic Writings of Sigmund Freud* (New York: Modern Library).

Gaebelein, J. W. (1973) 'Third party instigation of aggression: An experimental approach', *Journal of Personality and Social Psychology*, 27, 389–395.

Gaertner, S. L. and Dovidio, J. F. (1977) 'The subtety of white racism, arousal and helping behaviour', *Journal of Personality and Social Psychology*, 35, 691–707.

Gaertner, S. L. and McLaughlin, J. P. (1983) 'Racial stereotypes: Associations and ascriptions of positive and negative characteristics', *Social Psychology Quarterly*, 46, 23–30.

Geen, R. G. (1968) 'Effects of frustration, attack and prior training upon aggressive behaviour', *Journal of Personality and Social Psychology*, 9, 316–21.

Geen, R. G. and Donnerstein, E. (eds) (1983) *Aggression: Theoretical and Empirical Reviews* (New York: Academic Press).

Geen, R. G. and Stonner, D. (1971) 'Effects of aggressiveness habit-strength on behaviour in the presence of aggression-related stimuli', *Journal of Personality and Social Psychology*, 17, 149–53.

Gentry, W. D. (1970) 'Effects of frustration and attack and prior aggressive training on overt aggression and vascular processes', *Journal of Personality and Social Psychology* 16, 18–25.

George, G. M. (1991) 'State or trait: Effects of positive mood on prosocial behaviours at work', *Journal of Applied Psychology*, 76, 299–307.

Gibbons, F. X. (1990) 'Self attention and behaviour: A review and a theoretical update', *Advances in Experimental Social Psychology*, 23, 249–303.

Gilbert, D. T. (1989) 'Thinking lightly about others: Automatic components of the social inference process', in J. S. Uleman and J. S. Bargh (eds), *Unintended Thought* (New York: Guilford Press).

Goffman, E. (1967) *Interaction Ritual: Essays on Face-to-face Behaviour* (Garden City, NY: Doubleday).

Goldberg, P. (1968) 'Are some women prejudiced against women?', *Trans-Action*, 5, 28–30.

Granberg, D. (1987) 'Candidate preference, membership group and estimates of voting behaviour', *Social Cognition*, 5, 323–35.

Gray, J. S. and Thompson, A. H. (1953) 'The ethnic prejudices of white and Negro college students', *Journal of Abnormal and Social Psychology*, 48, 311–13.

Gruber, E. R. and Kersten, H. (1995) *The Original Jesus: The Buddhist Sources of Christianity* (Shaftesbury: Element).

Grusec, J. E and Skubiski, S. L. (1970) 'Model nurturance, demand characteristics of the modeling experiment, and altruism', *Journal of Personality and Social Psychology*, 14, 352–9.

Grusec, J. E. and Redler, E. (1980) 'Attribution, reinforcement and altruism', *Developmental Psychology*, 16, 525–34.

Grusec, J. E., Kuczynski, L. Rushton, J. P. and Simutis, Z. M. (1978) 'Modelling, direct instruction, and attributions: Effects on altruism', *Developmental Psychology*, 14, 51–7.

Guimond, S. and Dubé-Sinard, L. (1983) 'Relative deprivation theory and the Québec Nationalist Movement: The cognitive–emotion distinction and the personal–group deprivation issue', *Journal of Personality and Social Psychology*, 44, 526–35.

Haas, F. J. and Fleming, G. J. (1946) 'Personnel practices and wartime changes', *Annals of the American Academy of Political and Social Science*, 244, 48–56.

Halpin, A. W. (1966) *Theory and Research in Administration* (New York: Macmillan).

Haney, C., Banks, C. and Zimbardo, P. (1973) 'Interpersonal dynamics in a simulated prison', *International Journal of Criminology and Penology*, 1, 69–97.

Hardin, G. (1968) 'The tragedy of the commons', *Science*, 162, 1243–8.

Hargreaves, D. (1967) *Social Relations in a Secondary School* (London: Routledge).

Harris, M. B. (1974) 'Mediators between frustration and aggression in a field experiment', *Journal of Experimental Social Psychology*, 10, 561–571.

Harrison, A. A., Clearwater, Y. A. and McKay, C. P. (eds) (1990) *From Antarctica to Outer Space: Life in Isolation and Confinement* (New York: Springer-Verlag).

Hatfield, E. (1987) 'Love', in R. J. Corsini (ed.), *Concise Encyclopaedia of Psychology* (New York: Wiley).

Hatfield, E. and Walster, G. W. (1981) *A New Look at Love* (Reading, Ma: Addison-Wesley).

Hayes, N. (1993) *Principles of Social Psychology* (Hove: Lawrence Erlbaum Associates).

Hayes, S. (1994) *Foundations of Psychology* (London: Routledge).

Hays, R. B. (1985) 'A longitudinal study of friendship development', *Journal of Personality and Social Psychology*, 48, 909–24.

Hays, R. B. and Oxley, D, (1986) 'Social Network development and functioning during a life transition', *Journal of Personality and Social Psychology*, 50, 305–13.

Hayward, S. (1996) *Biopsychology* (Basingstoke: Macmillan).

Hazan C and Shaver, P. (1990) 'Love and work: An attachment-theoretical perspective', *Journal of Personality and Social Psychology*, 59, 270–80.

Hazan, C. and Shaver, P. (1987) 'Romantic love conceptualized as an attachment process', *Journal of Personality and Social Psychology*, 52, 511–24.

Hebb, D. O. (1949) *The Organisation of Behaviour* (New York: Wiley).

Heider, F. (1946) 'Attitudes and cognitive organisation', *Journal of Psychology*, 21, 107-12.

Heider, F. (1958) *The Psychology of Interpersonal Relations* (New York: Wiley).

Heider, F. and Simmel, M. (1944) 'The experimental study of apparent behaviour', *American Journal of Psychology*, 57, 243–59.

Hersh, S. (1970) *My Lai: A Report on the Massacre and its Aftermath* (New York: Vintage Books).

Hess, E. H. (1962) 'Ethology', in R. Brown, E. Galanter, E. H. Hess and G. Mandler (eds), *New Directions in Psychology* (New York: Holt).

Higgins, E. T. (1987) 'Self-discrepancy: A theory relating self and affect', *Psychological Review*, 94, 319–40.

Hill, C. T., Rubin, Z. and Peplau, L. A. (1976) 'Break-ups before marriage: The end of 103 affairs', *Journal of Social Issues*, 32 (1), 147–68.

Hill, R. (1945) 'Campus values in mate selection', *Journal of Home Economics*, 37, 554–78.

Hill, T., Lewicki, P., Czyzewska, M. and Boss, A. (1989) 'Self-perpetuating development of encoding biases in person perception', *Journal of Personality and Social Psychology*, 57, 373–87.

Hofling, K. C., Brontzman, E., Dalrymple, S., Graves, N., and Pierce, C. M. (1966) 'An experimental study in the nurse/physician relationship', *Journal of Mental and Nervous Disorders*, 43, 171–8.

Hogg, M. A. (1992) *The Social Psychology of Group Cohesiveness: From Attraction to Social Identity* (London: Harvester Wheatsheaf).

Hogg, M. A. and Vaughan, G. M. (1995) *Social Psychology: An Introduction* (Hemel Hempstead: Prentice-Hall/Harvester Wheatsheaf).

Holmes, J. G. (1989) 'Trust and the appraisal process in close relationships', in W. H. Jones and D. Perlman (eds), *Advances in Personal Relationships*, Vol. 2 (Greenwich Ct: JAI Press).

Homans, G. C. (1958) 'Social behaviour and exchange', *American Journal of Sociology*, 63, 597–646.

Homans, G. C. (1961) *Social Behavior: Its Elementary Forms* (New York: Harcourt Brace and World).

Homans, G. C. (1974) *Social Behaviour: Its Elementary Forms*, rev edn (New York: Harcourt Brace Jovanovich).

Hornstein, G. A. (1970) 'The influence of social models on helping', in J. Macaulay and L. Berkowitz (eds), *Altruism and Helping Behaviour* (New York: Academic Press).

Hovland, C. I. and Sheif, M. (1952) 'Judgemental phenomena and scales of attitude measurement: Item displacement in Thurstine Scales', *Journal of Abnormal and Social Psychology*, 47, 822–32.

Hsu, F. L. K. (1985) 'The self in cross-cultural perspective', in A. J. Marsella *et al.* (eds), *Culture and Self: Asian and Western Perspectives* (London: Tavistock Publications).

Hudson, J. W. and Henze, L. F. (1969) 'Campus values in mate selection: A replication', *Journal of Marriage and the Family*, 31, 772–5.

Huesmann, L. R., Eron, L. D., Lefkowitz, M. M. and Walder, L. O. (1984) 'Stability of aggression over time and generations, *Developmental Psychology*, 20, 1120–34.

Hui, C. H., Triandris, H. C. and Yee, C. (1991) 'Cultural differences in reward allocation: Is 'collectivism' an explanation?' *British Journal of Social Psychology*, 30, 145–7.

Insko, C. A., Smith, R. H., Alicke, M. D., Wade, J. and Taylor, S. (1985) 'Conformity and group size: The concern with being right and the concern with being liked', *Personality and Social Science Bulletin*, 11, 41–50.

Isen, A. M. (1987) 'Positive affect, cognitive processes and social behaviour: The warm glow of success', *Journal of Personality and Social Psychology*, 15, 294–301.

Janis, I. L. (1982) *Groupthink: Psychological Studies of Policy Decisions and Fiascos*, 2nd edn (Boston, Ma: Houghton Mifflin).

Janis, I. L. and Mann, L. (1977) *Decision Making* (New York: Free Press).

Jason, L. A., Rose, T., Ferrari, J. R. and Barone, R. (1984) 'Personal versus impersonal methods of recruiting blood donors', *Journal of Social Psychology*, 123, 139–40.

Jellison, J. M. and Green, J. (1981) 'A self-representation approach to the fundamental attribution error: The norm of internality', *Journal of Personality and Social Psychology*, 40, 643–9.

Jemmott, J. and Locke, S. (1984) 'Psychosocial factors, immunologic mediation and human susceptibility to infectious diseases: How much do we know?', *Psychological Bulletin*, 95, 78–108.

Johnson, D. W. and Johnson, F. P. (1987) *Joining Together: Group Theory and Group Skills*, 3rd edn (Englewood Cliffs, NJ: Prentice-Hall).

Jones, E. E. and Davis, K. E. (1965) 'From acts to disposition: The attribution process in person perception', in L. Berkowitz (ed.), *Advances in Experimental Social Psychology* (New York: Academic Press).

Jones, E. E. and Harrris V. A. (1967) 'The attribution of attitudes', *Journal of Experimental Social Psychology*, 3, 1–24.

Jones, E. E. and McGillis, D. (1976) 'Correspondent inferences and the attribution cube: A comparative re-appraisal', in J. H. Harvey, W. J. Ickes and R. F. Kidd (eds), *New Directions in Attribution Research*, Vol. 1 (Hillsdale NJ: Erlbaum).

Jones, E. E. and Nisbett, R. E. (1972) 'The actor and the observer: Divergent perceptions of the causes of behaviour', in E. E. Jones, D. E. Kanouse, H. H. Kelley, R. E. Nisbett, S. Valins and B. Weiner (eds), *Attribution: Perceiving Causes of Behaviour* (Morristown, NJ: General Learning Press).

Jones, E. E. and Sigall, H. (1971) 'The bogus pipeline: A new paradigm for measuring affect and attitude', *Psychological Bulletin*, 76, 349–64.

Jones, E. E., Davis, K. E. and Gergen, K. J. (1961) 'Role playing variations and their informational value for person perception', *Journal of Abnormal and Social Psychology*, 63, 302–10.

Jorgensen, B. W. and Cervone, J. C. (1978) 'Affect enhancement in the pseudo-recognition task', *Personality and Social Psychology Bulletin*, 4, 285–8.

Josephson, W. L. (1987) 'Television violence and children's aggression: Testing and priming, social script and disinhibition predictions', *Journal of Personality and Social Psychology*, 53, 882–90.

Joule, R. V, Goullioux, F. and Weber, F. (1989) 'The lure: A new compliance technique', *Journal of Social Psychology*, 129, 741–9.

Judd, C. M. and Park, B. (1988) 'Out-group homogeneity: Judgements of variability at the individual and group levels', *Journal of Personality and Social Psychology*. 54, 778–88.

Kahn, A., O'Leary V. E., Krulewitz, J. E. and Lamm, H. (1980) 'Equity and equality: Male and female means to a just end', *Basic and Applied Social Psychology*, 1, 173–97.

Kandel, D. B. (1978) 'Similarity in real-life adolescent pairs', *Journal of Personality and Social Psychology*, 36, 306–12.

Kaplan, M. F. (1987) 'The influence process in group decision making', *Review of Personality and Social Psychology*, 8, 189–212.

Kaplan, M. F. and Miller, C. E. (1987) 'Group decision making and normative versus informational influence: Effects of type of issue and assigned decision rule', *Journal of Personality and Social Psychology*, 53, 306–13.

Karuza, J. Jr and Brickman, P. (1978) *Preference for Similar and Dissimilar Others as a Function of Status* (Paper presented at meeting of Mid-Western Psychological Association: Chicago, May 1978).

Katz, D. and Kahn, R. L. (1976) *The Social Psychology of Organisations* (New York: Wiley).

Kelley, H. H. (1967) 'Attribution theory in social psychology', *Nebraska Symposium on Motivation*, 15, 192–240.

Kelley, H. H. (1973) 'The process of causal attribution', *American Psychologist*, 28, 107–28.

Kelley, H. H. and Thibaut, J. W. (1978) *Interpersonal Relations: A Theory of Interdependence* (New York: Wiley Interscience).

Kelley, H. H., Berscheid, E., Christensen, A., Harvey, J. H., Huston, T. L., Levinger, G., McClintock, E., Peplau, L. A. and Peterson, D. R. (1983) *Close Relationships* (New York: Freeman).

Kelly, G. A. (1955) *The Psychology of Personal Constructs* (New York: Norton).

Kerckhoff, A. C. and Davis, K. E. (1962) 'Value consensus and need complementarity in mate selection', *American Sociological Review*, 27, 295–303.

Kilham, W. and Mann, L. (1974) 'Level of destructive obedience as a function of transmitter and executant roles in Milgram's obedience paradigm', *Journal of Personality and Social Psychology*, 29, 696–702.

Kinder, D. R. and Sears, D. O. (1981) 'Prejudice and politics: Symbolic racism versus racial threats to the good life', *Journal of Personality and Social Psychology*, 40, 414–31.

Kirkpatrick, L. A. and Shaver, P. R. (1988) 'Fear and affiliation reconsidered from a stress and coping perspective: The importance of cognitive clarity and fear reduction', *Journal of Social and Clinical Psychology*, 7, 214–33.

Knox, R. E. and Inkster, J. A. (1968) 'Post decisional dissonance at post time', *Journal of Personality and Social Psychology*, 8, 319–23.

Konečni, Y. J, (1975) 'Annoyance type and duration of post-annoyance activity and aggression: The "cathartic" effect, *Journal of Experimental Psychology General*, 104, 76–102.

Kramer, R. M. and Brewer, M. B. (1984) 'Effects of identity on resource use in a simulated commons dilemma', *Journal of Personality and Social Psychology*, 46, 1044–57.

Kramer, R. M. and Brewer, M. B. (1986) 'Social group identity and the emergence of cooperation in resource conservation dilemmas', in H. Wilke, D. Messick and C. Rutte (eds), *Psychology of Decisions and Conflict*, Vol. 3 (Frankfurt: Verlag Peter Lang).

Krebs, D. L. and Miller, D. T. (1985) 'Altruism and aggression', in G. Lindsey and E. Aronson (eds), *Handbook of Social Psychology*, 3rd edn, Vol. 2 (New York: Random House).

Kronhausen, F. and Kronhausen, P. (1964) *Pornography and the Law*, rev edn (New York: Ballantine).

Kutchinsky, B. (1973) 'The effect of easy availability of pornography on incidence of sex crimes: The Danish experience, *Journal of Social Issues*, 29 (3), 163–81.

La France, M. and Mayo, C. (1976) 'Racial differences in gaze behaviour during conversations: Two systematic observational studies', *Journal of Personality and Social Psychology*, 33, 547–52.

La Piere, R. T. (1934) 'Attitudes versus actions', *Social Forces*, 13, 230–7.

Lamm, H. and Kayser, E. (1978) 'The allocation of monetary gain and loss following dyadic performance: The weight given effort and ability under conditions of high and low intradyadic attraction', *European Journal of Social Psychology*, 8, 275–78.

Landy, D. and Sigall, H. (1974) 'Beauty is talent: Task evaluation as a function of the performer's physical attractiveness', *Journal of Personality and Social Psychology*, 29, 299–304.

Langer, E. J. (1978) 'Rethinking the role of thought insocial interaction', in J. H. Harvey, W. J. Ickes and R. F. Kidd (eds), *New Directions in Attitude Research*, Vol. 2 (Hillsdale, NJ: Erlbaum).

LaPiere, R. T. (1934) 'Attitudes versus actions', *Social Forces*, 13, 230–7.

Latané B and Darley, J. M. (1970) *The Unresponsive Bystander: Why doesn't He Help?* (New York: Appelton-Century-Crofts).

Latané, B. and Darley, J. M. (1976) 'Help in a crisis: Bystander response in an emergency', in J. W. Thibaut and J. T.Spence (eds), *Contemporary Topics in Social Psychology* (Morristown, NJ: General Learning Press).

Le Bon, G. (1908) *The Crowd: A Study of the Popular Mind* (London: Unwin) (first published 1896 by Ernest Benn).

Leavitt, H. J. (1951) 'Some effects of certain communication patterns on group performance', *Journal of Abnormal and Social Psychology*, 46, 38–50.

Lerner, M. J. (1977) 'The justice motive: Some hypotheses as to its origins and forms', *Journal of Personality*, 45, 1–52.

Lerner, M. J. and Miller, D. T. (1978) 'Just-world research and the attribution process: Looking back and ahead', *Psychological Bulletin*, 85, 1030–51.

Lesnik-Oberstein, M. and Cohen, L. (1984) 'Cognitive style, sensation seeking and assortative mating', *Journal of Personality and Social Psychology*, 46, 112–7.

Levitt, E. and Klassen, A. (1974) 'Public attitudes towards homosexuality: Part of the 1970 national survey by the Institute for Sex Research', *Journal of Homosexuality*, 1, 29–43.

Leyens, J.-P., Camino, L., Parke, R. D. and Berkowitz, L. (1975) 'Effects of movie violence or aggression in a field setting as a function of group dominance and cohesion', *Journal of Personality and Social Psychology*, 32, 346–60.

Leyens, J.-P., Herman, G. and Dunand, M. (1982) 'The influence of an audience on reactions to filmed violence', *European Journal of Social Psychology*, 12, 131–42.

Liebart, R. M. and Schwartzberg, N. S. (1977) 'Effects of mass media', in M. R. Rosenzweig and L. W. Porter (eds), *Annual Review of Psychology*, Vol 28 (Palo Alto, Ca: Annual Reviews).

Liebert, R. M. and Sprafkin, J. (1988) *The Early Window: Effects of Television on Children and Youth*, 3rd edn (New York: Pergamon Press).

Likert, R. (1932) 'A technique for the measurement of attitudes', *Archives of Psychology*, 140 (6).

Linssen, H. and Hagendoorn, L. (1994) 'Social and geographical factors in the explanation of European nationality stereotypes', *British Journal of Social Psychology*, 23, 165–82.

Linville, P. W. (1987) 'Self complexity as a cognitive buffer against stress-related depression and illness', *Journal of Personality and Social Psychology*, 23, 165–82.

Lipetz, M. E., Cohen, I. H., Dworin, J. and Rogers, L. (1970) 'Need complementarity, marital stability and marital satisfaction', in T. L. Huston (ed.), *Personality and Social Behaviour* (New York: Academic Press).

Lippitt, R. and White, R. (1943) 'The social climate of children's groups', in R. G. Barker, J. Kounin and H. Wright (eds), *Child Behaviour and Development* (New York: McGraw-Hill).

Lippman W. (1922) *Public Opinion* (New York: Harcourt, Brace & World).

Litton, I. and Potter, J. (1985) 'Social representations in the ordinary explanations of a "riot"', *European Journal of Social Psychology*, 15, 371–88.

Lloyd, B. B. and Duveen, G. (1992) *Gender Identities and Education: The Impact of Starting School* (Hemel Hempstead: Harvester Wheatsheaf).

Lorenz, K. (1937) 'The companion in the bird's world', in W. Sluckin (ed.), *Imprinting and Early Learning* (London: Methuen).

Lorenz, K. (1966) *On Aggression* (New York: Harcourt, Brace & World).

Luce, R. D. and Raiffa, H. (1957) *Games and Decisions* (New York: Wiley).

Lysack, H., Rule, B. G. and Dobbs, A. R. (1989) 'Conceptions of aggression: Prototype or defining features', *Personality and Social Psychology Bulletin*, 15, 233–43.

Maccoby, E. E. and Jacklin, C. N. (1974) *The Psychology of Sex Differences* (Stanford, Cal: Stanford University Press).

Major, B. and Adams, J. B. (1983) 'Role of gender, interpersonal orientation and self-presentation in distributive justice behaviour', *Journal of Personality and Social Psychology*, 45, 598–608.

Major, B. and Deaux, K. (1982) 'Individual differences in justice behaviour', in J. Greenberg and R. L. Cohen (eds), *Equity and Justice in Social Behaviour* (New York: Academic Press).

Malamuth, N. M. and Donnerstein, E. (1982) The effects of aggressive pornographic mass media stimuli', in L. Berkowitz (ed.), *Advances in Experimental Social Psychology Vol 15* (New York: Academic Press).

Malamuth, N. M. and Donnerstein, E. (1984) *Pornography and Social Aggression* (New York: Academic Press).

Malim, T., Birch, A. and Wadeley, A. (1992) *Perspectives in Psychology* (Basingstoke: Macmillan).

Malim, T., Birch, A. and Hayward, S. (1996) *Comparative Psychology. Human and Animal Behaviour: A Sociobiological Approach* (Basingstoke: Macmillan).

Mann, L., Newton, J. W. and Innes, J. M. (1982) 'A test between deindividuation and emergent norm theories of crowd aggression', *Journal of Personality and Social Psychology*, 42, 260–72.

Mann, R. D. (1959) 'A review of the relationship between personality and performance in small groups', *Psychological Bulletin*, 56, 241–70.

Mantell, D. M. (1971) 'The potential for violence in Germany', *Journal of Social Issues*, 27, 101–12.

Marks, G. and Miller, N. (1988) 'Perceptions of attitude similarity: Effect of anchored versus unanchored positions', *Personality and Social Psychology Bulletin*, 14, 92–102.

Markus, H. (1977) 'Self-schemata and processing information about the self', *Journal of Personality and Social Psychology*, 35, 63–78.

Markus, H., Crane, M., Bernstein, S., and Siladi, M. (1982) 'Self-schemas and gender', *Journal of Personality and Social Psychology*, 42, 38–50.

Marsh, P., Rosser, E. and Harré, R. ((1978) *Rules of Disorder* (Milton Keynes: Open University Press).

Marshall, G. O. and Zimbardo, P. G. (1979) 'Affective consequences of inadequately explained physiological arousal', *Journal of Personality and Social Psychology*, 37, 970–88.

Maslach, C. (1979) 'Negative emotional biasing of unexplained arousal', *Journal of Personality and Social Psychology*, 37, 571–7.

Matthews, K. A. (1982) 'Psychological perspectives on the Type A behaviour pattern', *Psychological Bulletin*, 9, 293–332.

Maxwell, G. M. and Coeburgh, B. (1986) 'Patterns of loneliness in a New Zealand population', *Community Mental Health in New Zealand*, 2, 48–61.

Mbiti, J. S. (1970) *African Religions and Philosophy* (New York: Doubleday).

McAdams, D. P., Healy, S. and Krause, S. (1984) 'Social motives and patterns of friendship', *Journal of Personality and Social Psychology*, 47, 828–38.

McCauley, C. (1989) 'The nature of social influence in groupthink: compliance and internalization', *Journal of Personality and Social Psychology*, 57, 250–60.

McClintock, C. G. and McNeel, S. P. (1966) 'Reward level and game playing behaviour', *Journal of Conflict Resolution*, 10, 98–102.

McDougall, W. (1920) *The Group Mind* (London: Cambridge University Press).

McGinnis, R. (1959) 'Campus values in mate selection: a repeat study', *Social Forces*, 36, 283–291.

McGrath, J. E. (1984) *Group Interaction and Performance* (Englewood Cliffs, NJ: Prentice-Hall).

McGuire W. J. (1973) 'The ying and yang of progress in social psychology: seven koan', *Journal of Personality and Social Psychology*, 26, 446–56.

McGuire W. J. (1989) 'The structure of individual attitudes and attitude systems', in A. R. Pratkanis, S. J. Brerckler and A. G. Greenwald (eds), *Attitude Structure and Function* (Hillsdale, NJ: Erlbaum).

Mead, G. H. (1934) *Mind, Self and Society* (Chicago: University of Chicago Press).

Menges, R. J. (1973) 'Openness and honesty versus coercion and deception in psychological recearch', *American Psychologist*, 28, 1030–4.

Metts, S. (1989) 'An exploratory investigation of deception in close relationships', *Journal of Social and Personal Relationships*, 6, 159–79.

Middlebrook, P. N. (1980) *Social Psychology and Modern Life*, 2nd edn (New York: Knopf).

Midlarsky, E. and Midlarsky, M. (1973) 'Some determinants of aiding under experimentally induced stress', *Journal of Personality*, 1, 305–27.

Mikula, G. (1980) 'On the role of justice in allocation decisions', in G. Mikula (ed.), *Justice and Social Interaction* (New York: Springer-Verlag; Bern: Hans Huber).

Milardo, R. M., Johnson, M. P. and Huston, T. L. (1983) 'Developing close relationships, changing patterns of interaction between pair members and social networks', *Journal of Personality and Social Psychology*, 44, 964–76.

Milgram, S. (1963) 'The behavioural study of obedience', *Journal of Abnormal and Social Psychology*, 67, 371–8.

Milgram, S. (1965) 'Some conditions of obedience and disobedience to authority', *Human Relations*, 18, 57–76.

Milgram, S. (1970) 'The experience of living in cities', *Science*, 167, 1461–8.

Milgram, S. (1974) *Obedience to Authority* (New York: Harper & Row).

Milgram, S. (1977) 'A psychological map of New York City', in S. Milgram (ed.), *The Individual in a Social World* (Reading, Ma: Addison-Wesley).

Milgram, S. (1992) *The Individual in a Social World: Essays and Experiments*, 2nd edn (Reading, Ma: Addison-Wesley).

Miller, A. G. (1986) *The Obedience Experiments: a Case Study of Controversy in Social Science* (New York: Praeger).

Miller, A. G. and Lawson, T. (1989) 'The effect of an information option on the fundamental attribution error', *Personality and Social Psychology Bulletin*, 15, 194–204.

Miller, J. G. (1984) 'Culture and the development of everyday social explanation', *Journal of Personality and Social Psychology*, 46, 961–78.

Miller, N. E. and Dollard (1941) *Social Learning and Imitation* (New Haven Ct: Yale University Press).

Mills, J. and Clark, M. S. (1982) 'Exchange and communal relationships', *Review of Personality and Social Psychology*, 3, 121–44.

Moscovici, S. (1988) 'Notes towards a description of social representation', *European Journal of Social Psychology*, 18, 211–50.

Mullen, B., Salas, E. and Driskell, J. E. (1989) 'Salience, motivation and artifact as contributions to the relation between participation rate and leadership', *Journal of Experimental Social Psychology*, 25, 545–59.

Myerscough, R. and Taylor, S. P. (1985) 'The effects of marijuana on human physical aggression', *Journal of Personality and Social Psychology*, 49, 1541–6.

Newcombe, T. M. (1961) *The Acquaintance Process* (New York: Holt, Rinehart & Winston).

Ng, S. H. (1990) 'Androgenic coding of man and his memory by language users', *Journal of Experimental Social Psychology*, 26, 455–64.

Nisbett, R. E. and Ross, L. (1980) *Human Inferences: Strategies and Shortcomings in Social Judgement* (Englewood Cliffs, NJ: Prentice-Hall).

Nobles, W. W. (1976) 'Extended self: Rethinking the so-called negro self concept', in R. L. Jones (ed.), *Black Psychology* (New York: Harper & Row).

Novak, D. and Lerner, M. J. (1968) 'Rejection as a consequence of perceived similarity', *Journal of Personality and Social Psychology*, 9, 147–52.

Orne, M. T. (1969) 'Demand characteristics and the concept of quasi-controls', in R. Rosenthal and R. Rosnow (eds), *Artifact in Behaviour Research* (New York: Academic Press).

Osborn, A. F. (1957) *Applied Imagination*, rev edn (New York: Scribners).

Osgood, C. E., Suci, G. J. and Tannenbaum, P. H. (1957) *The Measurement of Meaning* (Urbana III: University of Illinois Press).

Palmarek, D. L. and Rule, B. G. (1979) 'Effects of ambient temperature and insult on motivation to retaliate', *Motivation and Emotion*, 3, 83–92.

Paulus, P. B., Dzindolet, M. T., Poletes, G. and Camacho, L. M. (1993) 'Perception of performance in group brainstorming: the illusion of group productivity', *Personality and Social Science Bulletin*, 19, 78–89.

Pennebaker, J. W. (1989) 'Stream of consciousness and stress: Levels of thinking', in J. S. Uleman and J. R. Bargh (eds), *Unintended Thought* (New York: Guilford Press).

Perdue, C. W., Dovidio, J. F., Gurtman, M. B. and Tyler, R. B. (1990) 'Us and them: Social categorization and the process of intergroup bias', *Journal of Personality and Social Psychology*, 59, 475–86.

Perry, D. G., Perry, L., Bussey, K., English, D. and Arnold, G. (1980) 'Processes of attribution and children's self punishment following misbehaviour', *Child Development*, 51, 545–51.

Pettigrew, T. F. (1958) 'Personality and sociocultural factors in intergroup attitudes: A crossnational comparison', *Journal of Conflict Resolution*, 2, 29–42.

Pettigrew, T. F. (1979) 'The ultimate attribution error: Extending Allport's cognitive analysis of prejudice', *Personality and Social Psychology Bulletin*, 5, 461–76.

Pettigrew, T. F. (1987) *Modern Racism: American Black and White Relations since the 1960s* (Cambridge, Ma: Harvard University Press).

Phillips, D. P. (1980) 'The deterrent effect of capital punishment: New evidence on an old controversy', *American Journal of Sociology*, 86, 139–48.

Piliavin, J. A., Dovidio, J. F., Gaertner, S. L. and Clark, R. D. III (1981) *Emergency Intervention* (New York: Academic Press).

Pomazal, R. J. and Clore, G. L. (1973) 'Helping on the highway: The effects of dependency and sex', *Journal of Applied Social Psychology*, 3, 150–64.

Pratkanis, A. R. and Greenwald, A. G. (1989) 'A sociocognitive model of attitude structure and function', in L. Berkowitz (ed.), *Advances in Experimental Social Psychology*, Vol. 22 (New York: Academic Press).

Przybyla, D. P. J. (1985) 'The facilitating effects of exposure to erotica on male prosocial behaviour', Ph.D thesis, State University of New York in Albany (NY).

Radloff, R. and Helmreich, R. (1968) *Groups under Stress: Psychological Research in SEA LAB II* (New York: Irvington).

Ramirez, A., Bryant, J. and Ziliman, D. (1982) 'Effects of erotica on retaliatory behaviour as a function of level of prior provocation', *Journal of Personality and Social Psychology*, 43, 971–8.

Ransford, H. E. (1968) 'Isolation, powerlessness and violence: A study of attitudes and participation in the Watts riot', *American Journal of Sociology*, 73, 581–91.

Raphael, B. (1985) *The Anatomy of Bereavement: A Handbook for the Caring Professions* (London: Hutchinson).

Raven, B. H. (1965) 'Social influence and power', in I. D. Steiner and M. Fishbein (eds), *Current Studies in Social Psychology* (New York: Holt, Rinehart & Winston).

Reicher, S. D. (1982) 'The determination of collective behaviour', in H. Tajfel (ed.), *Social Identity and Intergroup Relations* (Cambridge: Cambridge University Press).

Reicher, S. D. (1984) 'Social influence in the crowd: Attitudinal and behavioural effects of deindividuation in conditions of high and low in-group salience', *British Journal of Social Psychology*, 23, 341–50.

Reicher, S. D. (1987) 'Crowd behaviour in social action', in J. C. Turner, M. A. Hogg, P. J. Oakes, S. D. Reicher and M. S. Wetherall, *Rediscovering the Social Group: A Self-Categorisation Theory* (Oxford: Blackwell).

Rempel, J. K., Holmes, J. G., and Zanna, M. P. (1985) 'Trust in close relationships', *Journal of Personality and Social Psychology*, 49, 95–112.

Roberts, D. F. and Maccoby, N. (1985) 'Effects of mass communication', in G. Lindsey and E. Aronson (eds), *Handbook of Social Psychology*, 3rd edn, Vol. 2 (New York: Random House).

Roethlisberger, F. J. and Dickson, W. G. (1939) *Management and the Worker* (Cambridge, Ma: Harvard University Press).

Rogers, C. R. (1951) *Client-Centred Therapy* (London: Constable).

Rogers, C. R. (1961) *On Becoming a Person: A Therapist's View of Psychotherapy* (London: Constable).

Rokeach, M. (1948) 'Generalized mental rigidity as a factor in ethnocentrism', *Journal of Abnormal and Social Psychology*, 43, 259–78.

Rokeach, M. (1960) *The Open and Closed Mind* (New York: Basic Books).

Romzek, B. S. and Dubnick, M. J. (1987) 'Accountability in the public sector: Lessons from the *Challenger* tragedy', *Public Administration Review*, 47, 227–38.

Rosenberg, S. and Jones, R. A. (1972) 'A method for investigating a person's implicit theory of personality: Theodore Dreiser's view of people', *Journal of Personality and Social Psychology*, 22, 372–86.

Rosenberg, S. and Sedlak, A. (1972) 'Structural representations of implicit personality theory', *Advances in Experimental Social Psychology*, 6, 235–97.

Rosenfield, D., Greenberg, J. Folger, R., and Borys, R. (1982) 'Effect of an encounter with a black panhandler on subsequent helping for blacks: Tokenism or conforming to a negative stereotype', *Personality and Social Psychology Bulletin*, 8, 664–71.

Rosenhan, D. L., Salovey, P. and Hargis, K. (1981) 'The joys of helping: Focus of attention mediates the impact of positive affect on altruism', *Journal of Personality and Social Psychology*, 40, 899–905.

Rosenthal, R. (1966) *Experimenter Effects in Behavioural Research* (New York: Appleton-Century-Crofts).

Ross, L. (1977) 'The intuitive psychologist and his shortcomings', in L. Berkowitz (ed.), *Advances in Experimental Social Psychology*, Vol. 10 (New York: Academic Press).

Ross, L., Greene, D., and House, P. (1977) 'The "false consensus" effect and egocentric bias in social perception and attribution processes', *Journal of Experimental Social Psychology*, 13, 279–301.

Rotter, J. B. (1966) 'Generalized expectancies for internal versus external control of reinforcement', *Psychological Monographs*, 80, 1, whole no. 609.

Rotton, J. and Frey, J. (1985) 'Air pollution, weather and violent crimes: Concomitant time series analysis of archival data, *Journal of Personality and Social Psychology*, 49, 1207–20.

Rubin Z. (1973) *Liking and Loving: An Invitation to Social Psychology* (New York: Holt, Rinehart & Winston).

Rule, B. G. and Leger, G. J. (1976) 'Pain cues and differing functions of aggression', *Canadian Journal of Behavioural Science*, 8, 213–22.

Rule, B. G. and Percival, E. (1971) 'Effects of frustration and attack on physical aggression', *Journal of Experimental Research in Personality*, 5, 111–18.

Runciman, W. G. (1966) *Relative Deprivation and Social Justice* (London, Routledge & Kegan Paul).

Rushton, J. P., Fulker, D. W. Neale, M. C., Nias, D. K. B. and Fysenck, H. J. (1986) 'Altruism and aggression: The heritability of individual differences', *Journal of Personality and Social Psychology*, 50, 1192–8.

Rutter, M., Maughan, B., Mortimore, P. and Ouston, J. (1979) *Fifteen Thousand Hours* (London: Open Books).

Schachter, S. (1959) *The Psychology of Affiliation* (Stanford, Ca: Stanford University Press).

Schachter, S. and Singer, J. (1962) 'Cognitive, social and physiological determinants of the emotional state', *Psychological Review*, 69, 379–99.

Schaller, M. and Cialdini, R. B. (1988) 'The economics of empathetic helping: support for a mood management motive', *Journal of Experimental Social Psychology*, 24, 163–81.

Schank, R. C. and Abelson, R. P. (1977) *Scripts, Plans, Goals and Understanding: An Enquiry into Human Knowledge Structures* (Hillsdale, NJ: Erlbaum).

Scher, S. J. and Cooper, J. (1989) 'Motivational basis of dissonance: The singular role of consequences', *Journal of Personality and Social Psychology*, 56, 899–906.

Schroeder, D. A., Dovidio, J. F., Sibicky, M. E., Matthews, L. L. and Allen, J. L. (1988) 'Empathic concern and helping behaviour: Egoism or altruism?', *Journal of Experimental Social Psychology*, 24, 333–53.

Schwartz, S. H. (1977) 'Normative influences on altruism', in L. Berkowitz (ed.), *Advances in Experimental Social Psychology*, Vol. 10 (New York: Academic Press).

Schwartz, S. H. and David, T. B. (1976) 'Responsibility and helping in an emergency: Effects of blame, ability and denial of responsibility', *Sociometry*, 39, 406–15.

Scodel, A., Minas, J. S., Ratoosh, P. and Lipetz, M. (1959) 'Some descriptive aspects of two person non-zero sum games' I, *Journal of Conflict Resolution*, 3, 114–9.

Sears, D. O. (1986) 'College sophomores in the laboratory: Influences of a narrow data base or social psychology's view of human nature', *Journal of Personality and Social Psychology*, 51, 515–30.

Shanab, M. E. and Kahya, K. A. (1977) 'A behavioural study of obedience in children', *Journal of Personality and Social Psychology*, 35, 530–6.

Shaver, P. and Hazan, C. (1987). 'Being lonely, falling in love: Perspectives from attachment theory', *Journal of Social Behaviour and Personality*, 2, 105–24.

Shaver, P. and Hazan, C. (1988) 'A biased overview of the study of love', *Journal of Social and Personal Relationships*, 5, 473–501.

Shaw, M. E. (1964) 'Communication networks', in L. Berkowitz (ed.), *Advances in Experimental Social Psychology*, Vol. I (New York: Academic Press).

Shaw, M. E. (1978) 'Communication networks fourteen years later', in L. Berkowitz (ed.), *Group Processes* (New York: Academic Press).

Sheehan, P. W. (1983) 'Age trends and correlates of children's television viewing', *Australian Journal of Psychology*, 35, 417–211.

Sherif, M. (1936) *The Psychology of Social Norms* (New York: Harper).

Sherif, M. (1966) *Group Conflict and Cooperation* (Boston, Ma: Houghton Mifflin).

Sherif, M. (ed.) (1962) *Intergroup Relations and Leadership* (New York: Wiley).

Sherif, M., Harvey, O. J, White, B. J., Hood, W. R. and Sherif, C. W. (1961) *Intergroup Conflict and Cooperation: The Robber's Cave Experiment* (The University of Oklahoma Book Exchange).

Sherif. M. (1951) 'A preliminary experimental study of inter-group relations', in J. J. Rohrer and M. Sherif (eds), *Social Psychology at the Crossroads* (New York: Harper & Row).

Shettel-Neuber, J., Bryson, J. B., and Young, L. E. (1978) 'Physical attractiveness of the "other person" and jealousy', *Personality and Social Psychology Bulletin*, 4, 612–15.

Shuntich, R. J. and Taylor, S. P. (1972) 'The effects of alcohol on human aggression', *Journal of Experimental Research in Personality*, 6, 34–8.

Sigall, H. and Ostrove, N. (1975) 'Beautiful but dangerous: Effects of offender attractiveness and the nature of the crime on juristic judgement', *Journal of Personality and Social Psychology*, 31, 410–14.

Silva, M. L. (1990) 'Mate selection criteria' (unpublished manuscript: Mercer University).

Simpson, J. A., Campbell, B. and Berscheid, E. (1986) 'The association between romantic love and marriage: Kephart (1967) twice re-visited', *Personality and Social Psychology Bulletin*, 12, 363–72.

Skinner, B. F. (1953) *Science and Human Behaviour* (New York: Macmillan).

Smith, F. T. (1943) 'An experiment in modifying attitudes towards the Negro', *Teachers' College Contributions to Education*, No. 887.

Snyder, M. (1987) *Public and Private Realities: The Psychology of Self-Monitoring* (New York: W. H. Freeman).

Spears, R. and Manstead, A. S. R. (1990) 'Consensus estimation in the social context', *European Review of Social Psychology*, 1, 81–109.

Spence, J. T., Helmreich, R. L. and Stapp, J. (1974) 'The personal attributes questionnaire: A measure of sex role stereotypes and masculinity–femininity', *JSAS Catalog of Selected Documents in Psychology*, 4, 127.

Sprecher, S. (1986) 'The relation between inequity and emotions in close relationships', *Social Psychology Quarterly*, 49, 309–21.

Steele, C. M. (1988) 'The psychology of self-affirmation: Sustaining the integrity of the self', *Advances in Experimental Social Psychology*, 21, 481–91.

Steiner, I. D. (1972) *Group Processes and Productivity* (New York: Academic Press).

Steiner, I. D. (1976) 'Task performing groups', in J. W. Thibaut and J. T. Spence (eds), *Contemporary Topics in Social Psychology* (Morristown, NJ: General Learning Press).

Stephan, W. G. and Rosenfeld, D. (1978) 'Effects of desegregation on racial attitudes', *Journal of Personality and Social Psychology*, 36, 795–804.

Stephan, W. G. and Stephan, C. W. (1984) 'The role of ignorance in intergroup relations', in N. Miller and M. B. Brewer (eds), *Groups in contact: The Psychology of Desegregation* (New York: Academic Press).

Sternberg, R. J. (1986) 'A triangular theory of love', *Psychological Review*, 93, 119–35.

Stewart, J. E. (1980) 'Defendant's attractiveness as a factor in the outcome of criminal trials: An observational study', *Journal of Applied Social Psychology*, 10, 348–61.

Stewart, R. A. (1988) 'Habitability and behavioural issues of space flight', *Small Group Behaviour*, 19, 431–55.

Stogdill, R. (1974) *Handbook of Leadership* (New York: Free Press).

Stoller, R. J. (1976) 'Sexual excitement', *Archives of General Psychiatry*, 33, 899–909.

Stoner, J. A. F. (1961) 'A comparison of individual and group decisions including risk', *Masters Thesis*, Massachusetts Institute of Technology.

Storms, M. D. (1973) 'Videotape and attribution process: Reversing actor's and observer's points of view', *Journal of Personality and Social Psychology*, 27, 165–75.

Stroebe, M. S. and Stroebe, W. (1983) *Bereavement and Health* (New York: Cambridge University Press).

Stroebe, W., Lenkert, A. and Jonas, K. (1988) 'Familiarity may breed contempt: The impact of student exchange on national stereotypes and attitudes', in W. Stroebe, A. Kruglanski, D. Bar-Tal and M. Hewstone (eds), *The Social Psychology of Intergroup Conflict: Theory, Research and Applications* (New York: Springer-Verlag).

Strube, M. J., Turner, C. W., Cerro, D., Stevens, J. and Hinchey, F. (1984) 'Interpersonal aggression and Type A coronary-prone behaviour pattern: A theoretical distinction and practical implications', *Journal of personality and Social Psychology*, 47, 839–47.

Stryker, S. and Statham, A. (1985) 'Symbolic interaction and role theory', in G. Lindzey and E. Aronson (eds), *Handbook of Social Psychology*, 3rd edition, Vol. I (New York: Random House).

Sumner, W. G. (1906) *Folkways* (Boston, Ma: Ginn).

Swim, J., Borgida, E. and Maruyama, G. (1989) 'Joan McKay versus John McKay: Do gender stereotypes bias evaluation?', *Psychological Bulletin*, 105, 409–29.

Symonds, M. (1975) 'Victims of violence: Psychological effects and after-effects', *American Journal of Psychoanalysis*, 35, 19–26.

Szasz, T. (1967) *The Myth of Mental Illness* (London: Paladin).

Tajfel, H. (1978) 'Intergroup behaviour. II: Group perspectives', in H. Tajfel and C. Fraser (eds), *Intergroup Behaviour* (Oxford: Blackwell).

Tajfel, H. (1982) 'Social psychology of intergroup relations', *Annual Review of Social Psychology*, 33, 1–39.

Tajfel, H. and Turner, J. C. (1986) 'The social identity theory of intergroup behaviour', in S. Worchel and W. G. Austin (eds), *Psychology of Intergroup Relations*, 2nd edn (Chicago: Nelson-Hall).

Taylor, S. E. (1982) 'Social cognition and health', *Personality and Social Psychology Bulletin*, 8, 549–62.

Taylor, S. P. (1986) 'The regulation of aggressive behaviour', in R. J. Blanchard and D. C. Blanchard (eds), *Advances in the Study of Aggression* (Orlando Fl: Academic Press).

Taylor, S. P. and Gammon, C. B. (1975) 'Effects of type and dose of alcohol on human physical aggression, *Journal of Personality and Social Psychology*, 34, 938–41.

Taylor, S. P. Gammon, C. B. and Capasso, D. R. (1976) 'Aggression as a function of the interaction of frustration and physical attack', *Journal of Social Psychology*, 84, 261–7.

Taylor, S. P., Vardaris, R. M., Rawtich, A. B., Gammon, C. B., Cranston, C. W. and Lubethin, A. I. (1976) 'The effects of alcohol and delta-9-tetrahydrocannabinol on human physical aggression', *Aggressive Behaviour*, 2, 153–61.

Taynor, J. and Deaux, K. (1973) 'When women are more deserving than men: Equity, attribution and perceived sex differences', *Journal of Personality and Social Psychology*, 28, 360–7.

Tesser, A. and Paulhus, D. L. (1976) 'Toward a casual model of love', *Journal of Personality and Social Psychology*, 34, 1095–105.

Tesser, A., Gatewood R. and Driver, M. (1968) 'Some determinants of gratitude', *Journal of Personality and Social Psychology*, 9, 233–6.

Theoretical and Empirical Reviews (New York: Academic Press).

Thibaut, J. W. and Kelley, H. H. (1959) *The Social Psychology of Groups* (New York: Wiley).

Thibaut, J. W. and Kelley, H. H. (1978) *Interpersonal: A Theory of Interdependence* (New York: Wiley).

Tolman, E. C. (1948) 'Cognitive maps in rats and men', *Psychological Review*, 55, 189–208.

Triandis, H. C. and Vassiliou V. (1967) 'Frequency of contact and stereotyping', *Journal of Personality and Social Psychology*, 7, 316–38.

Triandris, H. C. (1971) *Attitudes and Attitude Change* (New York: Wiley).

Trivers R. L. (1971) 'The evolution of reciprocal altruism', *Quarterly Review of Biology*, 46 (4) 35–57.

Turner R. H. (1974) 'Collective behaviour', in R. E. L. Faris (ed.), *Handbook of Modern Sociology* (Chicago, Ill: Rand-McNally).

Turner, C. W. and Berkowitz, L. (1972) 'Identification with film aggressor (covert role taking) and reactions to film violence', *Journal of Personality and Social Psychology*, 21, 256–64.

Turner, M. E., Pratkanis, A. R., Probasco, P. and Leve, C. (1992) 'Threat, cohesion and group effectiveness: Testing a social identity maintenance perspective on groupthink', *Journal of Personality and Social Psychology*, 63, 781–96.

Tyerman, A. and Spencer, C. (1983) 'A critical test of Sherif's Robbers' cave experiments: Intergroup competition and cooperation between well-acquainted individuals', *Small Group Behaviour*, 14, 515–31.

US Riot Commission (1968) *Report of the National Advisory Commission on Civil Disorders* (New York: Bantam Books).

Valins, S. (1966) 'Cognitive effects of false heart-rate feedback', *Journal of Personality and Social Psychology*, 4, 400–8.

van Knippenberg, A. and Ellemers, N. (1990) 'Social identity and intergroup differentiation processes', *European Review of Social Psychology*, 1, 137–6.

Voissem, N. H. and Sistrunk, F. (1971) 'Communication schedules and cooperative game behaviour', *Journal of Personality and Social Psychology*, 19, 160–7.

Waddington, D., Jones, K. and Critcher, C. (1987) 'Flashpoints of public disorder', in G. Gaskell and R. Benewick (eds), *The Crowd in Contemporary Britain* (London: Sage).

Wadeley, A. (1991) *Ethics in Psychological Research and Practice* (Leicester: British Psychological Society).

Walker, I. and Mann, L. (1987) 'Unemployment, relative deprivation and social protest', *Personality and Social Psychology Bulletin*, 13, 275–83.

Walster, E., Walster, G. W. and Berscheid, E. (1978) *Equity: Theory and Research* (Boston, Ma: Allyn & Bacon).

Walters, R. H. and Brown, M. (1963) 'Studies of reinforcement of aggression III: Transfer of resourses to an interpersonal situation', *Child Development*, 34, 536–71.

Watson, J. B. (1913) 'Psychology as the behaviourist views it', *Psychological Review*, 20, 158–77.

Webb, E. J., Campbell, D. T., Schwartz, R. D. and Sechrest, L. (1969) *Unobtrusive Measures: Non-reactive Research in Social Sciences* (Chicago: Rand-McNally).

Wegner, D. M. (1986) 'Transactive memory: A contemporary analysis of the group mind', in B. Mullen and G. R. Goethals (eds), *Theories of Group Behaviour* (New York: Springer-Verlag).

Wegner, D. M., Erber, R. and Raymond, P. (1991) 'Transactive memory in close relationships', *Journal of Personality and Social Psychology*, 61, 923–9.

Weiner, B. (1979) 'A theory of motivation for some classroom experiences', *Journal of Educational Psychology*, 71, 3–25.

Weiner, B. (1985) '"Spontaneous" causal thinking', *Psychological Bulletin*, 97, 74–84.

Weiner, B. (1986) *An Attributional Theory of Motivation and Emotion* (New York: Springer-Verlag).

Weiner, M. J. and Wright, F. E. (1973) 'Effects of undergoing arbitrary discrimination upon subsequent attitudes towards a minority group', *Journal of Applied Social Psychology*, 3, 94–102.

Wheeler, L., Reis, H. and Neslek, J. (1983) 'Loneliness, social interaction and sex roles', *Journal of Personality and Social Psychology*, 45, 943–53.

White, J. W. and Gruber, K. J. (1982) 'Instigative aggression as a function of past experience and target characteristics', *Journal of Personality and Social Psychology*, 42, 1069–75.

Wilder, D. A. (1986) 'Social categorization: Implications for creation and reduction of intergroup bias', in L. Berkowitz (ed.), *Advances in Experimental Social Psychology*, Vol. 19 (New York: Academic Press).

Wilder, D. A. (1977) 'Perception of groups, size of opposition and social influence', *Journal of Experimental Social Psychology*, 13, 253–68.

Wilke, H. and Lanzetta, J. T. (1970) 'The obligation to help: The effects of the amount of prior help on subsequent helping behaviour', *Journal of Experimental Social Psychology*, 6, 488–93.

Williams, J. G and Solano, C. H. (1983) 'The social reality of feeling lonely: Friendship and reciprocation', *Personality and Social Psychology Bulletin*, 2, 237–42.

Wilson, E. O. (1975) *Sociobiology: The New Synthesis* (Cambridge Ma: Belknap Press of Harvard University).

Wilson, E. O. (1978) *On Human Nature* (Cambridge, Ma: Belknap Press of Harvard University).

Winch, R. F., Ktsanes, I. and Ktsanes, V. (1954) 'The theory of complementary needs in mate selection', *American Sociological Review*, 19, 241–9.

Wispé, L. G. (1972) 'Positive forms of social behaviour: An overview', *Journal of Social Issues*, 28, 1–19.

Worchel, S., Andreoli, V. A. and Folger, R. (1977) 'Intergroup cooperation and intergroup attraction: The effect of previous interaction and the outcome of combined effort', *Journal of Experimental Social Psychology*, 13, 131–40.

Zajonc, R. B. (1968) 'Attitudinal effects of mere exposure', *Journal of Personality and Social Psychology*, 9, 1–27.

Zillman, D. (1988) 'Cognition excitation interdependencies in aggressive behaviour', *Aggressive Behaviour*, 14, 51–64.

Zillman, D. and Bryant, J. (1982) 'Pornography, sexual callousness and the trivialization of rape', *Journal of Communication*, 32 (4) 10–21.

Zillman, D. (1979) *Hostility and Aggression* (Hillsdale, NJ: Erlbaum).

Zillman, D. and Cantor, J. R. (1976) 'Effect of timing of information about mitigating circumstances on emotional responses to provocation and retaliatory behaviour', *Journal of Experimental Social Psychology*, 12, 38–55.

Zillman, D., Bryant J, Cantor, J. R. and Day, K. D. (1975) 'Irrelevance of mitigating circumstances in retaliatory behaviour at high levels of excitation', *Journal of Research in Personality*, 9, 282–93.

Zimbardo, P. G. (1970) 'The human choice: Individuation, reason and order versus deindividuation, impulse and chaos', in W. J. Arnold and D. Levine (eds), *Nebraska Symposium on Motivation, 1969* (Lincoln, Ne: University of Nebraska Press).

Zimbardo, P. G. (1979) *Psychology and Life*, 10th edn (Glenview, Ill: Scott Foresman).

Zimbardo, P. G. and Leippe, M. R. (1991) *The Psychology of Attitude Change and Social Influence* (New York: McGraw-Hill).

Zimbardo, P. G., Banks, W. C., Craig, H., and Jaffe, D. (1973) 'A pirandellian prison: The mind is a formidable jailer', *New York Times Magazine*, 8 April, 38–60.

Zuckerman, M., Lazzaro, M. M. and Waldgeir, D. (1979) 'Undermining effects of the foot-in-the-door technique with extrinsic rewards', *Journal of Applied Social Psychology*, 9, 292–6.

Index

272   *Index*